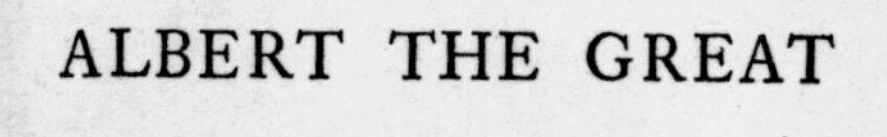
ALBERT THE GREAT

SANCTUS ALBERTUS MAGNUS ECCLESIÆ DOCTOR
From a fresco by Tommaso da Modena in the Chapter Hall of the old Dominican Priory, now a Seminary, in Treviso.

ALBERT THE GREAT

SAINT AND DOCTOR OF THE CHURCH

By

HIERONYMUS WILMS, O.P.

ENGLISH VERSION WITH ADDITIONAL NOTES AND APPENDICES, BY ADRIAN ENGLISH, O.P., S.T.L., B.Sc., AND PHILIP HEREFORD, A FOREWORD BY VINCENT McNABB, O.P., S.T.M., AND MANY ILLUSTRATIONS.

LONDON

BURNS OATES & WASHBOURNE LTD.

PUBLISHERS TO THE HOLY SEE

NIHIL OBSTAT:

FR. VINCENTIUS MCNABB, O.P., S.Th.M.,
FR. W. LEO MOORE, O.P., S.Th.L.

IMPRIMATUR:

FR. BERNARDUS DELANY, O.P.,
Prior Provincialis Angliae.

23 *Jan., in festo S. Raymundi,* 1933.

NIHIL OBSTAT:

JOANNES V. SIMCOX, D.C.L., M.A.,
Censor deputatus.

IMPRIMATUR:

✠ JOSEPHUS BUTT,
Vicarius generalis.

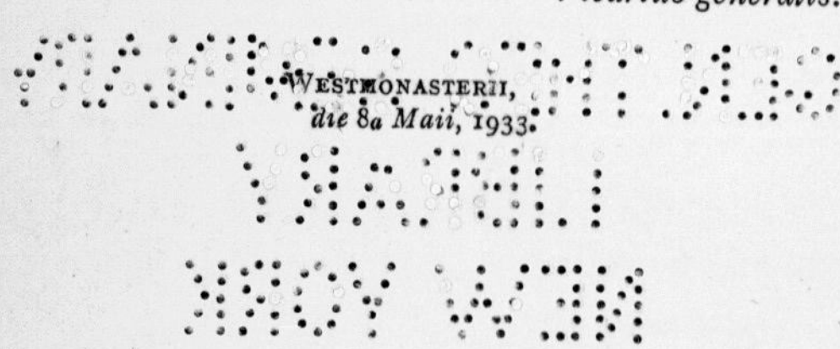

WESTMONASTERII,
die 8a Maii, 1933.

MADE AND PRINTED IN GREAT BRITAIN
1933

CONTENTS

LIST OF ILLUSTRATIONS

SANCTI ALBERTI MAGNI
Ordinis Prædicatorum
ELOGIUM

ALBERTUS *Deiparæ Philosophus,*
THOMAS *Verbi Theologus fuit,*
Bene hic de Filio, bene ille scripsit de Matre :
Uterque Magnus, sed ille Magister, hic discipulus ;
Uter plura sciverit ambiguum est,
Uterque aliquid scivit post omnia.
In ALBERTO *aliquid eminet unde supra alios Magnus est,*
Rudis ætate prima & ultima :
Parum debuit naturæ, ut omnia deberet gratiæ ;
Momento eruditus, momento indoctus,
Didicit omnia simul, omnia simul dedidicit,
Abstulit scientiam quæ dederat,
Ut sciret qui reddit, alienum esse quod redditur.

Bene usus Scientiis, quas acceperat commodatas,
Implevit Orbem octingentis Libris,
Satis unus omnibus Bibliothecis ;
Nec mirum si omnibus sufficit qui THOMÆ *discipulo satis fuit.*

Nec tantum erudivit orbem, sed correxit,
Emendavit in Guillelmo a sancto amore errores futuros,
Præparavit antidotum venenis venturis :
Fallaces Aurelii & Pseudo-Augustini
Expugnati sunt ab ALBERTO *diu antequam nati.*

Nulla opinio etiam falsa fefellit ALBERTUM,
Modum posuit Artibus curiosis ne ultra pergerent,
Ostendit ubi desineret natura unde inciperet gratia ;
Petiit a Virgine ne falli posset, addidit illa ne falleret,
Nemo erravit sub ALBERTO *Magistro, &* THOMA *Discipulo.*

Media ætas ALBERTI *illustris, omnis humilis fuit,*
Magister Sacri Palatii maluit Germaniam docere quam Romam,
Ratisbonenses Insulas sponte exuit, quas invitus acceperat ;
Vix inter suos provinciam regere voluit, qui Ordini regendo par erat,
Fundator Ordinis futurus, nisi Dominicus præcessisset.

Qui omnia didicit a Maria, nihil melius dedicit quam Mariam,
Scivit illam antequam aliquid disceret,
Illam scivit postquam omnia dedidicit,
Prima hæc vox erupit infanti, & ultima seni.

Denique dum ex Cathedra dictat, non tam verba quam oracula,
Obmutuit extemplo oraculum Orbis,
Et cujus memoria Sapientiæ promptuarium erat,
Id tantum tunc meminit se nihil amplius meminisse.
Nec mutum tamen ALBERTI *silentium fuit,*
ALBERTUS *senex & rudis adhuc Orbis Magister erat,*
Probabat immemor divinum esse quidquid memor dictaverat.
Obiit anno ætatis 87, clarus miraculis,
Ipse eruditus & rudis miraculum fuit,
Nec minore prodigio amisit Scientias quas accepit,
Beatus qui amittere Scientiam voluit, ut innocentiam retineret.

PETRUS L'ABBÉ *Societatis Jesu.*

FOREWORD

PERHAPS the highest praise of S. Albert is that he alone has received the title ' the Great ' amongst all the men of a century that may well be called ' the Great ' or even ' the Greatest.'

In offering to the English-reading world this Life of a great child of a great century, we are not mere *laudatores temporis acti*, asking our own age to praise and appraise a man of renown. Though his direct and indirect gifts to us would make this Life of the Saint some slender effort towards gratitude, the purpose of the book is propaganda rather than gratitude.

In frankly calling the book propaganda we feel no need to apologize either for the word or the thing. If Sir Alfred Ewing, from his Presidential Chair of the British Association, rightly sums up the state of the world by saying as of ' one who has gone a long way and finds he has taken a wrong turning,'[1] then true propaganda, i.e. the propaganda of truth, becomes not robbery with violence of man's intelligence but a needed mercy to his mind.

The simple frontier-line of what this mind won for all minds in the sphere of truths must make our contemporaries regret that many of these truths are not now considered true, or even considered. Albert the Great's discoveries and recoveries in the region of scientific ethics make few men of to-day feel themselves his debtors. Now as the best thanks-return for truth is to accept it as true, it is our hope in this book to requite the unbegrudging, unstinting mind of Albert by making a home in the minds of many for some of the truths he won only to share.

If in a world bewildered by tokens and untruths frank propaganda of truth is the only literary manner needing little apology, still less apology is needed for frank propaganda of the true attitude towards truth. It is in this

[1] Presidential Address, York, Aug. 31, 1932.

attitude towards truth that the great authentic child of a great century has no greater, not even his own authentic child, S. Thomas Aquinas. The century, which, in its thinkers, went East for wisdom as three centuries later the traders went West for gold, sought truth with a sincerity which is the unfading riches of the world. Indeed so supreme a quality is the hunger and thirst of men like Albert and Thomas for truth by whomsoever taught or wheresoever found—even by the Father of lying or in at the gate of hell—that were all their teaching found untrue their love of truth would canonize them amongst the heroes of the mind.

One last word is needed to introduce this Life of S. Albert to the many or few to whom its pages may be good tidings.

If the modern world is a world in bewilderment, it is a world in movement. Intellectually it is neither resting nor sleeping, though perhaps it is dreaming. But it is awake and astir ; and its dreams, if it has any, are of one who is awake. Even mid-Victorian headlongness at its best—and perhaps even at its worst—was a certain restless, childlike enthusiasm for putting into glass cases things it found, and building Crystal Palaces for the things it made. We that believed in God in those days of forgetfulness rather than denial still utter our old belief in a heartfelt thanks for the childlikeness which still exists amongst the modern Alberts of Science and makes them brother of Albert the Great.

VINCENT McNABB, O.P., S.T.M.

AUTHOR'S PREFACE

IN the year 1880, on the occasion of the celebration of the 600th anniversary of S. Albert's death, Hermann Cardauns wrote: 'It is a disgraceful fact that Germany still knows so little about the greatest of her mediæval sons.' These reproachful words were not without their effect. His exterior life has been investigated by researchers of the first rank. Thus Georg von Hertling wrote *Albertus Magnus, Beiträge zu seiner Würdigung*, which ran into a second edition. Paulus von Loë, O.P., brought out[1] a critical investigation of the chronological sources on Albert up to the fifteenth century and a catalogue of the *regesta* of Albert's works, and thus laid the necessary foundations for a worthy biography. Among other things he succeeded in proving beyond question the fact of Albert's presence at the Council of Lyons (1274). Emil Michael, S.J., has condensed his rich store of knowledge on Albertus Magnus in the third volume of his history of the German people.[2] In this work, as also in the *Zeitschrift für Katholische Theologie*,[3] he supported 1193 as the year of Albert's birth. J. A. Endres in the *Historisches Jahrbuch* for 1910 advanced the view that this should be 1207.[4] This writer has also investigated Albert's relation to the episcopal Castle Donaustauf, and furthermore has examined the question of Albert's second summons to the University of Paris.[5]

Albert's collected works were brought out by Jammy in the year 1651. In 1890 this uncritical and wholly unreliable text was reprinted by Borgnet, unfortunately without any

[1] P. von Loë, O.P.: *De vita et scriptis B. Alberti Magni.*
[2] E. Michael: *Geschichte des deutschen Volkes*, iii.
[3] E. Michael: *Wann ist Albert der Grosse Geboren?*
[4] J. A. Endres: *Das Geburtsjahr und die Chronologie in der ersten Lebenshälfte Alberts des Grossen.*
[5] J. A. Endres: *Albertus Magnus und die Bischöfliche Burg Donaustauf;* and *Eine beabsichtigte zweite Berufung Alberts des Grossen an die Universität Paris um Jahr* 1268.

essential correction. The foundations for a critical edition were laid by M. Weiss, who published a large collection of early documentary references to Albert's works under the title *Primordia novæ bibliographiæ beati Alberti Magni.* To this preliminary work Franz Pelster, S.J., contributed by his investigations on the scope and chronology of Albert's works. Two treatises, long ascribed to the Saint, the *De adhærendo Deo* and the *Philosophia pauperum*, have been shown by M. Grabmann to be spurious. According to him the former was compiled by Johann von Kastl, the latter by Albert von Orlamünde. Grabmann, however, in some way made up to Albert for their loss by the discovery and description of three unprinted parts of the Saint's *Summa de creaturis.* Following the example of C. Jessen, who had in 1867 brought out a critical edition of Albert's botanical work, *De vegetabilibus libri septem*, Hermann Stadler published his *De animalibus*, which appeared in two stately volumes in 1916 and 1921. Of the works not found in the collected edition, the commentary on Job was published by Melchior Weiss in 1904, and Mandonnet, in 1899, included in his volume on Siger of Brabant the treatise *De quindecim problematibus*, while Paulus von Loë in 1913 edited Albert's commentary on the *De divisione* of Boëthius.

Much special research has been devoted to the Saint's teaching. Leopold Gaul in his investigation of Albert's philosophy in its literary and historical aspects has thrown light on his relation to Plato. Arthur Schneider devoted two volumes to an account of his psychology. Anselm Rohner published a dissertation on the problem of creation as treated by Moses Maimonides, Albertus Magnus and Thomas Aquinas. Hermann Lauer examined the Saint's moral theology in its relation to the teaching of S. Thomas. Wilhelm Scherer made a compilation from Albert's various works of the teaching of the Church. This list could be considerably extended. Of the old vitæ of the Saint, the Bollandists published that by Luis de Valladolid, and Paulus von Loë the *Legenda Coloniensis* of 1483. In 1928 a new edition of the vitæ, which Rudolf von Nymegen composed in 1488, was brought out through the exertions of the Cologne Committee.

These and the many other works on Albertus Magnus which have appeared since 1880, but which cannot all be enumerated in a preface,[6] are a very gratifying sign of the ever-growing interest in the greatest German scholar of the Middle Ages. Although there is still a great deal of research to be done, a compendious account of the Saint's life and teaching may now be offered, with the aim of making Albert's extraordinary greatness intelligible to wider circles, and this not only in regard to his scientific importance, which Grabmann has excellently portrayed,[7] but also in his towering greatness in all things. The especial occasion of this book were the efforts, now happily crowned with success, of numbers of people in Germany under the leadership of Cardinal Frühwirth, to secure Albert the Great's inscription on the official roll of the Saints, and his elevation to the altars of the Church.

[6] But mention should be made of the contributions by Angelus Maria Walz, O.P., and Heribert Christian Scheeben, among others, whose works have appeared since this book was written. For details, see Appendix D [Ed.].

[7] Martin Grabmann : *Der Einfluss Alberts des Grossen auf das mittelalterliche Geistesleben.*

EDITORS' NOTE

THIS book on S. Albert the Great is, primarily, a translation of *Albert der Grosse*, by Hieronymus Wilms, O.P.

With the Author's consent some additional notes have been inserted, the chapter on science has been enlarged, a section added on the cult of the Saint, and supplementary matter has been dealt with in appendices. The Elogium printed at the beginning of this volume is taken from the first (1651) edition of S. Albert's works published by Petrus Jammy. For the illustrations we are indebted to Father Angelus Walz, O.P., and Dr. Heribert Chr. Scheeben. All controversy has been purposely avoided. The facts connected with the Saint's life and works bristle with difficulties and to discuss them in detail would have demanded another similar volume.

The work has been undertaken in order that English-speaking peoples may have in their own language a study of a great saint and man of vast learning, whose influence on the thought of Western civilization has been immeasurable, and in the hope that it may stimulate others to further research.

A. E., O.P.
P. H.

September 8, 1932.

AUTHOR'S INTRODUCTION

SAINT ALBERT, Dominican and Bishop of Regensburg, was called by his contemporaries Albertus Coloniensis or Albertus Teutonicus, to distinguish him from other Friars Preachers of the same name. M. Grabmann[1] makes the point that the appellation Albert of Cologne typifies the intimate relations which bound the learned South German prelate to the most important Dominican convent in the German province of the Order and to the metropolis of mediæval German learning, and that the name Albert the Teuton signifies not only the land of his birth but also the individuality of his intellectual life.

As Albert grew in influence and reputation new epithets were applied to him. Thus after attaining to the degree of Magister in Sacra Theologia at the University of Paris, many now called him rather 'Master Albert' or 'the celebrated Albert' or 'Albert the Theologian.' Thomas de Chantimpré, the Saint's contemporary, uses all three names.[2] Galguagnus de la Flamma says that after he had laid down his episcopal office he was called Dominus Frater Albertus.[3] Besides these shorter practical appellations, his contemporaries, as also the historians of the period following his, were not slow in bestowing laudatory titles on this extraordinary man. Girardus de Fracheto calls him in his *Vitæ Fratrum Ordinis Prædicatorum*, which he completed in 1260, 'a man of extraordinary reputation and great sanctity, Provincial of the German province of the Order, Brother Albertus Teutonicus, Master in Theology.'[4] Albert's

[1] M. Grabmann: *Der Einfluss Alberts des Grossen auf das mittelalterliche Geistesleben*, 5.

[2] Thomas Cantimpratanus, O.P.: *Bonum universale de apibus*, 141, 478, 583.

[3] Galguagnus de la Flamma, O.P.: *Cronica Ordinis Prædicatorum*, 99.

[4] Girardus de Fracheto, O.P.: *Vitæ Fratrum O.P.*, 187.

best-loved pupil, the learned Ulrich von Strassburg, remarks that because of his universal, almost divine knowledge he might well be called 'the astounding wonder of our time.'[5]

Cardinal Ehrle states that the title 'Magnus' cannot be proved to have been applied to Albert in the thirteenth and fourteenth centuries, and is of opinion that it came into use among the chroniclers and not in the Schools.[6] Grabmann was lucky enough to be able to trace the title without question to the middle of the fourteenth century.[7] He found it in the *Liber certarum historiarum*, by Johann von Victring. That the Schools also had a share in bringing this title into use is clear from the fact that Albert while he was still alive was called magnus philosophus, for instance by Raymund Martini.[8] Furthermore F. Pelster was able to prove that in a codex of the fourteenth century with questions to the Sentences of Peter Lombard, therefore a theological textbook, the phrase Albertus Magnus is repeatedly found.[9] It is quite true that this appellation did not come into general use until the fifteenth century. Henry of Hereford, who gives so much information on Albert that he may be regarded as the first biographer of the Saint, and who can never introduce sufficient epithets of praise to satisfy himself, calls him 'the most brilliant universal luminary of the whole of Christendom,[10] but had not yet, when he wrote, come across the particular title in question. Luis de Valladolid in his important vita does quote it.[11] Since then it has been universally used. Magnus is the precise expression for what all felt when thinking of this quite extra-ordinary man. The superabundance of his

[5] Petrus de Prussia : *Vita beati Alberti Magni*, 260.

[6] F. Ehrle, S.J. : *Die Ehrentitel der scholastischen Lehrer des Mittelalters*, 3.

[7] M. Grabmann, op. cit., 13.

[8] Raymundus Martini, O.P. : *Pugio fidei* iii, 445.

[9] Franz Pelster, S.J. : *Die Ehrentitel der scholastischen Lehrer des Mittelalters*, 43.

[10] Henricus de Hervordia, O.P. : *Liber de rebus memorabilibus sive Chronicon*, 196.

[11] Printed in *Catalogus codicum hagiographicorum bibliothecæ regiæ Bruxellensis*, 95–105.

learning, which simply overpowered his posterity, forced this expression into use.

Nowadays, when bibliophiles are not easily astonished by the sight of a stately row of volumes all by the same author, and do not halt at the first perhaps overwhelming impression, but test the value of the books in detail, it will be our task also to show in detail that Albert's learning does justify that title of honour. And we shall go on to show that on other grounds besides exceptional learning he justly deserved, and always will deserve, to be called the Great.

ALBERT THE GREAT

THE EXTERIOR GREATNESS

WHY is it that Albertus, the Dominican Bishop of Regensburg, bears the title Magnus? A simple, all too simple, explanation was given by the two scholars Vives and Heumann, who took Magnus to be the Latin version of the German family name de Grote.[1] In doing so they however overlooked the fact that Albert sprang from the noble family of the lords of Bollstädt.

Nor did Albert owe the title to his outward appearance, as was the case with Albert I, Duke of Braunschweig, who was called Magnus to distinguish him from his son Albert who was nicknamed Pinguis.[2] If the Dominican Albert's physical stature had been the cause of this appellation, he would have been given it by his contemporaries, and not first by scholars in the century following his death. Moreover, according to the best and most reliable of his biographers he was, if anything, small in stature. Thus Johannes Meyer[3] several times calls him 'the great Albrecht, great in intellect and small of person.' This smallness may at times have been merely used as a rhetorical embellishment, as in the legend, reported by Peter of Prussia, that Albert was so short that the Pope had at an audience begged him to stand up, under the impression that he was kneeling.[4]

[1] Fabricius: *Bibliotheca latina Mediæ et Infimæ Ætatis*, i, 113.

[2] Hermann Korner, O.P.: *Chronica novella*, 23.

[3] Johannes Meyer, O.P.: *Liber de viris illustribus Ordinis Prædicatorum*, 40. The references from Meyer's works have been grouped together by P. Albert in his *Zur Lebensgeschichte des Albertus Magnus*, 203–298.

[4] Petrus de Prussia: *Vita beati Alberti Magni*, 320.

Rudolf of Nymegen, relying on a statement by Humbert, the Master-General of the Order, makes the point that he was of an engaging figure.[5] Thomas de Chantimpré, Albert's pupil, repeats without questioning it the statement of Gavilus, the Augustinian Provost, who said that the sign by which he had recognized Albert was not the form of his body, but a mole on the eyelid.[6] Certainly Albert was strongly built; Humbert, the Master-General, alludes to this in the letter in which he tried to deter Albert from accepting the bishopric of Regensburg. He there speaks of the gigantic shoulders[7] on which he has borne the yoke of the Order. Rudolf, too, mentions his colossal strength in the shoulders. The medical report at the inspection of the relics of the Saint on November 12th, 1859, points to a powerfully built man of medium height.[8] The size of the chasuble which is shown in Cologne as having belonged to Albert, cannot be adduced as an argument against this, for in all probability it is not the one in which the Saint was originally buried.

If the title Magnus did not derive from Albert's bodily appearance, a certain exterior greatness can nevertheless be ascribed to him, insomuch as he belonged by descent to, and for a considerable time moved in, the circles frequented by those who are generally called the great of this world. Albert sprang from the family of the lords of Bollstädt, as Rudolf of Nymegen tells us.[9] The ancestral castles of these nobles lay six hours north of Lauingen. The castle is destroyed, but the village of the same name preserves its memory. The family did not belong to the high independent nobility, but to the official nobility, which was called 'ministerial' and had to fill certain imperial offices and posts of honour. It was one of these which Albert's father

[5] Rudolphus de Novimagio: *Legenda literalis de beato Alberto Magno*, 42.

[6] Thomas Cantimpratanus: *Bonum universale de apibus*, 143.

[7] Petrus de Prussia: op. cit., 255.

[8] Heinrich Goblet: *Der selige Albertus Magnus und die Geschichte seiner Reliquien*, 97.

[9] Rudolphus de Novimagio: op. cit., 8; but see Heribert Christian Scheeben: *Albertus Magnus*, 205, and his *Albert der Grosse: Zur Chronologie seines Lebens*, 5 *sqq*. [Ed.]

held in Lauingen, and it was here that in all probability the Saint first saw the light in the year 1193. This date, which is to-day still in dispute,[10] follows from the statement that Albert died in the year 1280, at the age of eighty-seven. That the lovely little Swabian town of Lauingen, which at that time was directly under the emperor, and only came under Bavarian rule in 1270, was his birthplace, is proved by the seal which Albert used before his elevation to the episcopate. He had had engraved on it the inscription, 'Sigillum Fr. Alberti de Lauging O.Pr.'[11] But very little information of his family circumstances has come down to us. We know for certain that his younger brother Henry, who also entered the Dominican Order, was Prior of the Convent at Würzburg at the time when Albert made his will, and was named as one of his executors.[12] According to tradition, a sister of Albert's is said to have been a nun in the Dominican cloister at Schwäbisch-Gmünd.[13] The Saint remembered the convent in his will, but he did the same for the Dominican convents of S. Mark in Würzburg and S. Catharine in Augsburg. The latter convent thought it also might claim to have had one of Albert's sisters as an inmate. There is documentary evidence relating to various members of the family in the thirteenth and fourteenth centuries, e.g. a Rudolf Bollstädter, a Siegfried Bollstädter, and Hans Bollstädter, who were all in the imperial service.[14] Their precise degree of relationship with Albertus Magnus cannot be determined. On the male side the family died out in the year 1607. No other member of the family has achieved any prominence.

Albert's parents were rich and pious. They gave their

[10] Franz Pelster, S.J.: *Kritische Studien zu den Schriften Alberts des Grossen*, 34–52. For a note on the chronology of the saint's life and on the dispute relative to the date of his birth, see Appendix C. [Ed.]

[11] Paulus von Loë, O.P.: *De vita et de scriptis Alberti Magni.*

[12] Joachim Sighart: *Albertus Magnus*, 248.

[13] Klaus: *Zur Geschichte der Klöster der ehemaligen Reichsstadt Schwäbisch-Gmünd.*

[14] Pfeifer & Platz: *Kurze Geschichte der Stadt Lauingen und des seligen Albertus Magnus*, 80 *sq.*

children an education and training proper to their position. It is uncertain whether Albert and Henry were privately educated or went to a convent school;[15] in any event their instruction was thorough, as we can see from what Albert accomplished. They took their recreation in hunting, and Albert himself tells how as a youngster he had gone after pigeons with dogs, and had been helped by wild falcons. Again the fight between an eagle and a swan which he so graphically describes, would seem to have been observed by him at that time near his home.[16] As a boy he may well have got from his father's huntsmen and labourers many of the stories of the animal world which he later inserted in his great book on natural history.

When he was about twenty years old, following the usual custom of the German youth of that day, he wandered forth across the Alps into Italy, in order to finish his studies there. An excursion to Paris in pursuit of his studies cannot be regarded as precluded, but there is no sure tradition on this point. It is certain, as we know from his own account, that he lived for some time in Venice and Padua. In the latter town it was the study of the liberal arts which chiefly claimed his attention. A kindly uncle watched over his career. Again, reports on natural phenomena observed in that place led him to make mention of his stay there. In Lombardy he experienced a prolonged earthquake.[17] In Venice some blocks of marble were being sawn up for the decoration of a church, and in one of them he saw the head of a man with a long beard and crowned with a royal crown. The only fault in it was its rather too high forehead.[18] Emil Michael sees in the fact that Albert was asked for an explanation of this phenomenon a proof that 'he was more assiduous than others in the study of the natural sciences and that his superior knowledge in this

[15] Dr. Schenz in his paper: *Altes und Neues über Albert den Grossen*, suggests S. Ulrich's convent at Augsburg.

[16] *De animalibus*, 617, 601. References to this work and to the *De vegitabilibus* will be to the new editions (Berlin, 1867, and Münster i. W., 1916, 1921, respectively), those to other of the saint's works in general to the Opera Omnia.

[17] *Meteororum*, lib. 3, tr. 2, cap. 9.

[18] *Mineralium*, lib. 2, tr. 3, cap. 1.

field was fully recognized.'[19] In Padua he saw a well which had long been closed up. When it was opened two men who descended into it were asphyxiated by the foul vapours which filled the shaft, while a third man who had only leant over the edge was stupefied and lay unconscious for two hours.[20]

Albert spent getting on for ten years studying in Italy, and then, in the year 1223, the great change took place in his life. Of this we have in the *Vitæ Fratrum Ordinis Prædicatorum* by Girardus de Fracheto an account which is said to be a report of what Albert himself told of the matter. The second Master-General of the Order of Preachers, Jordan of Saxony, made it his personal endeavour, by sermons and lectures delivered in the schools, to get recruits for the Order. His letters to Blessed Diana of Andalo, which have come down to us, give an insight into his activity. There are two letters for the year 1223 in which he joyfully announces that as a result of his sermons he has admitted forty-three candidates into the Order. Among them was Albert.[21] The report in the *Vitæ Fratrum* runs: 'A brother, a man of excellent reputation and great sanctity, who excelled in the sciences and was Provincial of the German province of the Order, and a Master in Theology, while he was still a very young man and was studying in Padua, had been led by the exhortation of the Friars and especially by the preaching of Master Jordan, to the desire to enter the Order, but nevertheless not yet quite seriously, since his uncle, who at that time was living there, was opposed to it. The latter even went so far as to make him promise under oath not to set foot in the house of the Friars within a certain period. When the time expired he was a frequent visitor at the Friars and in fact became more confirmed in his resolve than ever, but the fear that he might come out again made him again hold back. One night he dreamt that he entered the Order, but after a short time came out again. When he awoke he was

[19] Emil Michael: *Geschichte des deutschen Volkes*, iii, 71.

[20] *Meteororum*, lib. 3, tr. 2, cap. 12.

[21] Altaner: *Die Briefe Jordans von Sachsen*, 25; but see H. Chr. Scheeben: *Albertus Magnus*, 25 *sq.*

right glad that he had not entered, and said to himself: "Now I do see that what I feared would befall me, if I entered there!" On this very day it chanced that he was present at a sermon by Master Jordan, and the latter spoke among other things of the assaults and snares of the Devil. Jordan said in his sermon: "There are those who have a mind to forsake the world and to enter the Order, but the Devil deludes them in a dream that they would come out of it again, or they see themselves mounted on a charger or clothed in scarlet or utterly alone or among their dear ones, and all this only to inspire fear of entering it, as if they would not be able to persevere, or, if they have already entered, to strike terror and confusion into them." At this the young man was astonished beyond measure, and after the sermon went to the preacher and said to him: "Master, who has laid bare my heart to you?" Then he set forth before him all his thoughts as above reported and the dream. But the Master had a robust trust in God, and armed him in sundry ways against temptation of this kind. The latter was wholly transformed by his words, made an end of all hesitation, and entered the Order. This was related by the brother who added that the thought of the promise of that holy man was of singular help to him against all the temptations, whether from the Devil or the world, which assailed him in the Order.'[22] To all appearances his entrance took place in Padua, though Johannes Meyer suggests Cologne.[23] For the pursuit of his theological studies Bologna was the appropriate place, though Cologne could also be considered. Relying on a passage in Thomas de Chantimpré, Emil Michael is inclined to accord to Paris the honour of having introduced Albert to theology.[24] The Saint himself is said to have related that in Paris a brother had tried to persuade him to desist from study. Since such an attempt could hardly have been made with a professor, such as in later years Albert was in Paris, it is natural to think of him as being there as a student. This

[22] Girardus de Fracheto: *Vitæ Fratrum Ordinis Prædicatorum*, 187*sq*.
[23] P. Albert, op. cit., 7; H. Ch. Scheeben, op. cit. See also Appendix C.
[24] E. Michael: op. cit., iii, 74.

assumption receives some corroboration in the fact that the Paris house of studies was the most famous, and that from all the Provinces the most gifted were sent there to pursue their studies.

After ordination to the priesthood and the completion of these studies Albert was at once employed in teaching. In about 1228 he started on this work which was to occupy the greater part of his long and fruitful life. Henry of Hereford mentions that Albert held the post of Lector first in the Hildesheim convent, then in Freiburg im Breisgau, then for two years in Regensburg, and after that in Strassburg.[25] As the convent at Hildesheim was founded in 1233, it is probable that Albert was the first Lector of this house. At that time there had to be a Lector in every Dominican convent, whose duty it was to deliver lectures. The subject they taught was Holy Scripture or moral theology. Since the office of Lector in any given convent was as a rule held for one year only, and the convent at Freiburg was not founded till 1235, Albert must either have been employed in the interim in other houses or held the office in one or more convents for several years. Pelster thus sums up the results of his researches on this point: 'We must content ourselves with the conclusion that Albert taught in Hildesheim after 1233, in Freiburg after 1235, in Cologne in any case in 1244–1245 and perhaps for some considerable time previous to this. The Regensburg and Strassburg periods fall between 1236 and 1244.'[26] In Cologne the Saint delivered a series of critical lectures on the sentences of Peter Lombard; and it was hither that, in 1244 or at latest 1245, Thomas Aquinas, as an eighteen-year-old youth, was sent by the Master-General, John the Teuton, to be his pupil.[27] In the long years of his teaching activity many eager and gifted students sat at Albert's feet; we have only to think of Ambrose Sansedonius, Ulrich of Strassburg, Thomas de Chantimpré; but not one of them was so gifted as this young cadet of a noble Neapolitan family, in not one of them did Albert see his

[25] Henricus de Hervordia: op. cit., 201.
[26] F. Pelster: op. cit., 84.
[27] Guillelmus de Tocco: *Legenda sancti Thomæ Aquinatis*, 662.

hopes realized so immeasurably as they were in Thomas Aquinas. The relations between the two were very intimate. The discerning teacher soon recognized the capabilities of this silent pupil, who was misjudged by so many, and got them publicly recognized, and furthered them with all his might and main. Tradition has it that they occupied adjoining cells and shared one another's most intimate thoughts. Albert was summoned to Paris in 1245 to deliver the lectures necessary to the acquisition of a doctor's degree, and many historians therefore assume that Thomas accompanied him thither. This assumption is not necessary, for Albert returned to Cologne in 1248, and, since Thomas studied there for nine years, he could in any case have had the benefit of Albert's direction for four or five years.[28]

In Paris the Saint lectured on the subject he had already twice treated in Cologne, with such learning and address that he filled everyone with wonder. The title Doctor of Theology in his case really answered to the facts. The esteem in which he was held, in what was at that time the chief centre of learning, is shown by the invitation he received to take part as an expert in the examination of the Talmud, which the Papal Legate, Odo, Bishop of Tusculum, had put in hand. In the findings of this Commission Albert is expressly cited, and for the first time, as Doctor of Sacred Theology.[29] The Dominican Order had the wisdom to appreciate Albert's capabilities. The Chapter-General held in Paris in June 1248 had decided that a Studium Generale, modelled on that at Paris, should be instituted in four other provinces of the Order.[30] For Germany they had Cologne in view, and the execution of this plan was entrusted to Albert. The reputation which the house of studies in Cologne at once acquired, justified the confidence of the Order in its Regent. The highest secular and ecclesiastical circles in Germany held the new Master in honour and appreciated his importance. At the beginning of the year 1249 King William of Holland came

[28] Michael: op. cit., iii, 77; Pelster: op. cit., 80.
[29] *Chartularium Universitatis Parisiensis*, i, 209 n., 178.
[30] *Acta Capitulorum Ordinis Prædicatorum*, i, 41.

to the metropolis of the Rhineland and, according to an old tradition, visited our Saint in the Dominican convent on the feast of the Epiphany. Legend has invested this event with a magical significance and would have it that Albert by a spell transformed a winter landscape into a blossoming, sunny, springlike garden.[31] As a mark of royal favour the completion of the convent at Utrecht was guaranteed to the Order. At Albert's request Archbishop Conrad of Hochstaden on May 7, 1249, conferred various privileges on the burghers of Cologne.[32] It is probable that it was immediately after his return from Paris that he was asked to inspect the old remains of the building which had been exposed in excavating the foundations of the new cathedral. Albert himself speaks of this inspection and cannot refrain from expressing his admiration for the ground plan and magnificence of those old buildings, which could still be recognized from the ruins.[33]

Albert remained Regent of Studies in Cologne till 1254, fully occupied with his lectures and literary work. His growing influence outside the Order is most clearly seen in his relations with the Papal Legate, Hugo of S. Cher, for whom he acted on several occasions. It was with him that he was appointed joint arbitrator in the dispute between the citizens of Cologne and the Archbishop.

His own German province showed its very great trust in him by electing him Provincial at the Chapter held in Worms in 1254. This province was at that time the largest in the whole Order, including as it did all countries of German speech. Albert brilliantly met all its expectations. He not merely held regularly every year a Provincial Chapter, and was zealous in visiting the individual houses, but he also promoted the true spirit of the Order everywhere, by admonition, by punishment where necessary, by encouragement, and by praise. Above all he sought to keep alive the spirit of voluntary poverty, and failings on this

[31] Paulus Maria von Loë, O.P.: *Kritische Streifzüge auf dem Gebiet der Albertus Magnus-Forschung*, 119.

[32] Paulus von Loë, O.P.: *De vita et de scriptis Alberti Magni*, ii, 285.

[33] *De causis elementorum*, lib. i, tr. 2, cap. 3.

point were inexorably punished according to the severe code of those days. A brother on whom money was found after his death was refused burial in consecrated ground.[34] Even the Priors of Minden, Trier, and Krems, who, contrary to the spirit of poverty, had without due need used animal transport, did not escape, but were punished by scourgings, fasts, and recitation of the penitential psalms.[35] Albert sought to instil into superiors great care for and charity towards their subordinates. He himself gave to all the best example of devoted, unwearying, self-sacrificing charity. Begging his way, he traversed the German-speaking countries on foot from the Rhine to Silesia and from the North Sea to the borders of Hungary. The writings which he composed in the various houses he left behind him as mementoes.

Albert likewise did all he could for the extension of the Order within his jurisdiction. Three houses for men were started during his rule, at Strassburg (1254), Seehusen (1255) and Rostok (1256),[36] while the Paradise nunnery in Soest, the foundation of which was begun by the Master-General, John the Teuton, was completed during Albert's term of office. Albert himself received the vows of the first twelve sisters and preached to the little band with as much animation as if they had been a multitude. He commended to them above everything faithful observance of the closure and holy poverty, and warned them against receiving unsuitable members.[37]

As if the heavy obligations of his office were not enough even for a man of Albert's strength, we find him being saddled with work from outside. The exceedingly complicated difficulties which existed between the town of Cologne and Archbishop Conrad of Hochstaden, were submitted to him for adjustment. The dangers threatening the activity of members of the Order at the Paris University, and in the last resort the very existence of the Mendicant

[34] Petrus de Prussia : op. cit., 212. [35] Ibid., 205.

[36] P. de Loë : *De vita, etc.*, 285.

[37] J. Suitbert Seibertz : *Quellen der Westfälischen Geschichte*, 4–13 ; and by the same : *Geschichte der Stiftung des Klosters Paradies bei Soest*, 267–290.

Orders, which were being stirred up by the Paris professors, were averted by Albertus Magnus. The arguments of their adversaries were set out by the canonist professor, William of Saint-Amour, in his book, *De novissimis temporum periculis*. The dispute was referred to the Pope, who summoned the parties to the Papal Court, which at that time was at Anagni. The case for the Mendicant Orders was stated by the Master-General of the Franciscans (John of Parma), the Master-General of the Dominicans (Humbert de Romanis), Thomas Aquinas, and Albert. According to the trustworthy report of Henry of Hereford,[38] it was not Thomas but Albert who played the chief rôle at the sittings of the Conference. Immediately on his arrival he had got hold of a copy of the book referred to above, had it copied, and utilized the twenty-four hours before the Consistory met to master its contents. When the book was read out at the sitting Albert was able to make such telling replies in refutation, that the opposing side ignominiously subsided. On October 5, 1256, Pope Alexander IV declared the book to be 'irrational and detestable,' and ordered it to be burnt. Thomas collected Albert's arguments in his opusculum, *Contra impugnantes Dei cultum et religionem.* Albert's stay at the Curia seems to have been somewhat protracted, for mention is made of lectures on S. John's Gospel which he is said to have delivered before the Cardinals at that time.[39] He is therefore sometimes also referred to as Master of the Sacred Palace.

This journey to Anagni and his stay there made it difficult for him properly to look after the affairs of the German province of the Order, and on this ground, and also we may take it at Albert's own urgent request, he was relieved of his office as Provincial at the Chapter-General held in Florence in 1257. He seems, however, to have continued to discharge his duties until the following year.

[38] Henricus de Hervordia : op. cit., 197.

[39] Thomas Cantimpratanus : op. cit., 141. It was perhaps during this stay at the Curia, but more probably during his second stay in 1261–2, that Albert made the journey to Greece, of which there is a tradition, possibly to consult with William of Moerbeke about new translations of Aristotle's works he was undertaking, probably at Albert's instance. See Appendix C. [Ed.]

His hope to be able to devote himself undisturbed to scientific work in the Studium Generale in Cologne was realized for but a short time. The diocese of Regensburg had been brought into utter disorder through the bad administration of Bishop Albert, Graf von Pöttigau. Pope Alexander removed the unworthy prelate from his office and looked round for a man who should be capable of restoring peace and order in the diocese. Albertus Magnus was personally known to the Pope, and Alexander IV in this extremely difficult situation set his hopes on him, and on January 5, 1260, without further ado appointed him to the bishopric of Regensburg.[40] Humbert, the Master-General, tried to put a stop to this, for he wished to keep such a force for the Order, but it was in vain.[41] On March 29, 1260, Albert repaired to Regensburg as bishop. An old chronicler describes the state of the episcopal Curia thus : 'Albert found no gold in the treasury, not a drop of wine in the cellars, and in the barns not a grain of corn.'[42] This describes the distressful material state ; the spiritual and religious conditions were no better. However, Albert set to work with his usual energy, and soon succeeded by rigid economy and wise management in settling the greater part of the debts and in putting a stop to the worst of the distress. He intervened with the greatest severity against those who were injuring the Church in regard to her temporal possessions ; to the poor and oppressed he was open-handed in his generosity. He kindled his clergy by precept and example to live a life of purity and piety and to be faithful in their care of the souls entrusted to them. By his persevering efforts he succeeded in a very short time in restoring the whole diocese. He himself, however, even in pontifical vestments and crowned with the mitre, remained the same simple, pious, industrious Religious. The stout shoes which he had formerly worn on his wanderings he still used as bishop, and they earned him the nickname of the bishop 'cum bottis.'[43] In the following

[40] J. Quétif and J. Echard, O.P. : *Scriptores Ordinis Prædicatorum*, i, 168.

[41] Petrus de Prussia : op. cit., 252 *sqq*.

[42] Orfele : *Rerum Boicarum scriptores*, 207.

[43] Rudolphus de Novimagio : op. cit., 46.

SCHIMMELTURM (WHITE HORSE TOWER) AND MEMORIAL TO THE SAINT IN THE ALBERTUS MAGNUS PLATZ IN HIS BIRTHPLACE, LAUINGEN

year Albert went to Rome to beg the Pope to relieve him of his episcopal office; and on February 25, 1262, he is for the last time designated Bishop of Regensburg. On May 11 of the same year Urban IV sanctioned the choice of Dean Leo as Albert's successor in the See of Regensburg. Albert, however, was not able immediately to return to the cloister as a simple Religious; he was retained at the Curia and soon after was appointed to preach the crusade in the German-speaking countries, and in this service he spent the following years travelling over the whole of Germany. The Franciscan Berthold helped him in this important work, which dragged on for several years. After this, Albert seems to have made his headquarters first in the Dominican house at Würzburg, where his brother Heinrich was probably Prior, and then in Strassburg, where his beloved pupil Ulrich was Lector. In the year 1270 he returned to Cologne, and from then on, save for a few short journeys which took the tireless man away, he remained in that city engaged in teaching, writing, and the care of souls. Only two greater events broke the repose of his old age. In 1274 he attended the Council of Lyons[44] and secured the recognition of Rudolf of Hapsburg as ruler of Germany. In 1277 he was again in Paris for a time, in order to defend the teaching of his pupil Thomas Aquinas, who had preceded him to eternal life.[45] Returning to Cologne, he devoted his last years and his dwindling powers solely to pious practices. On November 15, 1280, he died peacefully in his cell, sitting in an arm-chair, surrounded by his praying brethren.

Although by birth Albert belonged to the great of this world, although for a great part of his long life he frequented the circles in which they lived, and though he accomplished great things in all the positions which he held, yet the outward course of his life is not so out of the ordinary as to be a ground for the title of Magnus.

[44] Paulus von Loë: *Albert der Grosse auf dem Konzil von Lyon, 1274.*

[45] *Acta Sanctorum Martii*, i, 714.

THE INTERIOR GREATNESS

I. THE INTELLECTUAL GREATNESS OF ALBERT AS SCIENTIST

OUR age justly boasts of its achievements in the exact sciences; indeed at no period has scientific interest been centred in the study of nature to such an extent as it is to-day. If, however, its magnificent discoveries must be unreservedly recognized, it has to be admitted that never were the methods pursued in the field of natural science so unscientific as they were in the days of Häckel, Fellerbach, Büchner, when the learning of a host of naturalists culminated in the attempt to prove that they, with the rest of us, had been evolved 'from jelly-fish, through fishes, amphibians, and reptiles to the more developed mammals, and thence through the apes to the finished product Man.'[1] A biogenetic principle of such a kind, which runs counter to established facts as well as to the laws of accurate thinking, could only have been advanced by the modern scientific temper which is inimical to the Faith, with the result that it has ranged itself at a level far lower than the much-abused Middle Ages, when, though unfortunately natural science was neglected, it was at any rate not profaned.

This neglect was to some extent due to circumstances. Mediæval man was heir to two important legacies: the treasures of the Græco-Roman culture and the Christian faith. With correct judgement he lavished on the latter, as being the more important, his whole enthusiasm; since, too, it supplied, what all the wisdom of Greece and Rome could never do, the answer to the most fundamental problems of existence, and a conception and rule of life which alone could satisfy the mind. In consequence

[1] Robert Kosmas Lewin: *Apostaten-Briefe*, 271.

of the conditions prevalent in the Middle Ages, with wars raging almost all the time, with the nations striving for some settled form of government, with the masses in a state of dependence, and the great ones of the earth preoccupied by military affairs, it was only the clerics who devoted themselves to the study of the sciences, with the natural consequence that theology dominated everything, and from the inheritance from antiquity only that was taken which would best serve towards the understanding and development of that science.

Mediæval man was for the most part occupied out of doors, whether as soldier, peasant, fisherman, or hunter, and since modern means of communication were not open to him, he was, on his journeyings and pilgrimages, almost of necessity brought into the closest relation with the exuberant life of the countryside of those days. He had, too, in general, a good practical knowledge of the objects around him, and for more than this he had no desire. If such a desire were aroused in him, he satisfied it with what was offered him by the clergy, who used natural objects to explain the supernatural mysteries of the Faith.

The textbook in common use was the *Physiologus.* In this work, information, mainly in the form of fairy tales and fables, was collected about animals, serpents, and stones, and their good or bad influence on the fortunes of human beings. The pagan nucleus in all this, greatly enlarged by Christian additions, had developed into a kind of religious natural history. In the *Physiologus*, too, may be seen the source of that rich symbolism which found expression in the architecture of the Middle Ages. Even in Albert's day the statements in this book were accepted by such naturalists as Vincent de Beauvais and Thomas de Chantimpré, while Albert himself did not quite shake himself free from its influence, though he often rightly and severely criticized its teaching. His merit lay in the fact that he went back beyond this popular book to the scientific labours of the Ancient World, and in particular to the writings of Aristotle on the natural sciences, and by establishing contact with them furthered the progress of true science.

We can hardly be surprised that in a man like Albert

the study of the profound works of Aristotle should have aroused the greatest enthusiasm for the Greeks of antiquity. That, however, he considered natural science as conterminous with the knowledge of Aristotle, as Hertling[2] seems to hint, is opposed to all the facts. Albert recognized the authority of the Greek, but he was also aware that no one man can know everything from personal experience, nor can he even verify everything, but must primarily take his stand on the previous work of others. For him the work of Aristotle was such preliminary labour. It is thus that his oft-quoted saying must be understood, that 'in matters concerned with faith and morals the greatest authority attaches to Augustine, with medicine to Galen, and with natural science to Aristotle.'[3] It frequently happens that where Albert has investigated a subject for himself, he differs from Aristotle. Thus the Greek had declared that a lunar rainbow only occurs twice in fifty years; to which Albert opposes the fact that such a rainbow had been seen twice within one year.[4] He states explicitly that to him the Greek is a man subject to error like any other man, and that only one who regarded him as God could suppose that he had never made a mistake.[5] Moreover, Albert could not have allowed unlimited authority to Aristotle without contradicting his own fundamental conception of natural science, for he is emphatic that the task of the natural philosopher does not lie in simply taking over the reports of others, but in investigating the causes operative in natural phenomena. Albert knew, and stressed the point, that the acquisition of such knowledge, which can only be the result of detailed observation, must often entail much time and trouble, since it is not sufficient to have made an observation in one way. It is only by repeating it under the most varied conditions, that the true cause underlying the phenomenon may be ascertained with any certainty.

In these principles Albert is in accord with the greatest

[2] Georg von Hertling: *Albertus Magnus, Beiträge zu seiner Würdigung*, 40.

[3] *II Sententiarum*, dist. 13, art. 2.

[4] *Meteororum*, lib. 3, tr. 4, cap. 11.

[5] *Physicorum*, lib. 8, tr. 1, cap. 14.

investigators of modern times. The same reverent awe was characteristic of him as inspired Linnæus, who strode through the wealth of natural forms merely classifying as he went. Albert was endowed with a singular gift for the investigation of nature ; a keen eye well adapted to the observation and determination of the slightest variation ; a calm judgement capable of excluding any but sure results ; above all a sensitive heart which embraced in its love the whole of nature down to its smallest elements. His own statements betray the interest which he took in all that went on in this field. The earliest information we have about his boyhood is connected with notes on occurrences in the animal and vegetable world ; for instance, the note on the sagacity of the hawks which helped him on his pigeon hunts and afterwards waited to get their share of the booty ; so, too, the note on the migration of fishes, which, according to Endres, he had observed as a youth ;[6] though it is true that most researchers assign these observations to the time when he was a bishop. The long journeys on foot which Albert made, while still a youth, to Italy, and in that country, offered him every opportunity to follow his inclination to investigate the secrets of nature. In Padua it was the asphyxiating gas in a choked-up well, in Venice the design in a block of marble, which arrested his attention. That he was asked to explain these is a clear proof of the regard in which he was held as a natural philosopher, even before his entry into the Order.[7] Nor when he was actually in the Order had these interests of his to be repressed, for the offices which he held as Regent of various convents, and still more as Provincial, when it was his duty to visit the widely scattered houses of the Order on German soil, took him again and again out of his cell into God's open country, and so into the field of his researches in natural history. This does not mean to say that he did not carry out personal observations in the cloister. His detailed report on the habits of spiders will have been made by himself from observations in his cell, while he had every

[6] *De animalibus*, 522 *sq.* ; J. A. Endres : *Albertus Magnus und die bischöfliche Burg Donaustauf*, 830.

[7] Michael : op. cit., iii, 71.

opportunity of observing bees at his leisure in the garden of his convent at Cologne.

In the natural sciences Albert held personal observation to be by far the best criterion ; what is taken over from the observations of others is of secondary importance. He makes this clear at the beginning of the sixth book of his treatise on botany : 'What I have to say on the various plant species is partly the result of my own observations, and partly taken from the reports of others, but only when I was convinced that these contained conclusions based on their own careful observation.'[8] He regarded Aristotle's reports as particularly reliable, whence his close correspondence with him. That Albert was acquainted with and used the works of later naturalists is probable ; and Stadler mentions the names of Anthimius, Alexander Nekam, Arnoldus Saxo, and the holy Abbess Hildegard von Bingen ; but it has not yet been established whether there is any close relation between their work and his.

As his collected works show, Albert treated almost the whole range of natural philosophy. Wimmer aptly remarks : 'Albert studied and described the whole cosmos from the stars to the stones.'[9] His motive for compiling these works did not lie in his teaching duties, as was the case with his theological, and later, after the revision of the order of studies, his philosophical writings ; for the natural sciences, even after this reform in the Dominican curriculum, were not officially pursued. Nor, again, was it the wealth of his personal knowledge seeking an outlet in this manner. Albert himself gives as his reason the persistent and reiterated pressure put on him by his brethren. 'Our object in these treatises on Natural Science is to meet, as far as lies in our

[8] *De vegetabilibus*, 340. Balss, in his *Albertus Magnus als Zoologe*, p. 7, remarks : 'Stadler, following the example of Jessen in the latter's edition of the *De vegetabilibus*, has done admirable work in separating the passages which are Albert's own property or in which his own words are used, from those in which he has slavishly followed his sources. Hence the older estimates of Albert by men like Pouchet, V. Carus, Bloch, Killermann, and others, no longer hold in the light of modern criticism, since they frequently saddle Albert with the views of his predecessors.'

[9] J. Wimmer : *Deutsches Pflanzenleben nach Albertus Magnus*, 7.

power, the wishes of the brothers of our Order, who now for several years have been begging us to compile such a book on the things of nature, as would give them a complete natural history, by means of which they could arrive at a sufficient understanding of Aristotle's writings. Though we do not consider ourselves to be equal to such a work, we could not resist the wishes of the brethren. Yielding to the supplications of some of them, we have at last consented, and have taken up the work, which we had often refused to do. We do this first to the honour of Almighty God, who is the source of wisdom, and the Creator, Orderer, and Sovereign of Nature; then for the benefit of the brethren and with them of all who may wish to read it and acquire a knowledge of nature from it. In this work our method will be to follow the arrangement and the views of Aristotle and to say what is necessary in explanation and demonstration, without, however, quoting the actual text. Besides this we shall make digressions in order to discuss the doubtful points which arise, and to supplement whatever remains obscure in this philosopher's teaching owing to a too concise presentation of the subject. We shall divide up the whole work into chapters. Where the title simply indicates the subject matter of a chapter, this will mean that this chapter is taken from Aristotle's works. Where, however, an addition is made to the title, we have there included matter of our own, supplementary to and in demonstration of the said subject. We shall also here and there fill up the gaps in defective portions of books, and occasionally make up the deficiencies in incomplete or missing books, which were either not written by Aristotle or have not come down to us. Where, however, this occurs, it will be made clear in the treatise which follows.'[10]

Albert remained true to this plan, and accordingly his works on the Natural Sciences are, as Stadler remarks, properly speaking only 'glossed paraphrases of the corresponding books of the great Stagyrite.'[11] The point must,

[10] *Physicorum*: lib. 1, tr. 1, cap. 1; also printed by Jessen in his edition of the *De vegetabilibus*.

[11] Hermann Stadler: *Albertus Magnus von Cöln als Naturforscher und das Cölner Autogramm seiner Tiergeschichte*, 4.

however, be made that Albert does not take up a position subservient to Aristotle, but by his side, that he criticizes, supplements, and corrects him. His own observations and rich experience serve him well in the explanation of what are often very meagre expositions, and since his examples are drawn from the natural life of his own Germany, they were brought more home to his countrymen and were the more easily intelligible. Albert has added so much of his own, and has pondered over, and himself experienced, what he has taken over to such an extent, that these writings are virtually original works.

Not only did Albert follow the method he had prescribed for himself, but he also actually gave an exposition of all the subjects which he had undertaken to treat. He wrote on astronomy, meteorology, climatology, physics, mechanics, chemistry, alchemy, mineralogy, anthropology, zoology, and botany. Here we shall only seek to appraise in some detail the services he rendered in the two branches of natural science which have in more recent times been the subject of particular investigation and exposition by specialists, namely botany and zoology.

1. *Albertus Magnus and the Flora.*

In investigating and describing the plant world Albert took as his text the pseudo-Aristotelian work *De plantis*, without, however, in any way blindly following its author. He enlarges the text by three books and adds several chapters to the five books of the original. He everywhere illustrates the text by his own observations and experiments, and is always pleased when he can substitute examples taken from the plant life of Germany for those drawn from other countries. In this way the old work is completely transformed and doubled in size. The experiences which Albert here sets out in all probability date from the years 1254–1257, when as Provincial of the German province of the Order he traversed the country in every direction on foot. In this connexion it is, however, certainly worthy of remark that the examples quoted in his botany are principally taken from Northern Germany.

MODEL OF THE OLD DOMINICAN PRIORY IN COLOGNE

This work of Albert's is the best which the whole of the Middle Ages produced in this field. Nevertheless with the passage of time it fell into almost total oblivion. Important researchers, such as Heller, Sprengler, etc., were in general ignorant of it,[12] and on the strength of some writings falsely ascribed to him, regarded Albert as a botanist of no importance whatever and hardly worthy of mention. It is true that Alexander von Humboldt did go back to the genuine works of the Saint, but it was Ernst Meyer who first recognized the whole importance of Albert's services to botany, and repeatedly drew attention to them. As early as the year 1836 he wrote : 'Prior to Albert we do not find a single botanist who can be compared to him with the exception of Theophrastus, whom he did not know ; and after him no one who had generally such a vivid conception of the nature of plants or had pondered over it more deeply, until we come to Conrad Gessner and Cesalpini. To the man, however, who was the complete master of all the learning of his day and definitely advanced it, who for three centuries was never equalled, let alone surpassed, the finest laurels are rightly due.'[13] In his celebrated history of botany Meyer returns to the subject of Albert and emphasizes the point that between Aristotle-Theophrastus on the one hand and Cesalpini (1583) on the other, that is to say over a period of more than two thousand years, Albert stands out as the solitary representative of a truly scientific theory of botany.[14]

With restless energy and at great personal sacrifices Meyer set himself the task of preparing the first critical edition of Albert's work *De plantis*. To this end he undertook a new critical edition of the pseudo-Aristotelian book which had formed the basis of Albert's work. This Meyer ascribed to Nicholas Damascene. It was only after completing this laborious task that he could go back to his main project, which unfortunately it was not reserved for him to finish. Carl Jessen carried on the undertaking, and in 1867 the critical edition of Albert's book on plants appeared.

[12] Karl Jessen in his preface to the *De vegetabilibus*, vi.
[13] Ernst H. F. Meyer : *Albertus als Botaniker*, 641–741.
[14] E. H. F. Meyer : *Geschichte der Botanik*, 9–84.

In his preface Jessen makes this boast for him: 'Albert was the first to give a scientific description of the flora of Germany.'[15] And in the words of his predecessor sets Albert on an equality with the greatest botanists in keenness of perception, sureness of observation, and practical knowledge of the plant life of his native country. He is of opinion that no greater botanist can be named in the period between Aristotle and Cesalpini. One might have thought that after all this the scientific world would have accorded to Albert his proper place, but, as Wimmer had regretfully to note, in spite of this extremely handy edition and of Meyer's and Jessen's warm recommendation, our modern specialists took little stock of Albert's book on plants; in fact one of them, J. Sachs, could talk disparagingly of Albert's botanical writings as being both rambling and unimaginative.[16]

Wimmer, who has gone very thoroughly into Albert's botany, calls him a true witness to the botanical knowledge of his day.[17] Stadler, who re-edited Albert's *De animalibus*, and has also made a careful survey of the other scientific writings of the Saint, insists that 'Albert in his observations and knowledge goes far beyond the *De plantis* of the pseudo-Aristotle, which was his source. Indeed he excels Theophrastus and Dioscurides, whom he only knew from hearsay.'[18]

Albert's masterpiece *De vegetabilibus* owes its perfection to four considerations: firstly to the independence with which he treated the subject, for all the respect he had for the reputed author of his source. As we have already seen, half of the valuable matter in the book was of his adding: moreover, he only had at his disposal an extremely imperfect text. Jessen[19] points out how Albert emended this, and, thanks to his own knowledge and independence of judgement, usually hit upon the right reading, as for instance in the description of the sycamore. In his treat-

[15] *De vegetabilibus*, Einleitung, v.

[16] J. Wimmer: op. cit., 8. Fellner, in his *Albertus Magnus als Botaniker*, had already, in 1881, refuted Julius Sachs's statement.

[17] Ibid.: op. cit., 9.

[18] H. Stadler: op. cit., 5.

[19] *De vegetabilibus*, 83.

ment on the sap of plants he makes the same additions as did Theophrastus, although he had never seen his work. He assigns to the conifers a gummy sap, and to the vine species a serous one.[20]

The second reason is the acuteness and range of his observations. Albert was the first to introduce spinach into Western literature,[21] and to call attention to the peculiar position of the grape cluster in relation to the vine leaf. He was the first to point out the difference between the tree buds enveloped by scaly coverings and the buds of plants which are without them. He was the first to describe the triple condition of the plant-germ in the pollen, an observation which Meyer compares with one of Cesalpini's.[22] He was the first to notice the influence of light and temperature on the growth of trees as affecting their height and spread. In regard to the latter Jessen remarks : 'Who can fail to admire this keen observation, of the need for which we have to remind many a naturalist even to-day.'[23] It was Albert, too, who first established that the sap in the roots is tasteless and that the higher it ascends the more palatable it becomes, 'a phenomenon which at the beginning of the nineteenth century was again noted by the English investigator Knight.'[24] Albert makes an apt comparison between a gash in the bark and a wound in an animal body. He acutely calls attention to the rarity of the dicotyledon, and clearly distinguishes between a thorn and a sting. It is only a keen and delicate eye that could make observations like these.

A third pre-eminent merit of Albert's work is seen in the clarity and precision of his description of individual plants and their parts. Wimmer gives prominence to the point that his description of the bulrush is very good, and that that of the corn-cockle, for which Albert has retained the mediæval name nigella, is exceedingly appropriate, as is also the representation of the chestnut tree in its similarity

[20] *De vegetabilibus*, 69.
[21] J. Wimmer : op. cit., 61 ; *De vegetabilibus*, 563.
[22] H. Stadler : op. cit., 6.
[23] *De vegetabilibus*, 279.
[24] Ibid., 115.

to, and difference from, the beech.[25] The mistletoe could hardly have been more clearly described than in Albert's words : 'High up in their branches there grows out of old trees a plant which shows the same form on every variety of tree. It has evergreen, leathery leaves, almost like those of the olive, but with a citron-yellow lustre, and in winter bears white berries. The structure of mistletoe is spongy and knotty like a vine ; the inner skin between the bark and the wood is, however, very sticky, and therefore serves for the preparation of bird-lime.'[26] He was also able to describe plants not indigenous to Germany, and this not merely by following foreign writers, but on the basis of his own observations made during his several stays in Italy and France. Thus in his treatment of the mandrake, which, though well known to the German people, is only indigenous to the lands bordering the Mediterranean, he goes far beyond his model. The sap of its ash-brown, sometimes black, roots he notes as poisonous ; mixed with wine it effects a complete narcosis, sufficient for the performance of the severest operations ; while the fact that after a too large dose apoplexy may intervene was not unknown to him. He also mentions the recovery of the celebrated oil of mandrake from the apple-like fruit of this plant.[27] In the cloister in the old days, at the end of the midday meal, fruit used to be passed round, in Germany usually apples. How Albert did not thoughtlessly enjoy this little addition to the meal, but here too carried on his observations, is shown by the fact that of all the things described in his book *De plantis*, not one has been so aptly presented as the apple. Wimmer thus expresses his admiration on this point : 'The exceedingly careful account of the apple from its rind to the core may be proclaimed a masterpiece of description.'[28]

A fourth merit in Albert's work is the attempt to lay stress on a systematic classification. He always sought to separate the essential from the non-essential. It was his

[25] J. Wimmer : op. cit., 56.
[26] *De vegetabilibus*, 252 ; J. Wimmer : op. cit., 32.
[27] *De vegetabilibus*, 535 *sq.* ; J. Wimmer : op. cit., 30.
[28] J. Wimmer : op. cit., 53.

endeavour to group together for treatment all plants which had essential characteristics in common, and thus to give the work a systematic structure. That he did not fully succeed can hardly be wondered at ; that he made the attempt at all is in itself worthy of recognition. He drew careful comparison between the leaves, blossoms, and fruits of the various species. He was the first to reduce their shapes to geometrical figures. In his celebrated second chapter, *de figuris florum*, he differentiates three basic forms in flowers : the bird, or wing-shaped, the bell-shaped, and, commonest of all, the star-shaped. Wimmer deplores the fact that Albert did not find time to pursue further the road which his genius had opened to him. In many a case the natural science of our day has completed the work which he began.[29] Albert took a serious stand against many ingenuous or actually superstitious notions of the Middle Ages, as for instance that house-leek has the power of warding off lightning or that catmint would fecundate cats.[30] He certainly himself paid toll to the backward state of knowledge in his day by accepting the principle of *generatio equivoca* and the truth of the report from the vineyard in Auvergne where, it was said, cuttings from an oak had become vines.[31] Such defects are mere shadows on the glorious picture of Albert, the greatest investigator of the flora of mediæval Germany, who, to borrow an expression from Franz Strunz, disposed of a knowledge of the vegetation of Germany which bordered on the marvellous.[32]

[29] Karl Jessen in his introduction to the *De vegetabilibus*, xvii ; J. Wimmer : op. cit., 29.

[30] *De vegetabilibus*, 544.

[31] Ibid., 314. Meyer, in his *Geschichte der Botanie* (iv, 64), says in his excuse : 'Albert's general Botany is the first of its kind. What Albert had to go upon, the two books of Nicolao's, were rather a hindrance to him than a help in his strictly scientific pursuit, and it was not till centuries had passed that a second work, only remotely comparable to his, appeared. Furthermore, the defects in his work are the fault of his age, its merits belong to him alone.'

[32] Franz Strunz : *Albertus Magnus. Weisheit und Naturforschung im Mittelalter*, 106.

2. *Albertus Magnus and the Fauna.*

(*a*) The Mammals.

In the first edition of Herzog's *Realencyklopädie der protestantischen Theologie* its judgement on Albert is summarily expressed in the words: 'What he says on natural history, as might be expected of a monk in his cell, follows Aristotle or is based on supposition.' How little this opinion fits the case is clear from the large number of experts who are lavish in their praise of Albert's independent judgement and practical experience in matters relating to natural science. Victor Carus called Albert 'the most important literary figure in the field of natural science in the thirteenth century,'[33] and Pouchet, Ehrle, and von Hertling held similar views. Wasmann considers Albert's merit as a naturalist to lie not merely in his reversion to Aristotle, but also in the fact that he did not blindly rely on authority but broke new ground by independent investigations of his own.[34]

Albert's most brilliant vindication came, however, through the new edition of the Saint's *De animalibus*, which was prepared by Professor Stadler and meets every modern requirement. Distorted views on Albert as a scientist were intelligible so long as there was only available the old edition, which, because of its defectiveness, was useless for any scientific work. Luckily the holograph of Albert's *De animalibus* has come down to us. It was formerly one of the most precious treasures of the old Dominican convent at Cologne, and it was from this original text that the new edition was prepared. Stadler had already communicated his results to wider circles. As early as March 20, 1905, he gave a lecture to the National History Society in Munich on Albert the Great as an independent natural philosopher,

[33] Victor Carus: *Geschichte der Zoologie*, 224; A. Pouchet: *Histoire des sciences naturelles au moyen-âge ou Albert le Grand et son époque considérée comme point de départ de l'école experimentale*; Card. F. Ehrle, S.J.: *Der selige Albertus Magnus*, 241 *sqq.*; G. von Hertling: op. cit., 42 *sqq.*

[34] Erich Wasmann, S.J.: *Die moderne Biologie und die Entwicklungstheorie*, 11. Heinrich Balss: *Albertus Magnus als Zoologe*, 141, expresses the same opinion.

and on September 21, 1908, at the eightieth gathering of German naturalists and physicians in Cologne, in a lecture on Albertus Magnus as naturalist and the holograph of his history of animals, he had again the opportunity of proclaiming Albert's merits. Wasmann supposes this to have been the first time for a gathering of German naturalists and medical men to be convened to do honour, in the name of modern natural science, to a mediæval Scholastic and Catholic Bishop and Beatus of the Church in Germany.[35]

All this appreciative recognition has had its influence on the new edition of the *Encyclopædia of Protestant Theology*. Nitsch has essayed to appraise the debt that the natural sciences owe to Albert, but could not refrain from remarking that the 'new discoveries' ascribed to Albert may well have been borrowed from some Arabic sources or other unknown to us.[36]

That this supposition may be ruled out in the case of a great deal of this new matter will be shown in what follows by a few examples from the section dealing with the mammals. Considering the interest Albert had in all natural phenomena and his many long journeys, he had plenty of opportunity for independent observation. Certainly many others had the same opportunities, but they did not use them, and it remains Albert's merit that he did use his and that he applied their results in his works.

As in botany so also in zoology Albert had a text which he followed, in this case the authentic work of Aristotle's, *De animalibus*. By the insertion of new matter he increased the scope of the nineteen books by about double, and added two independent treatises of a general nature and five books, in which, for the sake of his brethren, following the example of his pupil Thomas de Chantimpré, and using the latter's work as a basis, he enumerates and describes the individual animals in alphabetical order, inserting at the same time the early mediæval fabulous creatures. In this last part Albert shows far greater dependence on his model than in the first, and unfortunately it is on the second

[35] Erich Wasmann, S.J.: *Zur neuen Ausgabe der Tiergeschichte Alberts des Grossen*, 283.

[36] *Realenzyklopädie für protestantische Theologie*, I, 292.

part, as being the handier to use, that Albert's zoological knowledge has been for the most part estimated.

Stadler, who has gone more deeply than anyone into Albert's zoology, has established the fact that he was the first to describe the following mammals which are all to be found in Germany : the weasel, the two martens, the rat, the garden dormouse, and the common dormouse ; further, he is the first to mention the polar bear. He was also the first to employ in literature the German names (*Gemse*, *Hermelin*, and *Iltis*) for the chamois, the ermine, and the polecat.[37]

The description of the hound driving, or rather leading, her young to attack the wolf, which Albert incorporated in Aristotle's book, has a primitive German flavour : 'Those dogs, which are called Dalmatians and follow the sheep as watchers, vary greatly in size, but all go in pursuit of the wolf and seize him. In this chase it is the bitches who are prominent, and I myself saw a bitch actually training her young to hunt the wolf, inciting them to run and taking the lead herself. If, however, the wolf threaten to slip away, she holds fast to him until the puppies come up, when she lets him run again. And if the wolf bite the puppies she does not at once spring to their aid, as she wishes the puppies to become keen against the wolf. These dogs, however, vary greatly in size ; some are larger and stronger than wolves, others smaller. All belong to this breed, but are bigger and more courageous than other dogs.'[38]

It was in his German cell that Albert carried out the studies for his excellent description of the cat. He calls her modest, a lover of beauty, and given to biting.[39] He, however, remarks with regard to the first trait, that this is not the true modesty characteristic of man, but has a remote resemblance to it. 'Her colour is grey, like ice

[37] H. Stadler : op. cit., 6. [38] *De animalibus*, 572.

[39] The Saint's description is so racy that we quote a few lines of it : 'Cattus est animal a capiendo dictum, muribus infestum, ac dicitur esse moribus verecundum ac pulchritudinis amativum. . . . Est autem mordax valde in multis simile leoni secundam figuram, unguibus et dentibus armatum sicut leo.' *De animalibus*, lib. 22, tr. 2, cap 1. [Ed.]

in a hard frost; this is her natural colour. She gets others through accidental nourishment, especially the house cat.' In her general deportment he finds her like the lion with regard to teeth and claws, which she draws in and exposes exactly like a lion. Albert states that the cat, however much an enemy to the mouse she be, only kills, but does not eat, the small reddish-brown species called in North Germany the *Schermus* and in South the *Spicimus*, as if it were poisonous for her. Of this shrew-mouse he also adds that it makes a noise as if it were gnashing its teeth.[40]

Albert studied the ways of the squirrel in German forests and afterwards drew up his masterly description: 'The pirolus is an extremely lively little animal; it nests in the tops of trees, has a long bushy tail, and swings itself from tree to tree, in doing so using its tail as a rudder. When on the move it drags its tail behind him, but when sitting it carries it erect up its back. When taking food it holds it, as do the other rodents, in its hands, so to speak, and places it in its mouth. Its food consists of nuts and fruit and such-like things. Its flesh is sweet and palatable. In Germany its colour is black when young, and later reddish, in old age even partly grey. In Poland they are a reddish grey and in parts of Russia quite grey.'[41]

On the German meadowlands he could easily observe the lowland cattle and describes them as large and rich in milk. It was especially in Friesland, Holland, and Zealand that he found the cows very large, extraordinarily rich in milk, and almost all of them dappled, and he put down the exuberant proportions of this breed of cattle to the moistness of their rich pasturage. Besides domestic cattle he was acquainted with the wild stocks, the aurochs and the bison, and also the buffalo, of which he says: 'There is a black race of cattle, namely bufletus bubalus, which is tamed and has a ring put in its nose by which it is led about. It is called in the Romance and German tongue bufletus. It

[40] *De animalibus*, 20, 21, 548, 1371.

[41] Ibid., 1421; H. Stadler: *Zur Tiergeographie Deutschlands im Mittelalter*; Balss: op. cit., 35, says of this observation: 'Albert's description of the squirrel may be taken as an anticipation of the modern view of the geographical basis of specific variation.

has many wonderful characteristics. Its body colour is black and has but little hair, so that even at the tail it is almost hairless. Its head is small compared with the size of its body, its horns are short, almost like those of a goat. Sometimes these grow downwards round the throat towards the breast, sometimes also upwards. It is strong and draws the load of almost two horses. It has short and strong legs. The cheese made from its milk is rich and nourishing. It will not suffer the calf from another cow, but pushes it away if it be foisted upon it, since it notices from the smell that it is not its own. If, however, its dung is smeared on the calf it allows it to come to it as if it were its own. It suckles it and looks after it, since it has been deceived by the smell. It is excellently adapted for hauling heavy loads. First it makes a mighty plunge, sinks on its knees, stands up again, and then overcomes the load. It is very irascible. When angered it runs to the water and immerses itself up to the muzzle in the stream because of the heat of its excited blood. All classes of cattle have this trait in common, that in summer they crave for water in which to immerse themselves. It hates red or bright colours so much, that it tramples on anyone who is clothed in them. It defends itself with its hoofs with which it kicks violently, and it goes on kicking until whatever has roused its anger is pounded to pieces.'[42] The observations on which this description is based were probably made by Albert in his Italian period.

That Albert was thoroughly acquainted with the horse and the wild deer, and gave an accurate description of them from personal observation, may be taken for granted from his noble extraction. It is of more importance that we can from Albert's descriptions deduce what animals survived in the Germany of his day. Stadler[43] has carried out this work also, and has set down his conclusions in various detached notes, some of which we will here group together.

The beaver was still very common in several parts of Germany at that time ; the marmot was not infrequently

[42] *De animalibus*, 235, 236, 354.

[43] H. Stadler : *Albertus Magnus von Köln als Naturforscher*, 7.

to be found in the mountains ; the aurochs had been already exterminated in Germany proper ; the bison had been pushed back to the eastern borders, where it certainly still haunted the forests in large numbers ; the elk was leaving the country ; the fallow deer had not yet been introduced into Germany, and Albert in describing it from an alien source confuses the fallow deer with the gazelle.

(*b*) The Fishes.

Stadler also praises Albert's excellent knowledge of the fishes. As a Dominican, who practised perpetual abstinence, the almost daily consumption of fish was prescribed for him by the rule of the Order. What others partook of without further thought served him as an opportunity for scientific investigation. He himself narrates how once when eating oysters he found ten pearls at one meal.[44] His interest in investigations of this kind must very early have become known in wider circles, for in the year 1245 during his sojourn in Paris as teacher, 'there came to study in that town the son of the King of Castile. Once when the latter's cooks were buying fish, they got one fish, called in Latin "peccet," but in the vulgar tongue "pleis," which was very large. When it was cleaned there was found in its belly the shell of a fairly large mussel, which that prince was good enough to present to me. The mussel had on the smooth concave surface the image of three serpents with raised heads, so finely executed that the eyes were not wanting. On the rough outer surface more than ten were portrayed. These were bound together at the neck, but the heads and bodies were separated. On each image the opening in the mouth and tail of the snake was visible. I kept that mussel shell for a long time, and showed it to many people, and later sent it as a present to someone in Germany.'[45]

Albert was the first to write about the spook fish (aslec), and the first to point out the molar-like teeth in the gullet of the carp. The effect of a tinkling sound or the ringing

[44] *Mineralium*, lib. 2, tr. 2, cap. 11.
[45] Ibid., lib. 2, tr. 3, cap. 1.

of bells on fish was known to him.[46] He took an energetic stand against the old opinion on the fecundation of fish : 'I believe that there is no truth in it, for I have myself observed diligently, and have made investigations in the case of the oldest fishes in the sea and in rivers, and I have seen with my own eyes and heard with my own ears that fishes at pairing-time bring their bodies close together and on contact give out eggs and milk.'[47]

Albert had also precise knowledge of the German waters : where individual fishes occur or are to be found in larger numbers or of better quality. Thus he informs us that 'the fish which is called huso (royal sturgeon) has no bone or cartilage except in the head ; this fish is very numerous in the Danube, it is large and has a long snout like the common sturgeon.'[48] On the other hand he knows that there are no eels in the Danube, because this river draws the greater part of its water from the Alps, and in consequence its water is cold. The latter fish, however, flees the cold, because it likes warm, still water. With reference to the eel Albert corrects Aristotle, who has it that these fish live on slime. The Saint affirms : 'I have seen how it eats frogs, worms, and bits of fish, and how with bait such as these it is caught with a rod.'[49] That the Rhine, and especially the reaches in the neighbourhood of Cologne, yields the best salmon, is a fact well known to Albert, as also that at the mouth of the Rhine delta, where the Maas, the Rhine, the Ems, and the Elbe flow into the sea not far from one another, the greatest assemblage of fish is to be found.

Albert also gave his attention to the special characteristics of fishes. In the sea-devil he admires the cleverness with which this fish hides itself in the mud and catches smaller fish by means of its long eyebrows. The description is so vivid that one must suppose that Albert had actually handled this fish.[50] The effect of a blow from the electric ray he verifies by the report of a trustworthy man who had

[46] *De animalibus*, 1518, 1549 ; Stadler : *Zur Tiergeschichte Deutschlands im Mittelalter*, 72.

[47] *De animalibus*, 415.

[48] Ibid., 277, 1533.

[49] Ibid., 506, 1518.

[50] Ibid., 619.

tried the experiment on himself. He specifically classes seals and dolphins as mammals with firm bones instead of cartilage, bearing their young and breathing through wind-pipes instead of through gills. On this point he remarks : 'In these matters I pass over the accounts of the ancients in silence, for they do not agree with those of men of experience.'[51]

The Saint would appear to have had a special interest in the whale, for his accounts of this creature are unusually rich.[52] He was acquainted with a large number of species, all of which, however, he treats under the same designation, cetus. The walrus can at once be recognized in the northern animal with tusks an ell in length, with denticulated jaws and head covered with hair. The tusks serve him in climbing rocks. Thongs were cut from its hide and were to be bought in the Cologne market. The Greenland whale is identical with the cetus, of whose toothless mouth and extraordinarily strong beards he gives a graphic account. The most exhaustive descriptions refer, however, to the sperm whale. In the Saint's day two of these were caught, one in Friesland near Stauria. When its eye was pierced eleven jars of fat were obtained from its head. The jars were so heavy that a man could only carry away one with difficulty. Albert asserts that he himself saw the jars with the fat. The second was caught at Utrecht in Holland. Out of its head they recovered forty jars of fat. He remarks that the measurements given by the ancients for the size of this animal are incredible ; the dimensions which Albert sets out accord with modern observation. He was accurately acquainted with the manner of catching them. Even if he had never been actually present at the throwing of the harpoon, he nevertheless gives a very vivid description of it. Several fishermen get together and embark three to a boat. Two manage the boat, the third stands ready to throw. The javelin is made of a light wood and has a barbed head. In the shank at the end of the shaft a rope

[51] *De animalibus*, 310, 861 ; Stadler : *Albertus Magnus von Köln als Naturforscher*, 7.

[52] *De animalibus*, 1522 *sqq.* ; Stadler : op. cit., 6, and his *Zur Tiergeographie Deutschlands im Mittelalter*, 67, 98.

is made fast, which uncoils easily. When a whale appears they are all called together and throw their spears. If the whale make for the open sea the fishermen must cut the ropes as their trouble has been in vain ; if, however, he dive into the depths he will have been severely wounded. The blood which at once wells up marks the way the fish has taken towards the shore. The fishermen follow the way and renew their attack as often as the beast reappears until he is killed. In the other way of catching the whale a cross-bow is used which, being much stronger, is able to drive the weapon in deeper.

Albert gives a detailed account of a droll catch of a whale : 'He is most often caught when he too greedily follows the herring, and in doing so ventures too close inshore, so that he cannot get back into deep water again. This happened some time ago on the coast of Friesland. The inhabitants saw this and feared lest the tide should suddenly come in again and they would lose the fish. Accordingly they tied him with all the ropes which they could find on the island. They drove stakes deep into the ground and fastened the ends of the ropes to them and to stones and to the nearby houses and to trees. When the sea came in, however, the fish with the help of the water broke all these ropes, and taking them with him swam out again into deep water to the very great dismay of the inhabitants, who mourned the loss of the ropes. However, the fish had not had his fill, and on the third day after he again followed a shoal of herring and was stranded at the same spot as before. Then the people recovered their ropes and killed and cut up the fish. When they smashed in his head there was a crash as if a house had fallen in.'

In his account of fishes it is the almost universal opinion that some of Albert's observations date from the days when he was Bishop of Regensburg. 'The barbel collect, as I myself have observed on my property (villa) on the Danube, in the holes, which are there to be found in the rocks and walls, in such masses after the autumnal equinox, that one can catch them with the hand.'[53] As already remarked, Endres has urged weighty reasons for transferring this

[53] *De animalibus*, 523 ; J. A. Endres : op. cit., 829.

THE OLD DOMINICAN PRIORY OF S. BLAISE IN REGENSBURG

observation to Albert's youthful days. If so, one of the Saint's first observations in natural history which have come down to us refers to fishes. What we have cited will suffice to confirm Stadler's judgement that Albert had an excellent knowledge of fishes.

(*c*) The Birds.

Stadler starts his review of Albert's knowledge of birds with the words : 'I could now enumerate the whole bird world of Germany, for Albert is acquainted with three (or better four) swallows, five finches, three spotted woodpeckers, with, in addition, black, green, and grey woodpeckers, and two sparrows.'[54] We may add to this that he enumerates six kinds of eagle and three species of heron, while five different kinds of wild geese and three of wild duck are known to him. He establishes five kinds of goldfinch and enlarges on the differences in falcons as surely no one before him had done, not even Frederick II, to whose work he had access. He gives no less than ten kinds of falcon-gentle, and in addition three common and three mixed kinds. All these are cited with their characteristic markings, and their capabilities and merits are exhaustively appraised. Albert could acquire such knowledge the more easily, since at that time Germany was less thickly inhabited, had stretches of waste land to show, and above all still possessed extensive forests. In no other part of the work *De animalibus* do we come so often on the remark : 'I could establish the fact,' or 'I saw,' or 'I observed.' Nowhere else has he made so many and so thorough-going corrections in the texts he followed, or has so energetically dealt with the absurd and often superstitious views of the time. Strunz expresses this thought in his own way thus : 'It is a pleasure to meet with a naturalist in the far-off Middle Ages who, in the so-called golden age of superstition and credulity, had the courage, with clear and sure understanding, to scotch such gross miracle stories, and often took pains to overcome his religious prejudices in the matter.'[55]

The alphabetical grouping in the twenty-third book

[54] H. Stadler : *Zur Tiergeographie Deutschlands im Mittelalter*, 69.
[55] Franz Strunz : op. cit., 150.

begins with the eagle. Albert at once takes issue with the fable that the eagle proves its young to see whether they can look into the blazing face of the sun, and drives from the nest those who are not capable of doing so. He will not accept the statement of the philosophers that the golden eagle only lays two eggs, but that out of one of them two young ones are hatched, and submits: 'I have consulted many bird-catchers on this point, and in inquiries spread over many years I have never found the golden eagle to have more than one young one.'[56] He gives as a reason for this that it requires a great deal of nourishment, which the old birds have to bring from long distances. If, however, two young ones were to be occasionally found, this would be in northern regions near the sea and forests, where fish, birds, and small animals are plentiful as prey.

The tale told by the ancients of the eagle's curious sweat-cure and the renewal of its plumage is thus criticized by Albert: 'On this point I can only say, that there is much that is wonderful in nature, but what I have myself seen in two golden eagles in our country does not tally with this. They had been tamed and they moulted just like any other bird of prey.'[57] Pliny's statement that a certain eagle wraps its eggs in a wolf-skin and hangs this on a branch of a tree in the sun till the heat of the sun hatches the eggs out, is put down by Albert as being, according to his experience, *falsissimum*. He had for example never met with anything of the kind in Lithuania; on the contrary he had there seen that eagles hatched out their young in the normal way and fed them on fish, birds, and the smaller animals.

He labels as false and not in accord with his own experience Pliny's account of herons weeping blood; nor will he give any more credit to the existence of the one-eyed heron which Pliny mentions. 'This appears to be contrary to nature and false; for as the bird is matched with two wings and two legs, one on each side, so also is it with two eyes. It would be contrary to the law of nature that an eye should be formed on one side and not at the same time on the other. Pliny has in fact said a great deal that is false,

[56] *De animalibus*, 1434, n. 9. [57] Ibid., 1, 434, n. 10.

and therefore we ought not in this case to pay any heed to his pretensions.'[58]

The notion that the brent-goose grows like an apple on the trees and when ripe falls into the water, he regards as a fairy story, and appeals to his own experience as having seen the eggs of these birds, and observed the latter hatching out and rearing their young.[59] He disposes of a similar fable connected with the black-cock in the same way.

The swan had very early arrested his attention. 'It was in our time, and several of our companions were witnesses, that an eagle fought with a swan. They both soared to such a height that they became invisible to us. After about two hours they fell down before our eyes. The eagle had conquered the swan and now stood on him. Then our servant ran up, seized the swan, and the eagle flew off.'[60] Michael ascribes this tale to Albert's boyhood days; since, however, such a fight could hardly have taken place in Lauingen itself, we must suppose that Albert on occasion spent some time in the country, perhaps at the Castle of Bollstädt. With regard to the idea that the swan-song is a sign that death is to enter their ranks, he adds the remark that according to his experience swans always sing when in pain. Albert also supplemented what was known about the stork by being the first to mention the black stork.[61]

The widely accepted view of Hermes Trismegistus that the cock in old age lays an egg from which a serpent is hatched in the mud, is dismissed by Albert as incredible.[62]

The Saint gives a very vivid description of the kingfisher's plumage; but as against the assertion that if the skin of this bird is taken off and stretched on a wall it will change its feathers every year, he states that he has himself made the experiment, but without result, and that therefore this

[58] *De animalibus*, 1440.
[59] Ibid., 1441, n. 22, 1446, n. 30.
[60] Ibid., 600 *sq.*; Michael: op. cit., iii, 1; Killermann in *Die Vogelkunde des Albertus Magnus*, 84, says: 'What he [Albert] says about their singing is correct.'
[61] *De animalibus*, 1448, n. 35.
[62] Ibid., 1496, n. 116.

cannot be substantiated.[63] Experience shows, Albert insists, that just as little credence can be given to the statement that the osprey has its right foot taloned and its left webbed ; and he makes precisely the same criticism of the tale of the pelican opening its breast in order to nourish its young on its blood, which was such a favourite in the Middle Ages.

He defends the partridge against the charge of forgetfulness for which it is ridiculed, nor will he have anything to do with the iron-eating stork, since both are contrary to experience.[64] How acute his observation was is shown by his account of the nightingale : 'In the case of the nightingale I have observed how it flew up to good singers, to whose song it quietly listened, and then, as if to challenge them, started up its own song. In this way two nightingales mutually provoke one another to song.'[65]

Albert corrects Pliny's statement that no one has ever seen a vulture's nest by the remark that on the hills between Mainz and Trier such numbers of vultures nest yearly, that the whole countryside stank from the carrion which accumulated. Here again Albert reveals the keenness of his observation by remarking with reference to the vulture's clumsiness and voracity that it likes to rest on the ground, and must, before it can fly up, first take two or three hops. The Saint had himself caught a vulture which had overeaten itself.[66]

The falcons have received the most exhaustive treatment, and the reason for this lies in the interest with which these birds of the chase were regarded in the Middle Ages, when men were so well versed in the sport, and also in the excellent older works on the subject which he had at his disposal, while his own experience with falcons stretched back to his boyhood. After speaking of three kinds of hawks, of which one will only seize the pigeon in flight, another only when the bird is sitting on a tree, and a third only one which stays on the ground, he goes on to tell how, according to report, Trajan's hunters used to

[63] *De animalibus*, 1500, n. 123. [64] Ibid., 1507, 1510.
[65] Ibid., 1509 ; Strunz : op. cit., 151.
[66] *De animalibus*, 1513 ; Killermann : op. cit., 29.

employ wild hawks in hunting pigeons. Albert supplements this account with the following tale: 'As a youngster I had a somewhat similar experience with falcons. Sometimes I took dogs, which are called bird-dogs, with me in the fields. Falcons which were flying above me in the air followed us over the field and swooped down on the birds which the dogs had put up. The birds in their fright returned to earth and let themselves be caught by hand. When the hunt was over we gave each of the falcons a bird, and then they left us.'[67]

The caution with which Albert proceeds when an opinion, which he is not in a position to verify, seems to him questionable, is seen in his remarks on the common raven: 'The old view that ravens copulate by means of their beaks may be explained by the fact that with them coition takes place very early before dawn or at dusk in the evening, when they cannot be observed by people; the question has therefore up to now not been sufficiently examined. Pigeons may be seen billing, but because in their case coition normally takes place in the open, not a soul ever imagines that this is effected through their bills. The reason for this error about the raven is here again shown to be carelessness in the investigation of nature.'[68]

In spite of his great passion for research Albert did occasionally deceive himself, as for instance when, from the fact that a number of swallows had been found in the mould inside a hollow oak, he concluded that the migrants and birds of passage would not migrate but simply hide themselves.[69] His predilection for an ethical application

[67] *De animalibus*, 617 *sq.*; Strunz: op. cit., 152, supposes them to have been partridges.

[68] *De animalibus*, 1164; Strunz (op. cit., 146) aptly remarks on this and similar accounts of Albert's: 'Even the sexual element in human and animal life loses all unpleasantness in face of such delightfully frank truthfulness and reverent intimacy with nature. . . . In Albert we find the innocent, unaffected mind of the child and, for all that, of the sage.'

[69] *De animalibus*, 1448, 1449; Balss (op. cit., 104) remarks in this connexion: 'The observation may be correct. It would then be the case of a second, delayed brood, which could not fly away at the proper time.'

of animal traits may have been the cause of his taking seriously the account of the old, blind, and almost white hawk to whom two young hawks brought their prey, tore it into bits, and fed her with it.[70]

It may have been some youngsters in Cologne who took him in with the tale of the cheeky sparrow who had settled in a swallow's nest. The latter by its twittering invited the intruder to leave the nest, but the sparrow remained sitting. Thereupon the swallow raised such an outcry that all the swallows in the neighbourhood collected. They took clay in their beaks and walled the cheeky sparrow in, so that it had to die of hunger.[71]

(*d*) The Insects.

'Albert devoted special interest to insects,'[72] says Stadler, and indeed anyone who reads his treatises on them will imagine that he has found in him the prototype of the Scaribee in Oliver Wendell Holmes's tale. Albert observed spiders with extreme care at their work, namely spinning; he knows whence they draw the web, how they hold it in their feet, how they join it, how they pass the individual strands to and fro. He gives definite information as to which spiders do not spin, but jump (saltando) to catch flies and other small creatures. He knows too the spider custom by which the inert and clumsy male does not spin and hardly ever hunts, while the brisk and industrious female spins and hunts and feeds the male. He enumerates which kinds spread their nets on windows and which on the ground, and again those which set it up between the leaves of the trees. Of the latter he says that in Germany they are especially poisonous and harmful.

Albert knew also how the spider overworks, and how, spent with toil, she dies of exhaustion. 'They fall down, burst asunder in their fall, and infect with their fetid liquor whatever they alight on.'[73]

Since the spider won the Saint's special interest on account of her cleverness, we find the characteristics relating to this

[70] *De animalibus*, 618.
[71] Ibid., 1500.
[72] H. Stadler: op. cit., 8.
[73] *De animalibus*, 630, n. 140.

described with great minuteness. He sketches a graphic picture of the way she hunts, of the spider lurking as if in ambush in the corner, or in the middle of her web, of how she darts out as soon as some creature has been caught in it, how she bites it, wraps it up, kills it, drags it away, and sucks it dry, and how she will even overpower larger creatures. He had himself observed how a spider caught and took possession of a small lizard. 'When the little creature had got itself entangled, the spider at once came down and spun a web round its mouth so that she might not be injured that way. Then she settled down to the creature, and bit and stabbed it till it was dead or quite helpless. Then she went up to the net where she stored her provisions and drew her prey after her by a web. This I myself saw with my own eyes and marvelled at the ingenuity (solertia) of the spider.'[74] He also reports, as being credibly attested, that a spider had lowered herself on to a toad, and had sucked a serpent dry, and that she had even made the same attempt with human beings.

Again the great care with which the spider wraps up and watches over her eggs did not escape Albert. He is acquainted with numerous kinds, black, grey, green, large and small, long-legged and short, thick and thin, and seeks to set out the characteristics of the separate species. His treatment of the subject is so extended that the study of the spider might have been his sole occupation.

Albert gives a very striking description of the ant, depicting its small head and its eyes set in the projecting antennæ, its industry, a characteristic common to all species, and its regularity in keeping to its way and to times. He brings out very well how concerned the ant is about her eggs, even more than she is about herself. He considers the order preserved in ant-heaps to be wonderful, seeing that there is no one in supreme authority, and yet everything goes on in the most orderly manner. 'They all live together out of love of virtue and for the sake of natural goodness, and work for the common profit.'[75] He mentions too the acrid, blistering juice which the ant ejects on all who cause

[74] *De animalibus*, 630, n. 138; Balss: op. cit., 115 *sq*.
[75] *De animalibus*, 627.

them injury, though to be sure he says 'morsu suo'; he names also the odour which an ant-heap exhales, and knows its importance for the vine. He cites as the ant's born enemy the nightingale, who snatches at the ants and also their eggs, and, indeed, when ill, uses them as medicine.

The blinding of ants through the ripping off of their antennæ is known to him, and he tells how the blinded one attaches itself to other ants and thus finds its way back to the heap. Balss calls attention to this passage 'because of its fine observations.'[76]

Stadler considers that especial credit is due to Albert for having dispelled the mediæval conception of the ant-lion. Even Thomas de Chantimpré held it to be a further developed ant, '*ist amaizen geslähtes.*' As against this, Albert, supported by his personal experience, teaches that 'the ant-lion was not formerly an ant, as many say, for I have often observed, and have frequently shown to friends, that this creature is of the nature of a tick. It hides itself in the sand and digs in it a hemispherical hole of which its mouth forms the door. If now an ant passes over it in search of food it catches and eats it. I have often watched this.'[77]

Of all the insects, Albert treats the bee (apis) the most thoroughly. He knows of nine kinds, including the wasp, the bumble-bee, and the hornet, and calls attention to the virulence of the sting of the latter. According to the statement of peasants and shepherds, nine hornets would be enough to kill a horse.[78] In his circumstances Albert was not able to observe the life of these vespidæ to the extent that he could the ordinary bee. The interest was there but opportunity was wanting. He abstains from closer accounts of them with the argument: 'It is not known.'

Among the bees proper he again distinguishes three kinds and he describes them and their differences. How greatly this little creature interested him is shown by the remark: 'I have attempted to make an anatomy of the bee. At the back of the body behind the waist there is found a gleaming, transparent sack, and if it is examined

[76] Balss: op. cit., 113 *sq.* [77] *De animalibus*, 1586, n. 20.
[78] Ibid., 642, n. 169.

by taste, it yields a fine honey flavour. Otherwise there is found in the body only a thin, slightly convoluted intestine and thread-like tissue to which the sting is secured. Round about flows a sticky liquor. The legs are set in that part of the body which lies in front of the main section.'[79] By dissections such as these, which he frequently undertook, he arrived, as Jessen and Stadler remark, at a knowledge of the belly markings of the arthropoda, as appears from the following quotation from his botany : 'It must not be omitted that in animals there starts from the brain, or the substitute for a brain, a cord, called nucha, which runs the whole length of the body, either along the back, or below, through the breast and belly, as is the case in crabs, scorpions, and others.'[80]

Albert has described the bee-hive at its beginning, in its construction, and in its finished state. He has observed the queen bee and tells how she differs from the drones and workers. The order in a swarm is for him the ideal of a well-regulated state. He has followed individual bees in their flight under sunny and overcast skies, names their favourite flowers, and describes the difference when they are gathering honey or wax. He knows where the bee stows the honey it has collected, how before taking flight it tests whether the weight is not beyond its strength. He describes just as vividly the swarming, and the struggles incidental to it. It is with especial pleasure that he tells of a find he once made in a nest of wild bees, probably bumble-bees. He found in it three handfuls of honey, though he certainly adds : 'It was unfinished, inferior honey.'[81]

With the same love and care with which he described the dog among quadrupeds and the falcon among birds, so among insects he portrayed the bee. The reason will surely have been the cleverness which he found so remarkably displayed in these creatures.

[79] *De animalibus*, 390 ; Stadler : op. cit., 8.
[80] *De vegetabilibus*, 296, n. 18 ; Jessen remarks that he was the first to make this discovery.
[81] Ibid., 652.

3. *Albertus Magnus and the other branches of Natural Science.*

As has been already stated, Albert treated the other branches of natural science with the same thoroughness as he did the fauna and flora. Of these works, however, no critical editions have as yet appeared. Certain fields have indeed been specially examined ; for instance Strunz has given particular attention to Albert's chemistry and alchemy.[82] We shall here only refer to a few features which are generally singled out as being characteristic of the Saint's views.

Albert regards the earth as a sphere and accepts the reasons which Aristotle had already advanced for this, based on the form of the earth's shadow at an eclipse of the moon and on the conditional visibility of certain stars, but he goes further and deduces the fact from gravity. Since all parts of the earth are attracted to the centre, the earth must necessarily assume a spherical shape.[83] By this there were also solved for him all the difficulties which arise in regard to the question of the Antipodes. He defends the thesis that it is not only the northern zone but also the southern that is inhabited. In the further development of this thought of Albert's, Mandonnet, Michael, and others saw a foreshadowing of Laplace's theory.[84]

Following Aristotle, Albert in his *Liber meteororum* first describes the appearances of comets in the sky, their formation, and their influence on human destinies. With regard to the Milky Way he knows that, however much it may appear to be bands of white, it is in reality made up of a multitude of stars. In his explanation of hoar-frost, rain, and snow he goes far beyond his text, while his discussions on earthquakes, the genesis of thunderstorms, rainbows, the ebb and flow of the tides, and volcanoes are considered to be especially clear.[85]

[82] Balss (op. cit., 12) is of opinion that Strunz has done more justice to Albert's personality than to his scientific importance.

[83] *De cœlo et mundo*, lib. 2, tr. 4, cap. 9.

[84] P. Mandonnet, O.P. : *Les idées cosmologiques d'Albert le Grand et de saint Thomas d'Aquin et la découverte de l'Amérique ;* Michael : op. cit., iii, 450.

[85] *Meteororum*, lib. 2, tr. 1 ; Michael : op. cit., iii, 451.

The book *De natura locorum* was very highly regarded by Alexander von Humboldt. It contains a theory of zones to which he has appended a description of the influences which the sea, mountains, forests, and particular conditions of the soil exercise on the vegetable and animal worlds and also on human beings. Albert even holds that they have an influence on the dispositions and customs of the latter.[86]

The book *De mineralibus* is characterized by Strunz as very rich in historico-chemical material, while supplementary matter based on personal research is not wanting. Albert himself made distillations. He purified gold by cementation, and separated it from silver with nitric acid ; he investigated the combination of sulphur with metals and found that it attacked all of them except gold.[87]

The fame of Albert the Great is based principally on his achievements in natural science, and even to-day he still is recognized as an authority of the first rank in this domain. G. von Hertling, however, emphasizes the fact that in no field is it more difficult to form a judgement on merit of this kind, avoiding both depreciation and exaggeration.[88] In the old days the sight of heavy folios crammed with learning was enough in men's eyes to justify the esteem in which the teacher was held, and in fact in Albert's case this superabundance of learning was, and will always be, amazing. We have here a universality of knowledge such as is but extremely rarely met with even in the most gifted of scholars. However, if Albert had merely made a compilation of the material of others we should not consider he had the right to be called a distinguished natural philosopher.[89] Moreover, he made no epoch-making discovery leading to the development of the natural sciences as in the cases of Galileo, Newton, and Lavoisier, and yet he belongs to the ranks of the great scientists, and deserves the name in precisely the sense which we give it to-day.

[86] Stadler : op. cit., 4 *sq.*
[87] *Mineralium*, lib. 3, tr. 1, cap. 8 ; Strunz : op. cit., 100 *sq.*
[88] G. von Hertling : op. cit., 154.
[89] It is Stadler's and Balss's merit that they undertook the separation of the ideas Albert borrowed from others and those which were his own.

Albert, in fact, with a persistence and steadfastness which has no parallel, pointed the way to the fundamental principle of all true science, namely personal experimentation as opposed to derived conceptions. And the Saint did this at a time when, on account of the speculative tendency of the age, a view like this was opposed as being foreign to it and senseless. We saw at the beginning of this section how with him experience overrode Aristotle's dicta ; and he carried out this principle in practice. On almost every page of his numerous scientific works we meet with such an expression as *vidi*, or *expertus sum*, or *experimentum feci*, and in consequence his own additions to the texts of the genuine or pseudo-Aristotle have real scientific value. Among the individual results of his research some are of capital importance, as, for instance, the astonishingly apt description of stamens, and his first mention of the nerve fibres of the stomach in insects. However, of much greater importance is, and will ever be, his insistence on personal experiment. This is science's greatest debt to Albert, and it is because of this that a place among the greatest researchers in the field is due to him. It was not his fault that his example and precept found little or no response. The fact that he stood alone makes him appear all the greater. Of hardly any other scientist can it be said what Stadler has advanced on his behalf—and no one has come forward to contradict him : ' In any case he was an observer of the first rank, and, if the development of the natural sciences had proceeded on the lines laid down by Albert, the wrong road taken for three centuries might have been spared them.'[90]

Albert was reproached in the Middle Ages and right up to very recent times for his dependence on Aristotle, though earnest researchers have not been wanting who saw an advantage in this, inasmuch as the ground was laid in the first place for a systematic structure, and in the second for a teleological conception of natural science. As regards zoology Strunz candidly recognizes the former when he says : ' Aristotle's zoology is a system of wonderful grandeur. Despite the many mistakes, overhasty generalizations, faulty observation, and the author's credulity which so

[90] H. Stadler : op. cit., 9.

often made itself felt, what he wrote on this subject ranks with the best that was written until well into the sixteenth century and even later, until Linnæus, who was the first to surpass him as a systematizer. The genius of the Aristotelian system lies in the philosophical mastery of the biological foundations, and in the manner in which zoology, general biology, the history of development, the theory of abnormalities, and physiology are all united into an organic whole. He had seen nature largely, as Albert also did later ; and it is this which gives his picture of the world its serene effect. Aristotle as a zoologist—and here too Albert took his master's road—was the creator of a classification and organization of the sciences, of a truly scientific system, whose logical arrangement remains to this day a model of its kind. Aristotle's zoology is dominated by a scientific method of perception. He is the first scientist to write.'[91] A little further on the same scholar again stresses the same point : 'We have here a well-considered system with many ramifications which is still to-day a subject for scientific and historical study ; it is certainly no worthless relic of antiquity which has had its day.'[92]

No one has brought out the second advantage more sharply than Georg von Hertling.[93] He admits all the advantages which the modern view of nature offers, but he cannot spare the mechanistic way of thinking the reproach that with all the detached knowledge it offers, it yet leaves the last and most profound question unanswered, a question which concerns the scientist in the highest degree : why this or that thing of which the beginning and end, the formation and the influence, may be determined to a hair's breadth in the smallest detail, why this thing should be exactly so and not otherwise. It cannot tell us why everything in the world, the whole and the individual element, should exhibit that precise form and arrangement which is good, and best suited to it. The enumeration of all the factors which contribute to bring about this thing is not sufficient. We want to know the ultimate reason why this thing is as it is, to what end this is as it is. The

[91] Strunz : op. cit., 125 *sq.* [92] Ibid : op. cit., 130.
[93] G. von Hertling : op. cit., 156 *sqq.*

modern mechanistic view of nature shelves this question or answers it by arbitrary philosophical assertions which are opposed to common sense. Albert from his teleological standpoint could give an answer satisfying both the mind and the heart, and in doing so goes far beyond Aristotle. The whole universe is the work of God's hands. He gives not merely a Supreme Orderer but a Creator of all things. Wherefore in the last resort everything is, because God wills it, and everything is precisely the thing it is, because it best answers the purpose of the whole. The universe and every individual thing in it bears the imprint of the Creator on it, and speaks of His goodness and beauty.[94] To have pursued the natural sciences from the teleological point of view is the Saint's great merit. Neglect of this is the fatal error of most modern scientists. The mechanistic view in its true elements does not exclude the teleological. It is only when the two are united that we attain to a complete conception of nature. That Albert in his day, and as far as his powers extended, fostered this, redounds to his very great honour.[95] It has been said that if Albert's principles on *experience* had been followed, natural science might have spared itself a détour of three centuries. It can with equal right be maintained that if it does not now accept his teleological conception, it is destined to pursue a yet more fatal by-road. It is only in judging Albert with this teleological manner of observation in mind that his full service to natural science is revealed and the justification is seen for his title : the Great.[96]

[94] *Physicorum*, lib. i, tr. 1, cap. 1 ; printed by Jessen in his edition of the *De vegetabilibus*, xxvi.

[95] That for Albert the individual animal did not sink to being a mere machine is very finely brought out by Schneider in his *Die Psychologie Alberts des Grossen*, 484.

[96] 'If ever there were a man in the Middle Ages who was a scientist in the modern sense of the word it was that great Doctor.' (Pope Pius XI thus referred to Albertus Magnus in an address to the eight hundred delegates to the Physiological Congress held in Rome in September, 1932.) [Ed.]

4. *Retrospect.*

It may be well now to review in retrospect the whole field of science as investigated by Albert the Great and to give exact references, with quotations, in illustration of his claim to be 'the first scientist.'

It has become quite customary for certain modern historians of science to repeat *ad nauseam* that the *Physiologus* was representative of the thirteenth-century attitude towards nature. Again, we are as frequently told that S. Albert was a mere copyist, and simply handed on the writings of Aristotle in another form.

How truly mistaken both these ideas are may be further illustrated by a few extracts taken at random from S. Albert's writings on natural science. He was no mere narrator, or romancer, but he had a truly scientific mind. Furthermore, so true is this, that he might be called a scientific genius, for modern research has already proved that our Saint had anticipated by many centuries several of the more important theories which are the boast of modern science.

In order to substantiate these statements we proceed to quote but a few extracts from his own words, and then finally to give in outline a very brief synopsis of his achievements in the various branches of natural science.

S. Albert's idea of and attitude towards science will be seen from the following quotations :

'We must not seek in God's use of natural things for a miracle declaring his power but rather for the natural causes proper to the things he has created.' (*De cælo et mundo*, lib. 1, tr. 4, cap. 10.)

'There are some people who attribute all these things to divine order and say that we must not consider in them any other cause but the will of God. This in part we can agree to. Yet we do not say that he does this because of a natural cause of which he is the first mover, since he is the cause of all movement ; for we are not seeking a reason or explanation of the divine will but rather investigating natural causes which are as instruments through which God's will is manifested. It is not sufficient to know these things in a general sort of way ; what we are looking for is the cause of each individual thing according to the nature belonging to it. This is the best and most perfect kind of knowledge.' (*De causis proprietatum elementorum*, lib. 1, tr. 1, cap. 9.)

'We will not go into all that may be said about these things since this would not advance our knowledge of the science. It is not the business of natural science to accept implicitly whatever may have been said on the subject but to search for the causes proper to each natural thing.' (*De mineralibus*, lib. 2, tr. 2, cap. 1.)

'And therefore I think that Aristotle must have spoken from the opinions of his predecessors and not from the truth of demonstration or experiment.' (*Meteororum*, lib. 3, tr. 4, cap. 11.)

'In this sixth book *De vegetabilibus* we satisfy the curiosity of our students rather than that of Philosophy itself. Therefore we will propose certain things more known to us and leave others out altogether. Of those which we shall treat, some we shall prove from our experience, whilst others we shall leave to the dicta of men who, as we have ascertained, do not say things lightly but base everything on experience. This method alone can give certainty in such things.' (*De vegetabilibus*, lib. 6, tr. 1, cap. 1.)

'Following the principle of another book [i.e. Thomas de Chantimpré's], we shall here take the various species in alphabetical order according to their names. For though this method is not proper to philosophy, as we have shown above, because in this there must often be repetition ; yet because we have a duty to the unlearned as well as to the learned, we follow this and treat each species separately, as being the best way to instruct the rustic mind.' (*De animalibus*, lib. 22, tr. 1, cap. 1.)

'These are to be taken rather as tales than as philosophical proofs based on experiment.' (*De animalibus*, lib. 23.)

'This is what we have discovered about the nature of whales ; what the ancients have written on the subject we pass over, since it does not tally with our experience.' (*De animalibus*, lib. 24.)

'This is absolutely false as we have proved elsewhere.' (*De animalibus*, lib. 24.)

'That is more true which has been found by the experiments of philosophers. But if we follow the accounts given by those who report what they have heard from the common people rather than demonstrate the phenomena of nature from this personal experience, then, following Pliny and Solenius and some others . . . and these statements I consider not to be sufficiently well founded.' (*De animalibus*, lib. 25.)

'Nature does what is best in all things.' (*De animalibus*, lib. 25.)

'There are birds according to Solenius and Jorach which can fly into the flames of fire without being burnt in wing or body. But these philosophers tell many falsehoods and I think that this is one of them.' (*De animalibus*, lib. 23.)

'This we have already proved by experiments.' (*De animalibus*, lib. 23.)

'We found by experiment that after we had cut off its head it crowed for some time after.' (*De animalibus*, lib. 23.)

'When we have gone over these various points, that we may well and minutely understand what has been said, we must then make conjectures and experiments of our own so as to arrive at a knowledge of trees *per se*.' (*De vegetabilibus*, lib. 1, tr. 2, cap. 12.)

'But this is not proved sufficiently by definite experiment, as in the case of the rest which is written here, but is taken from the writings of the ancients.' (*De vegetabilibus*, lib. 6, tr. 1, cap. 30.)

'In their characteristics therefore the animals differ according to their various species; but we know less about the nature of the smaller animals than we do of the larger ones, for the former cannot be dissected and have not a long enough life to enable us to study them through experiments; whereas of the latter we have a greater knowledge since we can dissect their various parts and arrive at conclusions about their use and actions: and again their longer life gives us a better chance to observe them.' (*De animalibus*, lib. 8, tr. 1, cap. 1.)

'In this book as in the preceding ones of Aristotle I have not seen the tractate except in excerpts for which I had diligently to seek in various parts of the world. I will discuss therefore either those things which have been handed down to us by the philosophers or which I myself have experienced. For at one time when I was away from home I wandered far and wide to places where metals were to be found that I might discover their nature and properties. This is the best kind of inquiry and the most certain, for then a thing is known by the cause proper to it, and we have no uncertainty as to its accidentals.' (*De mineralibus*, lib. 3, tr. 1, cap. 1.)

'I saw and studied how they worked in copper in our parts, namely Paris and Cologne and other places in which I was.' (*De mineralibus*, lib. 4, tr. 1, cap. 6.)

'Furthermore, we can show the same thing by mathematical methods, for when we are considering the shape and size of the earth, which is also what Mathematicians deal with, though from a different point of view, we can employ mathematical demonstrations here because of the similarity of the matter under discussion. We may say therefore that the first sign proving that the earth is round is that which falls under our eyes in an eclipse of the moon. For if the earth were not round the shadow of the earth would not be round, and if the shadow were not round we should not see the eclipse in the form in which it is presented to our eyes, for this cannot be a mere optical illusion.' (*De cœlo et mundo*, lib. 2, tr. 4, cap. 11.)

To give but a list of his treatises in the Natural Sciences almost bewilders one—both in the range of subjects as well as in their number.

There are eight treatises on Natural Science, consisting of Commentaries on Aristotle's Physics and on the underlying principles of natural philosophy, and of energy and movement: four treatises concerning the Heavens and the Earth, which contain the general principle of the movement of the heavenly bodies. Besides there is a treatise on the

Nature of Places, consisting of a description of climates and natural conditions. This volume contains numerous suggestions with regard to ethnography and physiology. Then there is a treatise on the Causes of the properties of the elements, which takes up the specific peculiarities of the elements, according to their physical and geographical relations. To these must be added two treatises on Generation and Corruption ; four books on Meteors ; five books on Minerals ; three books on the Soul, in which is considered the vital principle ; a treatise on Nutrition and Nutritives ; a treatise on the Senses ; another on the Memory and the Imagination ; two books on the Intellect ; a treatise on Sleep and Waking ; a treatise on Youth and Old Age ; a treatise on the Motion of Animals, in two books, which concerns the voluntary and involuntary movements of animals ; a treatise on Life and Death ; a treatise in seven books on Vegetables and Plants ; and a treatise on Breathing Things ; finally a treatise on Animals in twenty-six books. Nearly seventy other works on a variety of subjects have been lost.

His originality and genius are shown in many ways. That he had anticipated many of the more important discoveries of modern science must be admitted if we take each branch in turn and see therein examples of S. Albert's scientific genius. These facts have been taken from experts working on the writing of our Saint.[97] It might be said, with a certain amount of truth, that no branch of science has caused more stir and called for more attention of late than that of Physics. It must be surprising to those who consider the Middle Ages as a period 'which distorted human thought'[98] to find that even here S. Albert had

[97] Hyacinth Casey, O.P., in *Irish Eccl. Record*, April and May, 1932 ; also in *Irish Rosary*, Feb., 1932 ; Sr. Mary Ellen O'Hanlon, O.P., in the *Torch*, 1932.

[98] 'Let us skip the Middle Ages to consider the modern age alone. For the Middle Ages of Europe were a period in which the natural course of development of human thought was distorted and overwhelmed by the dominance of the Christian Church with its authoritative claim to impose a supernaturally imposed religion.' (Prof. Wm. McDougall on 'The present chaos in Psychology,' in *Journal of Philosophical Studies*, July, 1920, p. 355.)

explained such things as Sound and Heat ; even the very analogies used by him might be taken from a modern textbook on these subjects.

For example, he says that sound is the vibration of the air produced by the percussion of two hard bodies, and that this vibration is propagated in the form of a sphere whose centre is the point of percussion. The sound-waves spread out from their source like ripples on the surface of water when a stone has been dropped into it. He also gives a perfect explanation of the phenomenon of the echo, as being merely the reflexion of the outgoing sound-waves.

That he was not unacquainted with the use of magnets is a well-known fact. He also knew the properties of mirrors and the laws concerning the reflexion of light, and notes accurately the effect of different angles of incidence of the sun's rays in heating the ground. Light, he says, is converted into heat on being absorbed by a body.

Perhaps the most surprising theory in this field of science is contained in one of his proofs that the earth is spherical —a theory which incidentally contains in embryo the nebular theory of Laplace. He states that the earth was formed by the condensation of particles brought about by the gravitational force contained in each. It is now a commonplace that all bodies attract each other gravitationally, and upon this fact was based the experiment performed some years ago to ascertain the weight of the earth.

In Anatomy we also find some striking remarks. He takes as the basis of structure the vertebral column, while the greater number of anatomists who succeed him always begin with the skull. But as a rational basis for the comparison of structures the vertebral column is certainly the more important. This system is followed in modern anatomy, but very little acknowledgement has been given to S. Albert as its initiator.

There is also the fact that he takes Aristotle to task as to the number of man's ribs. The Stagyrite held that man had eight ribs on either side : S. Albert disagreed with this opinion and said that 'man has seven true ribs and five false ribs on either side.'

In Architecture he is generally supposed to have drawn

the plans of the Cathedral at Cologne. This is probably not true; but the fact that it should have been thought so, proves that men were ready to accord to him skill in all the sciences. It is known that he planned the apse of the Dominican convent chapel in Louvain, and an interesting connexion with this is the apse of S. Dominic's Priory Church, Haverstock Hill, which was modelled on it.

Nor is Anthropology unrepresented in his works. He shows quite accurately and distinctly the effect of climate upon types of plants, animals, and men. We have a better and freer conception of the effect of terrestrial zones upon type. Whereas the classical world made every variation depend rigidly upon latitude, at the same time it had neglected the whole subject of the influence of level and aspect: both these errors, of excess and defect, find at least implicit correction in Albert.

In the realm of Astronomy—not forgetting the fact that he had no telescope nor modern means for proving his theories—his description of the movements of the heavenly bodies differs widely from the Aristotelian point of view; thus 'The heavens move from east to west carrying along with them their particular stars which move from west to east; something like a huge machine moved by God according to secret principles which the human intellect, however, can partly discover. Each star, in turn, is moved by a pure intellect, each having its own heavens with its particular motion; so that the circles of the stars are not concentric, as Aristotle on the authority of Eudoxus taught, but eccentric as in Ptolemy's system.' He has also an interesting comment to make upon the dark spots of the moon's disc. He shows that the theory of the ancients, which attributed them to the earth's shadow, is wrong, and gives as the true explanation the configurations of the moon itself, which is of the same nature as the earth.

It is extremely difficult to pick out his most important contribution to Biology. Everywhere the biological element and his own personality are prominent, and for this reason his writings form a sharp contrast to the dry book learning of the periods preceding and following his lifetime.

Perhaps enough has been said in a previous section with

regard to his observations in Botany. A small yet interesting fact might, however, be noted here, proving that he must have been very adroit in the use of the scalpel. He observes that fruits have three coverings, the epicarp, the mesocarp, and endocarp of modern botany. He is also careful to distinguish between the inner and outer bark of plants and of the rôle played by each in the plant economy. That he was also an expert in the art of plant-surgery may be gathered from his precise directions with regard to the ways of grafting.

Although it is now practically certain that the *Libellus de alchemia* has been falsely attributed to Albertus, yet there is, scattered throughout his other works, much that he contributed to the laying of the foundation for true chemical science. Here again he was 'original everywhere, even where he seems to copy.' He was familiar with many chemical processes and their operations. He was the first to state the metallic nature of arsenic, and by some historians he is given the credit of being the first one to isolate this element. He was the first to use the word 'affinity' in the sense that chemists use it to-day, and he certainly knew of the preparation of gunpowder from sulphur, saltpetre, and charcoal as early as the year 1250.

The theory of the transmutation of metals had for most scientific minds during the last century been quite enough of itself to stamp the generations of the Middle Ages who accepted it as utterly lacking, if not in common sense, at least in serious reasoning power. At the present time we are in the full tide of opinions that tend to make us believe not only in the possibility, but also in the actual occurrence, of the transmutation of metals.

Observations made with regard to radium have revolutionized all the scientific thinking on this matter. Radium has apparently been demonstrated as changing into helium. It has been shown that litheum, when acted upon by radium emanations, changes to some extent into copper.

He also has some striking remarks about embryos and fishes. We may select for a quotation a passage on the generation of fish, a subject on which some of Aristotle's

THE MASTER PROPHESYING THE GREATNESS OF HIS YOUNG PUPIL
S. THOMAS AQUINAS

Frontispiece to Rudolf von Nymegen's *Legenda literalis Alberti Magni*
Cologne, 1484).

most remarkable descriptions remained unconfirmed until modern times: S. Albert's description of the energies of fish and his accurate distinctions of their mode of development from that of birds, by the absence of allantoic membrane in the one and its presence in the other, must surely be startling.

In the later Middle Ages there was a momentous revolution in map science and in the art of navigation. It is no small wonder, therefore, that we find S. Albert treating of the subject of Geography in all its aspects. In his encyclopædic survey of the earth no fact seemed to escape his powers of observation. He has his theory of the formation of the earth's crust—a slowly cooling husk of a central world fire. He has no hesitation in describing the origin of mountain ranges as the results of upheaval, and most interesting of all, we find an excellent treatment of both latitude and altitude as influencing local climate. He even mentions his own maps (which have not come down to us), and it has been shown that his opinions were responsible, at least indirectly, for the discovery of America.

He treats as fabulous the commonly received idea that the region of the earth south of the Equator was uninhabitable, and considers that from the Equator to the South Pole the earth was not only habitable but in all probability actually inhabited; except directly at the poles, where he imagines the cold to be excessive. If there are any animals there, he says, 'they must have very thick skins to defend them from the rigour of the climate, and they are probably of a white colour.' Did he here anticipate the modern theory of Protective Coloration?

He also smiles with a scholar's freedom at the simplicity of those who suppose that persons living at the opposite regions of the earth must fall off, an opinion that can only arise out of the grossest ignorance, for when we speak of the lower hemisphere, this must be understood as relatively to ourselves.

It is also truly astonishing to find him tracing correctly the chief mountain chains of Europe, with the rivers which take their source in each; remarking on portions of coast which have in later times been submerged by the ocean, and islands which have been raised by volcanic action above the sea-level.

Although Geology is a very recent science, we also find that S. Albert was acquainted with fossil remains. He observed that some stones quarried near Paris contained shells of fish, and he ascribed this to the fact that the district had at one time been submerged under the sea.

That he probably wrote a treatise on Mathematics seems to be quite conclusive, as he often refers to his mathematical works, especially his fifteenth and sixteenth books of geometry ; but these works have not yet reached us. We know, however, that he placed mathematics between metaphysics and natural science. The object of mathematics is defined by him as 'the motion and material extension of natural objects independently of their essence and their fundamental causes.' The mathematician studies the straight line, for example, as it is materially illustrated in nature, but he does not consider the cause of the straight line or the particular matter which illustrates it.

In his books on minerals he gives the opinions of the ancients but disagrees with them very frequently, as when the facts of his own experience cannot be reconciled with them. He also shows that he was acquainted with the phenomenon of petrifaction, and that some water had the power of covering objects with a stony deposit. He gives a list of almost one hundred crystalline minerals, and to each he appends a short description, together with the medicinal and other qualities commonly ascribed to it by tradition ; but he is careful to include this latter information under the term 'dicitur.'

Scattered throughout his various works is a considerable amount of Physiology. But it is in the branch of Plant-physiology that S. Albert excels. He knew of the inability of plants to assimilate any complicated foods. These, he says, have to be first broken down by a process of digestion which takes place in the soil, which acts as a stomach for the plant. The roots then absorb the necessary nutriment which is conveyed by 'veins' to the various parts of the plant. He further explains that the term 'vein' is not to be used in the same sense of plants and animals.

Much importance has been given in modern times to the effect of the endocrine glands in formation of temperaments. The most recent findings have been compared with S. Albert's four classical temperaments and the characteristics of each. One cannot refrain from marvelling at what is almost verbal agreement between the two series of observations, the one belonging to the thirteenth century, the other to the twentieth.

Finally, as an example of S. Albert's sharp powers of observation, as well as his gift for accurate description even of the minutest detail, his account of the ostrich might easily be taken from a twentieth-century manual.

'The ostrich is a bird of the Libyan desert, but more often seen (by Europeans) in our country. When young it is ash-coloured, and completely feathered, but the feathers of its wings are not strongly developed ; in its second year, and thereafter little by little, it loses completely the feathers of the thighs, neck, and head, and exposes the body ; it is protected, however, from the cold by a tough skin, and the very dark feathers of the back become, as it were, like wool. The very strong hips and the fleshy legs have white skin, and the toes are arranged in the foot like a camel's ; it is called Camelon by certain Greeks, and Asida by others. Moreover, it is tall, perhaps five or six feet from foot to back ; it has a very long neck, a goose-like head, and a beak quite small, as compared to its body.

'It is said of this bird that it swallows and digests iron ; but I have not found this myself, because several ostriches refused to eat the iron which I threw them. However, they eagerly devoured large bones cut into small pieces, as well as gravel.

'This bird is said to be bound to the earth and unable to fly, but by extending its wings it somewhat hastens its course. It has a kind of spur in the elbow of its wings with which it strikes whatever it attacks.

'This bird lays its eggs in July and hides them in the coarse sand. These hatch in the heat of the sun, just as do many other eggs of animals. The ostrich does not return to the eggs, because its naked body is not able to incubate them. Sometimes, however, it guards them, keeping watch over the place where they lie ; and for this reason a false rumour has arisen that it hatches its eggs by looking at them. This is what I have observed concerning the ostrich, which seems to be not so much a bird as a creature half-way between a walking and a flying animal.'

Hence it may truly be said of him that while the encyclopædic character of his learning gained him from his contemporaries the title of Doctor Universalis, scientists certainly will not deny him the other contemporary title of the Great.

II. THE INTELLECTUAL GREATNESS OF ALBERT AS PHILOSOPHER

1. *Albertus Magnus and Aristotle.*

ALBERT was called *Magnus Philosophus* or *Maximus Philosophus* before the general title of 'the Great' was given him. In those days, it is true, the term 'philosophy' had a wider connotation than it has to-day; it embraced all purely natural knowledge and therefore also the natural sciences. In what follows we shall have to inquire whether his services in the field of philosophy, taken in its modern and narrower sense, also merited this epithet.

If we call a great philosopher not only one who for the first time expresses a new idea, and thus opens out new ways to research, but also that man who perceives the importance of, and obtains recognition for, an old and correct system, which has fallen into oblivion because its contemporaries and their successors did not grasp it, then without question Albert deserved the name of Great in philosophy, for he achieved this under the most difficult conditions in the case of a system of supreme genius.

In the purely natural field the wisdom of the ancient world unquestionably culminated in the philosophy of Aristotle. No one has thought more clearly and more correctly, more profoundly and at the same time more simply, on the problems of essence, existence, and act than did the Stagyrite; never were great truths stated more calmly and objectively than by him. His works exhibit relatively the highest achievements of the human reason when thrown on its own resources. It was his tragic fate that his own countrymen failed to understand his teaching, while the immediate pupils of the Master altered the principles in such a manner that the magnificent comprehensiveness of his system was lost. As time passed, the understanding of it became ever more confused and the disparity with the pure teaching of Aristotle more noticeable. When the glad tidings of the Gospel came to the world, Aristotle was almost forgotten, and what remained of his teaching no longer had any influence.

In its early days, owing to its struggles for existence with the might of the Roman state, Christianity had little time or opportunity to take up any definite attitude towards the existing philosophical systems ; but when under Constantine freedom was allowed it, and with it leisure and occasion to examine its attitude towards philosophy, and to enlist the truths of nature for the explanation and defence of the truths of the faith, the fashionable philosophy of the day was Neoplatonism. This system, because of its mystical atmosphere and extremely spiritual conception of man, and, above all, because of its teaching on the next world, seemed to be especially adapted for a scientific exposition of the truths of the faith. The Fathers of the Church made the attempt, and no less a one than Augustine devoted the whole perspicacity of his genius to bring about the desired result. The learned Bishop of Hippo achieved a great deal ; he was able to make direct use of many Platonic ideas for the exposition of the truths of the faith, while other conceptions only lent themselves to the problem after being subjected to more or less torsion ; but the compact and unified system for which they were looking would not result. No one, we may take it, suffered more than Augustine from the deficiencies of the Platonic philosophy. In spite of these, men in the succeeding centuries clung to the system, working along the same lines, hoping against hope to get what they were longing for. It must, to be sure, not be forgotten that in the immense upheavals in states and peoples due to the break-up of the Roman empire and the gradual entry of the Germanic tribes into the spirit of Christianity and of Roman culture, scientific undertakings naturally had to take a subordinate place.

The Aristotelian system had meanwhile experienced a revival and revision at the hands of Arabic and Jewish scholars, by which, though the original lines of thought of the great Greek remained obscured and confused, interest in them was awakened and a stimulus given to the study of his writings. When in the twelfth century, as a consequence of the Crusades and the founding of Universities, a period favourable to scientific research set in, Aristotle's writings gradually found their way into the centres of learning. As might be expected from the purely natural content of the works and the commentaries of the Jews and Arabs, it was the humanists who first directed their attention to this new acquisition to culture. The theologians maintained a cautious reserve, partly out of respect for the Fathers, who had unanimously held by Plato, partly, too, because of the many passages inimical to the faith which these new-found works, and especially the Judæo-Arabian commentaries, contained. True, out of the ranks of the theologians there were one or more who did occupy themselves with Aristotle's writings; they had been, indeed, directed to do so in the interest of the maintenance of the purity of the faith. Not a few also recognized the importance of one part or another of his teaching; but for their fundamental treatment they had to wait for Albert the Great. He it was who evoked a complete change of feeling.[1] Grabmann characterizes the introduction of Aristotle's philosophy as the greatest event of mediæval scholasticism.[2] And Michael says: 'It was Albert who for the first time threw open to the Christian world the whole philosophic system of Aristotle and made its treasury of knowledge available to scholasticism.'[3] Albert's significance as a philosopher lies in the fact that he was the first to recognize and to proclaim the full value of the Aristotelian philosophy, and, further, that he made the works of the Stagyrite accessible to his contemporaries by paraphrases, which remain of value even to-day, and thus made it possible for

[1] Arthur Schneider: *Die Psychologie Alberts des Grossen*, 15. The change had begun as early as 1200. Cf. Ueberweg und Geyer: *Geschichte der patristischen und scholastischen Philosophie*, 343, 346.

[2] M. Grabmann: *Der Einfluss Alberts des Grossen auf das mittelalterliche Geistesleben*, 2.

[3] Michael: op. cit., iii, 68.

them to verify his statements, and yet again in the fact that he treated the more important points in monographs, utilizing them finally in the creation of a Christian philosophy which could serve as a foundation for theology. What Augustine sought so eagerly, what he with his powerful genius might have accomplished had he had a better knowledge of Aristotle's writings, namely a Christian philosophy, was created by Albert. In saying this, there is no wish to detract from the merit of the preliminary labours accomplished by the Fathers and especially Augustine, nor is there any intention of belittling the services of later scholars in connexion with the development and treatment of certain individual parts ; it is only claimed for Albert that he was, properly speaking, the creator of that pregnant work, the *philosophia perennis*.

That Albert recognized the value of the Aristotelian system in the conditions of his time says extraordinarily much for him. It is true that the logical works of Aristotle had been known and used for a long time, but the metaphysical works, which in Albert's day were finding their way into the Christian world, were so distorted in the poor copies available, and by the commentaries of the Arabs and Jews, that theologians were at one in fearing them as a danger to the faith. The growing partiality of the humanists for the study of Aristotle increased still more the uneasiness of the theologians and only made them cling to Plato the more tensely. It was a great deal when one theologian or other, as for instance Alexander of Hales, brought himself to the point of utilizing some thesis of Aristotle's in the solution of a problem which could not be solved on Platonic principles. Albert did not rivet himself to one proposition, he was not concerned with any one particular problem, but with the system as a whole. He often enough differed with the Stagyrite on individual questions, but he never for a moment hesitated as between Plato and Aristotle ; his firm conviction was that it was not from Plato but from Aristotle that a Christian philosophy could be shaped. In this he found himself in opposition to the whole scientific world of the time, to the theologians because they clung to Plato, and to the humanists because he wanted another Aristotle than they did. When this conception first came to the great German scholar we do not know, nor can we tell whether it was a sudden intuitive vision or a divination to which the instinct of his genius led him. He stands before us with this conviction in him, and it is under this conviction that throughout the many days of his long life he studied, taught, and wrote, never taking rest, in order to force this conviction on his contemporaries. This was his life's work.

Albert did not reject Plato unheard. Gaul makes the specific point that the Saint, though he shared with his contemporaries many an error concerning certain particular doctrines of the Attic philosopher, nevertheless expressed in the happiest way the difference between the two systems, when he maintained that Plato starts from general principles (rationes universales) in order by them to explain particular phenomena, whereas Aristotle starts from the nature of things and deduced from this the general principles. When the same scholar goes on to say : ‘ It is clear that Aristotle's method must have appealed more closely than Plato's to the greatest or rather the only true scientist among the scholastics,'[4] he points to a congeniality between Albert and Aristotle, which certainly lightened the former's labours ; though, when all allowance is made for this, the amount he accomplished remains amazing. Only one who considers how hard it is even to-day to get at Aristotle's real meaning on certain points, and this in spite of editions of his works which meet every demand of scholarship, and notwithstanding splendid translations, will be able to measure the acuteness of mind which Albert must have displayed in order to recognize that element in the Stagyrite, which up to then had been lacking in the whole realm of knowledge. All the time he had at his disposal only defective copies, faulty transcriptions, and revisions bristling with errors ; but just as the falcon spies the prey it is seeking though it be lurking under thick undergrowth or luxuriant creepers, so did Albert discover under this husk the true kernel of his teaching, namely the system which could best serve his purpose.

Albert's genius shines out more clearly still when we

[4] Leopold Gaul : *Alberts des Grossen Verhältniss zu Plato,* 156.

remember that he never attended any philosophical course. According to the statements of some of the earlier writers he was quite young, in fact his sixteenth year is named, when he entered the Order. But if it be accepted, as is generally done, that he was getting on for thirty when he entered it, he at any rate never studied philosophy. Roger Bacon expressly says : ' He has never studied philosophy, nor did he attend lectures on the subject in the schools, he was also never in a studium solemne before he became a theologian ; he could not have received any instruction in his Order, for he was the first Master of Philosophy in it.'[5] Roger Bacon thus tries to make fun of one who would teach before he has learnt. Albert did not let himself be put out. He went on with his studies unremittingly and was soon able to lay before his contemporaries splendid results of his research in the paraphrases of Aristotle's works.

In the *Liber physicorum* Albert writes : ' Our purpose is to make all these parts [he is referring to Physics, Metaphysics and Mathematics] intelligible to Latinists.'[6] Roger Bacon sees presumption in this announcement, since he held the undertaking to be impossible of execution. Albert carried out what he had said he would do. First he looked round for a serviceable text, but the conviction was more and more forced on him that an entirely new translation was necessary. For this work Albert was confessedly not equal, since he was not versed in the Greek language, and at his age he had neither the time nor the opportunity to assimilate it ; but one of his brethren in the Order was capable of the task. William of Moerbeke had, in about the year 1242, been sent to Greece by the Chapter-General of the Order, where he worked indefatigably for the union of the Greek and Latin Churches. He died as Bishop of Corinth in the year 1281. This highly gifted Netherlander, who was thoroughly schooled in both philosophy and languages, completed in the years 1260–1270 a new transla-

[5] Roger Bacon : *Opera quædam hactenus inedita*, i, 327 ; J. A. Endres : *Das Geburtsjahr und die Chronologie in der ersten Lebenshälfte Alberts des Grossen*, 296 ; Endres : *Chronologische Untersuchungen zu den philosophischen Kommentaren Alberts des Grossen*, 97.

[6] *Physicorum*, lib. 1, tr. 1, cap. 1.

tion of Aristotle's works. The value of this version is still recognized. S. Thomas Aquinas is usually designated as having been the one to induce William to undertake the work, because he used his translation as a basis for his Commentaries. It is probable, however, that the instigation came from Albert, who was making his Commentary on the old version and, in doing so, saw at every step its defects, and became impressed with the absolute necessity of a better translation.

The Saint's work consisted in the elucidation of these writings. In this connexion Schneider remarks: 'His philosophical importance lies in the fact that he paraphrased the said works of Aristotle after the method of Avicenna, and thus not only gave his readers exact information on Aristotle's own views, but also, going far back historically, stated and criticized the pertinent teachings of the rediscovered Greek, Arabian, and Jewish writers. With extraordinary perspicacity he found his way through, and mastered, this immense range of scientific material and the multiform masses of ideas embedded in them.'[7] Albert's purpose was to reproduce in paraphrase as faithfully as possible the line of thought and meaning of Aristotle's works. That he succeeded in doing this is borne out by Ritter, who remarks that on many points Albert has understood Aristotle better than do the present-day philosophers.[8] It would, however, be perverse always to see in these works the personal ideas of the Saint. Albert found himself often obliged to take up a stand against such an impression. In the commentary on the *Politica* he says: 'It is not I who have said anything in this book; I have only set out what has been said, and stated principles and causes. Similarly in all the physical books I have never put forward my own opinion but have rather expounded as faithfully as I could the views of the Peripatetics. This I only say on account of some lazy people, who, seeking an excuse for their laziness, scrutinize the book for something they can find

[7] A. Schneider: op. cit., 16.

[8] Heinrich Ritter: *Geschichte der christlichen Philosophie*, iv, 186; Michael: op. cit., iii, 116.

fault with.'[9] Michael insists that Ritter had not adequately remarked this, otherwise he could not have maintained that Albert had not sufficiently freed himself from the emanation theory. 'The great interpreter of the great Greek only sets out to reproduce his train of ideas, and therefore repeatedly guards himself, sometimes in unusually acid terms, against the conclusion that he (Albert) is sponsoring a view simply because it stands in his paraphrase of Aristotle.'[10] By these expositions, which Albert was the first to give, on the complete works of Aristotle, the thirteenth century was in the position to acquire such a thorough understanding of the Stagyrite as was never the case before nor in the first centuries succeeding him.

In his treatment of the Nicomachean Ethics and the Politics, Albert altered his method. In the other works he makes special interpolations in which he discusses the views of the Arabs and Jews, and notes those which in his opinion express Aristotle's meaning most faithfully. These interpolations are recognizable as digressions. In the Ethics these discussions no longer stand out in the same way; we have, as it were, a transition towards an independent commentary. Albert never composed a commentary, properly speaking, on the Ethics, as Thomas later did, but only on the Politics. In this the text is rigidly separated from the explanation.

Opinions are divided as to the period when the Saint accomplished this work. While Loë[11] is of opinion that it fell after 1266, the general view is that it was much earlier. Endres[12] gives the years 1240–1256. It is certain that the two commentaries, which bear a special character, and would appear to have been influenced by Thomas's method, must be dated later than this.

[9] *Politicorum*, lib. 8, cap. 6 *in fine*.

[10] Michael: op. cit., iii, 117; cf. Schneider, op. cit., 4, and W. Arendt: *Die Staats- und Gesellschaftslehre Alberts des Grossen*, 80 *sqq*.

[11] P. von Loë: *Kritische Streifzüge auf dem Gebiete der Albertus Magnus-Forschung*, 126.

[12] Endres: *Chronologische Untersuchungen zu den philosophischen Kommentaren Alberts des Grossen*, 108. Mandonnet reached about the same conclusion in his *Polémique Averroeste de Siger de Brabant et de saint Thomas d'Aquin*.

2. *Albertus Magnus and Plato.*

The Saint's eager efforts for the elucidation and the dissemination of Aristotle's writings earned him the ill-will of his contemporaries, and he was called in mockery Aristotle's ape.[13] That Albert was no blind follower of the Greek may be seen by anyone who casts but a glance at the works. Moreover, he expressly emphasizes the fact that he does not hold Aristotle to be infallible. Whoever believes that Aristotle was a man and not God must expect to find in him errors and imperfections.[14] We shall see, especially in metaphysics and psychology, to what a searching criticism he subjected the theses of the Stagyrite. That Albert was not a fanatical adherent of Aristotle's is, moreover, clearly shown in the attitude he took up towards Plato. Dr. Gaul deserves great credit for having investigated the relationship. A result of his research is to establish the fact that Albert did not reject Plato's philosophy *a limine*, but made himself thoroughly acquainted with it. He certainly knew the Timæus, and, so far as Chalcidius had translated it, had studied it profoundly, and he also made the richest use of it in his own independent works. Whether he possessed other writings of Plato is doubtful, but it is certain that he was familiar with the contents of the Phædo, Meno, and Phædrus.[15]

Whatever judgement on Plato Albert allows to appear, varies completely according to the character of the work in which it occurs. Where, in a paraphrase of Aristotle, he hits out at Plato's ideas, he is following the Stagyrite. As the difference of opinion is often expressed very bluntly, he has been branded as an opponent of Plato's ; yet, as we have seen, his purpose throughout was not the exposition of his own view, but merely the most faithful possible reproduction of Aristotle's thought. In these works, therefore, where Aristotle is combating Plato's theses, Albert must also maintain a hostile attitude, and the sharpness of his attack varies as that of the Stagyrite's. Albert proceeds quite differently in his other works. In them he often has occasion to discuss Plato, and here, too, he not seldom

[13] Sighart : op. cit., 305.
[14] *Physicorum*, lib. 8, tr. 1, cap. 14.
[15] L. Gaul : op. cit., 29.

rejects his views, but never as bluntly as he does in the Commentaries. Sometimes he expresses himself as in agreement with Plato even in questions on which he has opposed him in the paraphrases. This change of attitude is explained by the different character of the various works. At one place, in the *Summa de creaturis*, for instance, Albert gives his own view, but this will not prevent him from admitting Plato's at another, if the latter's principles are sound. If he cannot accept some observation of Plato's in the form which he has before him, Albert will often essay a new interpretation in his own independent work, in an attempt to read a tenable meaning into the text. This he may have been led to do by the authority of the Fathers and especially S. Augustine. We may take as an example the definition of the soul from automatism. Albert made the mistake of supposing that Augustine had taken this from Plato's works, whereas it really derives from Alcuin. While, however, the Platonists understood this to apply to the activity of the soul, Albert referred it to the capacity to set the organism in motion. He is able to accept Plato's words on the presumption that they were supported by Augustine's authority, but he gives them an entirely new meaning. Gaul calls this case characteristic of 'Albert's method of synthesis.'[16] At any rate, an out-and-out opponent of Plato's would not have taken this course.

In the determination of the nature of the soul the Saint in certain details relies upon Plato. High as he rates the fact that Aristotle was the first to define the correct relation between soul and body, he nevertheless cannot follow him in everything. The soul is not merely the form, life, and activity in the body, but is independent of and superior to the body. Thus he remarks : 'To this we must answer, that when we are investigating the soul in itself we agree with Plato, but in so far as we are considering the form of the animation which it gives to the body, with Aristotle.'[17]

[16] L. Gaul : op. cit., 87.

[17] II *Summa Theologica*, tr. 2, q. 69. L. Gaul (op. cit., 91) remarks on this : 'Our investigations have, however, shown that Albert, despite all his previous attacks on Plato, pays him the tribute of having seen deepest into the nature of the soul, and in this respect of having an advantage over Aristotle.'

On the question of the immortality of the soul Albert cites Plato as *the* 'philosophical authority.'[18] He takes over three of his proofs without further change, while he recasts a fourth in such a way that he can say: 'Now that we have amended Plato's wording in this manner his demonstration is cogent and leads directly to the conclusion that the rational soul lives and continues to exist and does not perish with the body.'[19]

These are the two most important problems in which Albert keeps company with Plato; in many other cases what Gaul remarks holds: 'Where Albert is speaking in dependence on Aristotle, an unfavourable judgement on Plato is passed; where, however, he gives unfettered expression to his own opinion, he treats him with much greater deference.'[20] Albert's relation to Plato shows quite plainly that the Saint was not by any means a fanatical partisan of Aristotle and blind to everything else, but that in this case too he knew how to preserve his own broad sympathies and universality. His imitation of the Stagyrite did not bear the stamp of a slave but of a free man of independent, discriminating mind.

3. *Christian Philosophy.*

(*a*) Metaphysics.

In the philosophical field Albert's greatest importance rests on the fact that he recognized the value of Aristotle's teachings as a basis for a genuine Christian philosophy. Schneider expresses this thus: 'He was the first mediæval thinker of note not only to grasp the intrinsic value of Aristotle's scientific writings, but also to see clearly the great importance of his philosophy for the construction of a Christian dogmatic system.'[21] This will hold for the general fundamentals, for the superstructure, and for many individual details, but it does not hold in the sense that Albert took over without correction the whole body of his

[18] L. Gaul: op. cit., 97.
[19] *De natura et origine Animæ*, tr. 2, cap. 1.
[20] L. Gaul: op. cit., 144.
[21] A. Schneider: op. cit., 16.

teaching. It is for this reason that Hertling emphasizes the primary importance of demonstrating what Albert made of Aristotle's teachings, how he understood them, how he improved on them, and was able to fit them in as important factors in the sum of Christian knowledge.[22] Hertling himself took in hand this investigation in regard to metaphysics, and arrived at results exceedingly honourable to our Saint.

The fundamental problem of all philosophy, namely, the question of Universals, which intensely interested the eleventh and twelfth centuries, was not solved by Albert in Plato's sense. In this he took a decided stand on Aristotle's side. The Universal exists in a threefold manner: prior to the thing, in it, and posterior to it. Prior to the thing it exists in the divine intelligence; in it, it signifies that by which the thing has precisely its own nature proper to itself; posterior to it, it exists in the human understanding, which arrives at it by abstraction from the thing as the necessary and therefore proper object of science. Albert made a small correction in Aristotle by extending his definition to run: 'The Universal is *of* many things and *in* many things.'[23]

A second fundamental problem is the knowledge of God. Men disputed then as they do now over Aristotle's proofs of his existence, or, respectively, of the perception of God. The true bases for each are in any case to be found in Aristotle, and, as may be anticipated, Albert made them his own, and sought to bring them into connexion with what the dogmas of the Church and the speculations of the Fathers had established. The task was not easy, but, as Hertling insists, 'it is all the more interesting to see how Albert managed to bring this rich content into correspondence with Aristotle's conclusions in such a manner as to appear that the former is of necessity deduced from the latter.'[24]

Albert works out the relation of God to the world under the aspect of the threefold cause: the efficient, formal, and

[22] G. von Hertling: op. cit., 86.
[23] Ibid., op. cit., 92; I *Sententiarum*, dist. 19, a. 15.
[24] I *Summa Theologica*, tr. 3, q. 18, m. 1.

THE OLD CATHEDRAL IN COLOGNE, BURNT DOWN IN 1248
From the Hillinus Codex in the Cathedral Library Cologne.

final. In these questions he was left in the lurch by his master, whose statements on this point are often obscure and all too meagre. Ample material with which to fill up the gaps was offered by the Fathers, but here too the Saint did not content himself with merely tacking on the statements of the one to the principles of the other. Here also he strove after an harmonious whole, and to this end he collected passages from the various works of Aristotle which served to combine and unify the entire mass. The fundamental difficulty of this treatise is God's knowledge of things, and it is precisely here that Albert's genius is shown by his having solved this problem. He thus gave a classic extension to Aristotle's system.[25]

Faithfully following Aristotle's lead, Albert sees earthly things as composed of matter and form, and thereby, at any rate, elucidates and gives a closer definition to the conception which Aristotle had advanced on matter. According to another view, he fundamentally recast it and thus gave it the shape which we find in all scholastic philosophy in the succeeding period.[26] Certain it is that in this as in many other cases he sifted out and perfected the elements utilizable in a Christian philosophy and added them to the general stock of knowledge. Materia prima is for him the substratum common to all material things, an entity needing no further determination, yet not existing without this determination, or without the form postulated by it. It is by reason of its form that the thing is what it is. From its form it gets its existence and finally life and potency. Form is, however, not something added to the materia prima from without; it is educed from the materia by the efficient cause, in that the characteristics proper to it are called into being by the operation of the said cause. In this last explanation Albert transcends Aristotle, not on his own initiative, however, but resting on Averroes.[27]

[25] G. von Hertling: op. cit., 101–107; I *Summa Theologica*, tr. 15, q. 60.

[26] G. von Hertling: op. cit., 121.

[27] II *Summa Theologica*, tr. 1, q. 4, m. 2, a. 4; G. von Hertling: op. cit., 134.

The points we have cited may suffice to give us an idea of Albert's procedure in the creation of Christian metaphysics. Starting with Aristotle's fundamental ideas and utilizing the vast lines of this system, he recast them and extended them in the sense of the truths of Christianity. The fact that in making these corrections and additions he at times called other authors in council does not detract from Albert's merit, nor does it that some of these elements are to be found in Arabian and Jewish philosophers. It only shows him in his real nature, taking the good and the true wherever he found it. The effort to establish whence in every case Albert got the material for his structure has in many cases succeeded in demonstrating it to have been one of these Jewish or Arabic sources. That this has been successful everywhere, or that there would be any prospect of it being so in all cases, is not by any means established.[28] Moreover, it is not always justifiable to conclude that Albert borrowed a thought, merely because it may be found in some older writer. However, these researches have at any rate established one thing, that Albert took pains to assimilate the whole body of Arabic and Jewish knowledge. He did not simply reject these opponents of the Church without a hearing, but studied their writings thoroughly ; and if he found much that was objectionable in them, this did not prevent him from extracting from them everything that would serve his purpose and from incorporating it in his works. These researches prove that among all the Christian scholars of his day Albert had the fullest knowledge of the Arabic and Jewish philosophies.[29] This universality brings him into very close kinship with the science of our day, and if something of the fame of a discoverer is lost to him, there nevertheless remains to him the genius of a great builder. To have quarried the material suitable for the extension of Aristotle's philosophy in the spirit of Christianity from the works of the Arabians, Avicenna, Averroes, Costa-ben-Luca, Algazel, Alfarabi, Abubaker,

[28] Hence F. Nitzsch is quite inaccurate in saying that he [Albert], as is demonstrable, has borrowed almost every philosophical proposition.' (*Real enzyklopädie für protestantische Theologie*, i, 292.)

[29] M. Grabmann : op. cit., 21.

and Alkendi, and of the Jews Isaac Israel, Avencebrol, and Moses Maimonides, remains Albert's unchallengeable merit. This, again, is a revelation of his breadth of sympathy and keenness of intellect.[30]

(*b*) Psychology.

Schneider has made a thorough study of Albert's psychology, and in doing so has taken the opportunity of exploring its sources. The conclusion he arrives at is to the effect that the whole outline as well as the guiding principles, and, if not all the details, at any rate by far the greater part of the elements of the work, are taken from Aristotle's philosophy. Furthermore, the Arabs and Jews mentioned above are frequently allowed their say, while all the older philosophers, so far as their works were available to Albert, as also Augustine and the Fathers, were given consideration. Of the latter there are cited Jerome, Basil, Nemesius, John Damascene, and further the ecclesiastical writers Boëthius, Cassiodorus, Alcuin, Peter Lombard, Præpositivus, and William of Auxerre.[31] Albert utilized therefore all the material which in that age was in any way employable. So abundant and exhaustive are at times these historical references that Schneider does not hesitate to characterize Albert as a polyhistor, and to assign a very special historical value to one or other of these references. How these authorities were studied and utilized is shown in the treatment of the two central questions in Psychology, the nature of the soul and of the intellect.

On the first of these questions Albert sets out the views of philosophers as well as of theologians, allowing in his philosophical works the greater space to the former and in his theological works to the latter. The most ancient philosophers beginning with Thales are quoted and discussed in the Aristotelian spirit. He gives three definitions of Aristotle's with which he concurs, not indeed without qualification, but only under a definite aspect, whereby the soul is indicated as the form of the body.[32] The

[30] A. Schneider : op. cit., 9 *sq.* [31] Ibid. : op. cit., 364.
[32] II *Summa de creaturis*, q. 4, a. 7 ; II *Summa Theologica*, tr. 2, q. 69, m. 2, a. 2.

definitions of the Arabs, considered in the same sense, are likewise approved. In his philosophical works Albert supplements Aristotle's view by the definition of Isaac Israel, who sought to define the soul in itself on Neoplatonist mystical lines.[33] In the theological works Albert introduces a number of the Fathers and theologians and quotes definitions by Augustine, John Damascene, Bernard, Alcuin, Remigius of Auxerre, Alexander Neccam, Cassiodorus, and Seneca, whom with many of his contemporaries he held to be a Christian.[34] These also are approved by Albert, in so far as they give expression to the nature of the soul in itself. Yet none of these definitions could satisfy him, since none of them expressed both aspects of the soul. Instead, however, of independently formulating a correct definition, Albert contents himself with combining those which he has ready to hand.

The second problem, that of the intellect, again offered the Saint ample opportunity to draw upon the various views which had up to that time been advanced on the subject. No other question was to the same extent a centre of controversy among Albert's contemporaries and in the generation immediately preceding. We shall confine ourselves here to the true cognitive intellect (intellectus possibilis). Albert here sets out the different views of the more important Greek and Arabic philosophers with a thoroughness which borders on prolixity.[35] He examines each one in detail, exposes their errors, and measures everything by the true scale which he believed to have discovered in Aristotle's view, and which he had made his own. First he takes his stand against Alexander of Aphrodisias, who would have the intellect to be a product of the most complete compound of the elements. 'Magister Alexander,' Albert here proceeds, 'though much that he says is correct, has on this matter gone further astray than any of the others, for it follows from his words that the soul

[33] A. Schneider: op. cit., 17; II *Summa Theologica*, tr. 12, q. 69, m. 2, a. 2.

[34] A. Schneider: op. cit., 368; II *Summa Theologica*, tr. 12, q. 69, m. 1.

[35] *De anima*, lib. 3, tr. 2; A. Schneider: op. cit., 190.

perishes with the body, and as the body is changed so is the soul, and many other things which are absurd and little worthy of a celebrated philosopher; and therefore his teaching must be rejected.'[36] Albert regards Theophrastus and Themistius as being the very antipodes of Alexander, but though he finds their teaching much more reasonable, he has to reject it because of palpable exaggerations.

The Saint uses very sharp language in attacking Averroes, who regarded the intellect not as a faculty of the individual but as a transcendental, cosmic, universal potency.[37] Albert had picked this Arab out as his proper scientific opponent, and shrank from no pains to overthrow him. He saw, of course, with his own eyes, the great damage his teaching was doing in the faculty of arts at that precise time; and in the fierce conflict which raged, it was not Thomas Aquinas nor William of Auvergne but our Saint who stood out as champion.[38] Hence the severity and the force and the prolixity of his words when he has to speak on this writer's views. The Arabs Abubaker and Avempace got less severe treatment at his hands, for they at any rate allowed man an intellect identified with the phantasy. Still more mildly did he judge Avicenna, who recognized the intellect proper as the spiritual faculty of the individual, even if he did have a distorted conception of the active intellect and makes the act of cognition a passive one.[39] Albert has a similar respect for Avencebrol as he has for Avicenna. He was the first Dominican to make a thorough study of this Jew, though he cannot share his views on the perceptive faculty, since Avencebrol would define it as of the nature of primary matter.[40] On this question he is also at odds with the Platonists, and finds himself obliged

[36] *De anima*, lib. 3, tr. 2, cap. 4.

[37] A. Schneider: op. cit., 201. *De natura et origine Animæ*, tr. 2, cap. 4.

[38] M. Grabmann says: 'Albert the Great seems to have been the first among the theologians of the thirteenth century to disprove this Averroistic Monopsychism by philosophical argument based on a thorough and detailed investigation.' (*Die Wissentschaftliche Mission Alberts des Grossen.*)

[39] A. Schneider: op. cit., 208.

[40] Ibid.: op. cit., 211, 213.

to reject their view, as, too, that of his contemporaries, the Latin philosophers, whom, following the custom of the time, he does not cite by name. They were members of the Franciscan Order who had Platonist leanings.[41]

It will have been seen from these examples how abundant Albert's historical knowledge in the philosophical field was. That here and there a few errors crept in is not surprising, when we think how vast was the range of the material and how restricted the means, for practically no one had worked in the field before him. Occasionally the Saint reveals a very keen detective sense, as, for instance, when in his commentary on the Sentences he expresses himself with great reserve on the subject of Hermes Trismegistus, in fact actually doubts his historical existence. All he is concerned with is the truth, and he wants to hear every view that has been previously advanced, so that he may then form an independent judgement. His procedure seems to be rather historico-critical than exclusively philosophic ; but in this connexion it must be noted that his decision is not affected by the number or fame of those who champion a given opinion, but is based on its intrinsic value.[42]

With this method of procedure it was of advantage to him that he never took up a generally hostile attitude to any teacher. However wholeheartedly and sharply he may have combated some one view of a philosopher, this never prevents him from approving some other opinion of his. In fact we frequently find him letting pass an opinion which at first he had thought necessary to reject absolutely, but which he had afterwards considered from another point of view, or on which he had imposed certain limitations. In the *Summa de homine*, for instance, Albert had bluntly rejected the theory of the pre-existence of the soul before it is united to the body. In the *Summa theologiæ*, nevertheless, he makes the attempt, by a very original interpretation, to rid this theory of its objectionable features.

[41] J. Bach : *Des Albertus Magnus Verhältnis zu der Erkeuntnislehre der Griechen, Lateiner, Araber, und Juden*, 182 ; A. Schneider : op. cit., 218.

[42] A maxim of Albert's runs : ' Nobis de dicto potius, quam de dicente est quæstio.' (*De animalibus*, 281.)

The Saint takes the same course with the Platonic view of the transmigration of souls. At one point he rejects it, in another passage he gives it an allegorical interpretation, as if Plato had only meant to infer a moral degradation of the human being to the animal.[43] We find him also giving deference to the Arabians, Avicenna and Alfarabe, and again to the Jew Avencebrol. It was S. Augustine, however, who stood highest in Albert's regard ; and he strives in every way to defend and safeguard the views of this Father. In the problem of the origin of the soul, in which Augustine had actually taken a position oscillating between creationism and traducianism, Albert refrains from calling attention to the fact, and thus makes it appear as if the Bishop of Hippo had supported the view of the creation of the soul.[44]

In one point at any rate Albert has shown himself to be historico-critical : he coins no new terms, nor does he formulate any new definitions, but uses those which lie to his hand, even when they are wanting in precision, and he has to invest them with a new interpretation in order to make them serve his end. In another way Albert has paid tribute to his philosophical forerunners. The Platonic-Arabic theory of the ascent of the human intellect to the Highest Intelligence, that central point of pagan mysticism, seems to have roused the Saint's special interest. It is no longer the dispassionate philosopher but the inspired mystic who, in those parts dealing with the intellectus assimilativus, sets out to teach that the intellect may be called assimilative in so far as the man rises by its means to the divine intellect, up to the limit possible and permitted to him. This is said then to take place when the intellect, now in act according to its whole natural tendency, rises step by step through self-knowledge, and through the light of the Intelligences[45] to the simple divine intellect. He would therefore attain through the light of his practical understanding to the light of the Intelligences ; and through this

[43] II *Summa Theologica*, tr. 12, q. 72, m. 4, a. 3 ad. 8 ; A. Schneider : op. cit., 426.

[44] II *Summa de creaturis*, q. 17, a. 3 ; A. Schneider : op. cit., 434.

[45] 'Intelligentia proprie significat actum intellectus, et aliquando significat substantias separatas, scilicet angelos' (v. S. Thomas, I *Summa*, q. 79, a. 10). [Ed.]

to the intellect of God. In this exposition Albert's only intention was to set forth the natural tendency of man to be raised to a supernatural state and to final beatitude in the contemplation of God.[46]

Philosophy has to thank our Saint for many riches added to its store, among other things, for the relations between speech and thought, which he was the first to apprehend, for he stresses the point that general principles when expressed orally become more fully and accurately known.[47] In his explanation of the operation of sight Albert went far beyond Aristotle and was in many important points much closer to the modern view.[48] He also made the relationship of the individual sense to the sensus communis clear. Schneider remarks in this connexion: 'As regards precisely this problem of the sensus communis, it must be acknowledged that Albert operated with great skill and has given a satisfactory solution to those questions which in the exegesis of Aristotle's works have, right up to our own day, afforded the greatest difficulties.'[49] Again his decisive rejection of the doubtful material which was still being preserved by the champions of the old school had a most happy influence on the further development of philosophy.

Most of Albert's philosophical works consist of paraphrases interspersed with independent digressions of his own. Consequently the arrangement of the matter and the general plan in these writings was given, while the new elements, which the Saint had taken from the Jews and Arabs or had himself discovered, were inserted, mostly in the form of digressions, at their appropriate places. Albert does not seem to have attempted to collect and work up into one system the whole mass of the philosophical matter, to the exclusion of the theological, though he did make the attempt in respect to certain individual parts. He had already in his early teaching days treated the ethical truths in such a manner, and the result may be found in the still unprinted portion of the *Summa de creaturis* entitled *De bono*

[46] A. Schneider: op. cit., 361; cf. H. Doms: *Die Gnadenlehre Alberts des Grossen*, 55.

[47] *De apprehensione*, V, n. 10.

[48] A. Schneider: op. cit., 113. [49] Ibid.: op. cit., 137.

sive de virtutibus. Grabmann has pronounced this and, in addition, two other parts of the same *Summa*, to be authentic works of Albert's, and in particular praises the treatise under consideration as 'a systematic ethic written a good twenty years before the *Secunda* of S. Thomas, which deduces the whole of moral philosophy from the idea of the bonum.'[50] Albert also made a similar attempt in connexion with psychology in his *Summa de homine*. 'Here he had set himself the great task of demonstrating that the Aristotelian-Peripatetic psychology could well be brought into accord with that adopted by Augustine and his disciples in the early Middle Ages; and that their fundamental dogmas, however contradictory they might here and there appear to be, were adaptable to the formation of a uniform system.'[51] He was not so successful in his execution of this as he was in his ethics. The task was decidedly more difficult. The synthesis often remained a mere surface one, the juxtaposition of incompatible elements, or even an agreement effected by purely dialectical and pedantic discussion and interpretation of the definitions. This defect stands out most glaringly in the treatment of the vires motivæ. In spite of all this the whole does not merely give the effect of an ingenious attempt, it is as a matter of fact an extraordinarily bold achievement, which stands alone in the history of philosophy. For all its faults the direction lines were given and the catenation effected. The development in detail, the complete working out of the plan, could be left to others. While the Master was yet alive his still greater pupil solved this problem. Schneider appreciates Albert's achievement as follows: 'We must, if we are to judge him justly, steadily bear in mind that the plan to build up a thorough synthesis between the Aristotelian and Augustinian systems implied an extremely daring and gigantic undertaking, and that naturally numerous difficulties obstructed the realization of this plan. Even if, his strength failing him, Albert sometimes stumbled, he nevertheless not only pointed the road to his successors, but he also himself overcame the main obstacles, cleared

[50] M. Grabmann: op. cit., 16.
[51] A. Schneider: op. cit., 532.

the ground of stones and undergrowth, dug the foundations, and prepared the stone, the shafts, and the cross-beams for the building which his pupil completed.'[52]

The defects in Albert's work have been often and strongly stressed, too strongly even by Schneider. Only one who can bring home to himself the prodigious work which the Saint accomplished will be able to understand them rightly. We see him surrounded by such a colossal mass of material as had never been brought together before. We see him testing and appraising individual views and statements. He knows right well that many are inconsistent, and yet he divines a truth in both. In his hurry to push on with the work he cannot tarry too long on detailed investigation, nor does he want to discard any of the valuable matter. So he sets them out in juxtaposition and leaves the decision to a less burdened mind.

In any case in the philosophical field Albert's merit in connexion with the elucidation of Aristotle will always have to be recognized. What he wrote at the beginning of the Physics: 'Our object is to make all these works [of Aristotle] intelligible to Latinists,' he accomplished. If he had only done this, a place of honour among the great philosophers would have been assured him. But Albert also mastered the entire philosophic knowledge of his time. He knew, as no other did, the Arabians, the Jews, and the Latins. Grabmann extols in him the 'universality of his knowledge of the sources.' Further, Albert conceived the idea of linking together all the truths residing in the various systems. He attempted this task and worked at it in monographs and other treatises, taking Aristotle always as his basis. By these purely philosophical essays he founded a self-sufficient Christian philosophy. True, this was regarded as the handmaid of theology, but it was treated separately. These are achievements which justify the honourable title Magnus in philosophia. Indeed in the framework of his period we have every ground for calling him, as he was called by his contemporaries: 'Maximus in philosophia.'[53]

[52] A. Schneider: op. cit., 533.
[53] P. de Loë: *Statistisches über die Ordensprovinz Teutonia*, 23.

III. THE INTELLECTUAL GREATNESS OF ALBERT AS THEOLOGIAN

ALBERT was by natural inclination a naturalist, by conscious effort a philosopher, and with his whole devout soul, from the bottom of a heart which glowed with charity, a theologian. He was so much a theologian that this finds utterance in all that he did.[1] His works on the natural sciences have all a teleological, one might indeed say a theological, direction.[2] Everything is conceived and set out in relation to God, the ultimate cause. He entered the ranks of philosophy as a theologian, for it was in accordance with the principles of the faith that he adapted and corrected Aristotle's works ; and it was in the interest of the exposition of the faith, that is to say that Aristotle's philosophy might render service to theology proper, that he introduced it into the humanities of his day.[3] However, in spite of the sharp relief into which

[1] Wilhelm Arendt in *Die Staats-und Gesellschaftslehre Alberts des Grossen*, 86, though he does not mean it as praise, praises him thus : ' Albert never thinks otherwise than as a theologian.'

[2] Balss, in *Albertus Magnus als Zoologe*, 140, writes : ' The name of God, which we might have expected Albert, as a Dominican, to introduce here, occurs in the whole book only at the end (*Physicorum*, xxi, 51), where he thanks God for his help in enabling him to finish it. Albert is therefore a biologist in the present day sense of the word, and we can, with Zannick, rightly call him the pre-renaissance zoologist.' This, however, in no way disproves our assertion, for Albert at the beginning of all these books (*Physicorum*, lib. 1, tr. 1, cap. 1) determines the relation of all that follows to God. Furthermore, in these books he patently wished to investigate the order of the secondary causes.

[3] Cf. Grabmann's magnificent description in his *Die wissentschaftliche Mission Alberts des Grossen.* Because of the dangers of the times Albert saw himself faced with the problem of collecting and incorporating in a Christian philosophy based on Aristotle the many truths contained in the Greek, Arabic, and Jewish philosophies.

this theological character is thrown, Albert's definite and surpassing greatness does not lie in the domain of theology, but in the two fields previously named. In theology Albert was during his lifetime excelled by a greater than he.

Thomas Aquinas cannot compare with Albert as a natural philosopher, for Aquinas never cultivated this field. As a philosopher Albert competes with Thomas for the palm ; indeed in extent of historical learning, knowledge of the sources, genius and daring of scheme, and in number of works, he is certainly the superior, though he is surpassed by his pupil in keenness of perception and clarity in exposition. As a theologian, however, Albert takes a second place to Thomas, though not in the sense that he wrote less. Both treated the same subjects. Their principal works are the Commentary on the Sentences and the *Summa theologica*. The former work both of them finished, but not the latter. In the matter of bulk of theological writings Albert probably exceeds Aquinas, but, as what matters here is the keenness of intellect which will select the right principles, and thus bring into existence an enduring, universal synthesis, our Saint must take second place. But in this field, too, his is the undisputed merit of having pointed out the road to his pupil, of having accomplished the very difficult preliminary work of collecting the materials, of determining the lines on which to work, and of attempting a synthesis, though in the latter he was only partly successful. Without a due appreciation of Albert's preliminary labours, Thomas can never be rightly estimated. There is, moreover, much that is Albert's own in his theology, which was never made use of by Thomas, yet which was of importance in the development of theology and has still a value even to-day. Thus his greatness is assured in this field also, and it will be worth our while to follow him in the several branches of the theological sciences which he has treated.

1. *Albertus Magnus as Exegete.*

We cannot apply the standard of the exegesis of to-day to that of the Middle Ages, for this is now become a special science, ranking with archæology, patrology, etc., and entirely divorced from dogmatics and moral philosophy. It endeavours to arrive at the correct original text and the most faithful verbal elucidation of the Holy Scriptures by the aid of the most far-reaching knowledge of languages, on the basis of biblical geography and topography, by the study of comparative religion, and by weighing the results of special research into the dependence of the biblical accounts on Syrian, Assyrian, Babylonian, Egyptian, perhaps even Chinese and Indian sources, writings, and inscriptions. Mediæval exegetes did not possess these rudiments, and above all lacked the insight into the human side of the Sacred Books. To them Sacred Scripture was first and last a divine book, the book of books, out of which lessons were to be learnt and taught, that book, the knowledge of which sufficed the theologian.

Even if in Albert's day the Bible was no longer the actual textbook in the schools, because the instruction linked with it was not systematically enough arranged, if, too, the Sentences had already been adopted as a general primer and were preparing the way for the various *Summæ*, great weight was still laid on the study of the Sacred Scriptures, and the most distinguished professors lectured on them, and all had to attend. This instruction still continued on the old lines; it was dogmatic and moral. It would, however, be a mistake to deny mediæval scholars all interest in the sciences auxiliary to biblical study, which have been so enormously developed to-day. Interest in the languages of the Bible was without question present, and occupation with the writings of Aristotle and of the Jews and Arabs had promoted this still further. The schools founded by Raymund of Pennafort[4] corroborate this. Further evidence is provided by the decree of Clement V, that wherever the Roman Curia might be situated, and further at the Universities of Paris, Oxford, Bologna, and Salamanca, two professors of the biblical languages must be installed.[5] Interest in the topography and geography of the Holy Land was also not wanting.

[4] The primary object of these foundations was to train suitable missioners for the conversion of the Jews and Moors.

[5] H. Denifle, O.P.: *Dei Universitäten des Mittelalters*, I, 306.

The Crusades and the many pilgrimages to the holy places testify to the contrary. The means necessary to the satisfaction of these interests were largely lacking, as were, too, the indispensable rudiments. Thus, as Michael says, 'the school men still lacked the rudiments necessary for an elucidation of the texts on grammatical and historical lines. Philology, chronology, archæology, and history were still in all too undeveloped a state; but above all they had not an eye for the contemplation of the human side of the Bible which in our day is widely taken as a matter of course. For all this it is undeniable that a deeper search into the treasures of the Sacred Books was being made.'[6] In Albert's time a new division into chapters was arranged. The earlier division had proved itself unsuitable, since some chapters were unduly long and others again very short. The new division, which has persisted to this day, may in all probability be ascribed to the professor of logic at Paris, Stephen Langton, who afterwards became Cardinal Archbishop of Canterbury. It was made in about 1200, was adopted in the Paris Bible, and so came into general use.

The second important service contributed to Bible study in Albert's time consisted in the textual emendations which were being undertaken. People felt, as they did in S. Jerome's time, the disturbing effect of the many copyists' errors, which almost of necessity multiplied, and the want of a uniform edition in which one could impose full trust and from which errors could be corrected. The Paris Bible represented the attempt at a standard text, but it had so many and obvious defects that the call for a more correct text only resounded the louder. Rules for such emendation, which evidence a critical sense and which have some importance even to-day, were drawn up by the Dominican, Hugo of S. Cher.[7] Although he himself went too far in the application of these rules, there nevertheless was made under his influence a set of corrections which, from the fact that Thomas and Albert both availed themselves of

[6] E. Michael: op. cit., iii, 115.

[7] H. Denifle, O.P.: *Die Handschriften der Bibel-Korrektorien des 13 Jahrhunderts*, 292.

them, acquired a great importance, and which also as a matter of fact did introduce real improvements.

The third benefit accruing to the study and also to the general use of the Bible lay in the appearance of Concordances. The first of these important compilations, which made it possible to verify any text whatever of the Holy Scriptures, provided but one word in it was known, was the work of Hugo of S. Cher. This undertaking was of no particular moment to Albert individually, since he had a quite unusual knowledge of the Bible. His exegetical works give the impression of an artistic texture woven from the most widely different passages of Holy Scripture ; but in spite of this the Concordance may have occasionally been of use to him in order to verify the precise wording of a given passage. That Albert himself had some sort of share in the compilation of this work cannot be vouched for, though it is not improbable that he had, for the relations between the two men were very close, and their collaboration in other undertakings is well attested.

The earliest biographers of the Saint, Petrus de Prussia and Rudolf of Nymegen, state that Albert had commented on the whole of the Scriptures : 'Scripsit super totam bibliam per modum postellæ.'[8] Actually we only possess a Commentary on the Psalms, which fills three volumes in the Paris edition, one on all the Prophets, the major and the minor, and Commentaries on the four Gospels, the Apocalypse, and the Book of Job. The latter work was not included in either of the collected editions ; it was, however, published by M. Weiss in 1904 in an edition meeting every modern critical demand. We may also reckon among his exegetical works the *Liber de muliere forti*, where he takes the woman as a symbol of the Church. This is to be found in the collected works. Further, there belongs here a Commentary on the Canticle of Canticles which is catalogued under Albert's name in the municipal library in Zwettl,

[8] Petrus de Prussia : op. cit., 283. He cites, however, only those exegetical works which are also known to us to-day. So, too, Rudolphus de Novimagio : *Legenda*, 60. Cf. Mandonnet : *Travaux des Dominicains sur les saintes écritures* (*Extrait du Dictionaire de la Bible*, ii, 4, n. 3).

but has so far not been published, and also the Commentaries on the Pauline Epistles, which are lost, or at any rate have not yet been discovered. Among the manuscripts in Munich and Münster there is a moving Commentary on the Ave Maria also bearing Albert's name; but this, as Grabmann remarks, ought to be subjected to closer examination. If the claim of the earliest biographers that 'scripsit super totam bibliam' is, from what has come down to us, not to be taken literally, enough material remains for an investigation of his exegetical activity and to explore his influence in this direction.

If we are to estimate correctly the value of Albert's Commentary on the Psalms we must bear in mind that in the very earliest days of Christendom a twofold method of elucidating the text came into practice. In the course of time there were developed out of this two main currents, which were at times almost hostile to one another, namely the Alexandrian and the Antiochian. The former, principally represented by Origen, having regard for the divine origin of Holy Scripture, laid emphasis on the allegorical sense, a deeper sense, therefore, than the words in their primary meaning would bear. By this method it was an easy matter to get over many a difficulty, whose solution would otherwise have involved considerable labour. The Antiochian method on the contrary insisted strongly, sometimes too strongly, on the literal meaning; too strongly, because it thus held to this sense too exclusively. The Fathers avoided this exclusiveness; but though they made use of both manners of exposition, some, of course, preferred the literal sense, while others were more concerned with the allegorical interpretation. The West in general was more inclined to the allegorical method, as the works of SS. Ambrose, Augustine, and Gregory show. They wrote for the faithful, and therefore utilized everything in the Bible in order to bring to memory over and over again the precepts of the moral law and the truths of the faith.[9] In his Commentary on the Psalms Albert followed entirely this method of the Western Fathers, for he had the same end in view. It was his wish so to set forth the official

[9] Michael: op. cit., iii, 212 *sqq.*

prayers of the Church, which were then much more the common property of the whole community than they are now, that both clerics and the laity might be benefited in their devotions at the office in choir. Albert succeeded in this, and even to-day the pious reader will find in this work a fitting stimulus to the devotional recitation of the Psalter. In view of the liturgical movement of the present day this work might well receive greater attention.

In his Commentaries on the Prophets the Saint strikes a far more prosaic note. Here he first stresses the literal meaning, and only when he considers that he has abundantly treated this, does he pass on to the allegorical explanation of particular passages. This work bears therefore a far more scientific character. The reason for this procedure may be that Albert had the Jews in view. These played at that time, especially in Spain, an important rôle, for through their commentaries on Aristotle they had made a name for themselves in the world of scholarship. Under the leadership of S. Raymund of Pennafort the Dominicans were at pains to confute these men, but also to convert them. An allegorical exposition of the Sacred Books could bear no fruit with these dispassionate scholars, but much might be hoped from a clear, objective commentary on the Prophets as guide-posts to Christ. In his effort to establish the literal sense, Albert let himself be guided by the Fathers. The Constitutions of his Order, indeed, prescribed the same course, for in the year 1236 the Order had ordained that no one might read any other meaning into the Prophets than that which the Fathers had taught.[10] Such an admonition at a time when the Jewish philosophers were sponsoring a vaguely rationalistic interpretation, was not without significance in an Order which was concerned with apologetics. Among the Fathers Albert gave quite open preference to S. Jerome. That Albert in ascertaining and explaining the literal sense had not the same measure of success as is possible to-day, with all the help derived from historical and archæological research, is very intelligible ; yet it will ever be to his credit that he expressly points the way to this method of regarding the problem. However,

[10] *Acta capitulorum generalium O.P.*, i, 16.

he never contented himself with the mere determination of the thoughts ; he invariably estimates their value as applied to practical life. This moral keynote runs through all his exegetical writings.

In his Commentary on the four Gospels Albert hardly touches on the allegorical side, so that the literal meaning is thrown all the more into the foreground. He thus brings out the significance of these books as the historical source of Christianity. Even the strictest follower of the Antiochian tradition could not have proceeded more soberly. We do not possess any historical writings by Albert, but the manner in which he treats the Gospels lets us see that he had a gift for such work. Michael praises these commentaries in the following terms : 'The text is analysed from the objective point of view ; the individual words and clauses are conscientiously and dispassionately weighed in their intrinsic meaning, the context closely examined, difficulties arising out of the apparent discrepancies with the account of one of the other evangelists exposed and solved, and the dogmatic import of the texts, as applied to the older and newer heresies, extracted.'[11] One does not know which to admire more : the strictly logical analysis of the text or the calm, lucid explanation of the words, or the superabundance of the passages at his command to make Scripture intelligible by means of the Scriptures. His treatment of the sublime prologue to S. John's Gospel is regarded as a jewel of articulation : 'Only a Scholastic could have thus written, one in whose mind unity and lucidity reigned, and to whom his methodical training had given the power of elucidating in all its aspects a vast subject from the points of view which shall contribute best to the purpose of pertinent investigation.'[12] Among the Commentaries on the four Gospels that on Luke stands out conspicuously. The earliest biographers of the Saint sought words with which to set it in its proper light. Petrus de Prussia reports that in the compilation of this work Albert, in the opinion of many, was illuminated by the Holy Spirit in a quite special manner.[13] He himself sets

[11] Michael : op. cit., iii, 219. [12] Sighart : op. cit., 104.
[13] Petrus de Prussia : op cit., 265.

THE DOMINICAN PRIORY IN AUGSBURG
Detail of the plan of the town by Wolfgang Kilian, 1626.

this down to the sweet aroma of supernatural grace which the book exhales. According to tradition, the Saint is said to have composed this book during the time which he spent at the Castle of Stauf recuperating from his episcopal labours; but Hochwart, who had seen the manuscript, which was then the treasured possession of the Dominican library in Regensburg, declares that it seems to him impossible that a man should have written such a book within the space of a year, even if he had nothing else to do. In the ethical parts of this comprehensive work Albert attacks even more energetically than in his other writings the failings and disorders of the time; the consciousness of his duty as a bishop may have occasioned this more serious tone. Doms, who, in his exposition of Albert's teaching on grace, has drawn very freely on his Commentaries on the Gospels, is enthusiastic in their praise: 'Here the current of Albert's own thoughts and his mystically inclined disposition find their freest expression, and at times in passages of great nobility and sublime genius, passages which must surely rank with the greatest and most profound in the religious literature of all time.'[14]

The method employed in the Commentary on the Book of Job corresponds with that on the Gospels. Here, too, the desire predominates to get hold of the literal sense, and to make the passages intelligible by means of other texts of Holy Scripture or of quotations from the Fathers. To this end in explanation of the first chapter alone he cites no less than one hundred and thirty-eight biblical passages, and in the same section he quotes Gregory the Great seventeen times, Ambrose twice, the Pseudo-Dionysius twice, Basil, Chrysostom, Augustine once each; in addition he cites Aristotle, Plato, and Ovid once each; furthermore, Eustratius, Priscilian, and the *Glossa interliniaris* are each mentioned once, and an opinion of Maimonides, described by Albert as an *erroris fabula*, to which three other Jewish philosophers had subscribed, is also noted. The modern edition of this Commentary by M. Weiss brings out this method of exposition very graphically. Even if this method is no longer to the general taste, it certainly met with

[14] H. Doms: op. cit., 6.

approval in those days, and it does reveal a rare familiarity with the Scriptures and the Fathers.

The Saint did three great services to exegesis: by strongly insisting on the literal meaning, by a systematic analysis of the text, and by tracing the progressive development of revelation. We have already said enough on the first point. Here we will only note that Albert, with the means at his disposal at that period, strove to arrive at precisely the same thing which the modern results of historical and archæological research and all the other studies auxiliary to biblical study make possible to us, namely the exact determination of the literal sense. Albert started from the idea that regard must be paid to every sentence, indeed to every word, and this not only in its isolation, but also in its relation to the whole, and that only in this manner could its full import be disclosed. The analysis which he undertook, and which seems to us to-day with its many divisions and subdivisions to be somewhat finical, was contrived to the same end, and also did him good service. That he often went astray owing to the faultiness of his text and through his insufficient knowledge of languages can hardly be wondered at. These are defects which do not essentially detract from the greatness of the undertaking. 'The scholastic idiom being once understood, the student will be surprised at Albert's keenness of perception, at the certainty with which he masters his material, and of the wealth of ideas compressed into a few pages, qualities against which some singularities in etymology and the all-too-minute subdivision of his matter, which in the case of a mind of less intellectual force would have a disturbing effect, weigh little in the scale.'[15]

The third and last service he rendered was his tracing of the progressive development of revelation. His words have been understood as if he did not regard all the books of Holy Scripture as divinely inspired; but only an utter misapprehension of his standpoint could lead to such a view. To Albert every book of Scripture, yes, every word in them, is inspired. The judgement as to what properly belongs to Holy Scripture and as to the meaning of the

[15] Michael: op. cit., iii, 221.

same is the property, as he clearly teaches, of the Church. Whoever refuses to accept her decision is a heretic. With this, however, he held fast to the opinion that many mysteries were not revealed to man in their entirety at one time, but that gradually they were made clearer and clearer. This thought, which implied a certain progression in revelation, was a novel one in Albert's day. With it he opened an entirely new field for exegesis, which was left for the future to develop. The Saint had pointed out the road.

For all this, Albert, if measured by modern standards, does not occupy a place of any special importance in biblical science ; if, however, we consider its historical development, Albert's position within the circle of mediæval exegesis is one of extraordinary importance. Michael makes this point very emphatically when he says : 'Albert the Great is the best-known exegete of the thirteenth century,' and in 1473, in the preface to the *Mariale*, he was called 'famosissimus sacræ paginæ interpres.'[16]

2. *Albertus Magnus as Moral Theologian.*

In now attempting to form a judgement on Albertus Magnus in regard to his influence on moral theology, we shall have to confine ourselves to the investigation of the speculative branch of that science. This is not because the practical side of moral science was at that time neglected : moral questions were handled then as they are to-day, as many *summæ confessariorum* which have come down to us prove. The present investigation is limited to the scientific, speculative field because it is almost exclusively from this point of view that Albert treated the subject. Only here and there when the opportunity is thrust upon him, does he become practical in his expositions and allow himself to go into a detailed discussion of particular cases.

Until recently, for any investigation of Albert's influence on moral science only the printed works came into question ; for of further writings of the Doctor Universalis pertinent to the subject there were only vague reports but no sure information. It follows that many scholars, and chief of

[16] *Mariale*, 1 a. Cf. *Gesammtkatalog der Wiegendrucke*, i.

them Dr. H. Lauer in his excellent book, *Die Moraltheologie Alberts des Grossen mit besonderer Berücksichtigung ihrer Beziehungen zur Lehre des heiligen Thomas*, confined themselves to Albert's printed works. Even with this limitation the material available is copious, for the Saint discussed moral problems in the most diverse works. He did not, it is true, in any of his works set out the whole subject of morals as a self-contained system; he followed the method of his contemporaries who lumped together theology, dogma, and moral philosophy, and treated them in commentaries on the Sentences or in *Summæ*. Thus, too, Albert provides abundant material in his Commentary on the Sentences, his *Summa theologica*, and the *Summa de creaturis*. The Commentaries on Aristotle's Ethics can only be used with reserve, for, as Albert himself has explained in regard to these writings, they do not contain his own views, but his attempts to set forth the true teaching of the Stagyrite.

Of the three works of Albert's enumerated, Lauer classes the Commentary on the Sentences as the most important. 'It must generally be regarded as the most admirable of Albert's works, for in it the range of subjects taught by the Church is wider and they are handled with comparatively greater independence than in the others. The work is nothing less than an elucidation in the strict sense of the word. The Sentences of Peter Lombard only determine the arrangement of the material, not the form which Albert's teaching takes. The Lombard's heading is always given at the beginning, and this is as regularly followed by an introduction. His own teaching Albert has incorporated in 'Articles' within the 'Distinctions.' The Articles themselves have no further subdivisions. The order and distribution of the material leave a good deal to be desired. In the fourth part Albert would seem to have given space to much which, from its subject matter, ought to have been treated earlier.'[17]

The second main work, the *Summa theologica*, was written later than the Commentary on the Sentences. From a note in the work itself Albert must have been engaged on it in the year 1274; however, the undertaking, planned on a

[17] Hermann Lauer: *Die Moraltheologie Alberts des Grossen*, 20 *sq.*

large scale to embrace the whole of theology classified from a new point of view, remained unfinished.

A comparison of the two works shows a striking revolution in many points of doctrine. He explains that there was a considerable interval of time between the composition of the books, and that he had now another purpose. The Commentary on the Sentences represents Albert's attempt to make Aristotle's principles applicable to the development of theology. For this reason he often in this work travels quite new paths and reveals himself as the forerunner of Thomas Aquinas. The *Summa* was intended for the teaching brethren and those of them who took part in scientific disputations.[18] In this latter work Albert appears much more conservative ; the tradition of the Church is given prominence, the exposition is more dispassionate and calmer. Albert in this work aimed at a new arrangement of the material, but this reveals many defects. Lauer mentions particularly the minute division of the matter, the whole work being cut up into parts, these in their turn into sections and questions, the questions into membra, these again into articles, which are sometimes yet again divided into sub-questions. In spite of this very minute dissection of the matter there are no clear boundary lines between dogmatic and moral theology, nor any separation between general and particular moral philosophy. It must be admitted, however, that a definitive judgement cannot be passed on the work, since it remained a torso.

The importance of the third book, the *Summa de creaturis*, is summed up by Lauer in the words : 'The *Summa de creaturis* is of importance especially for the information given on many doctrines in the field of moral philosophy. It was composed about the same time as the Commentary on the Sentences and therefore stands in close relationship with it in subject matter.'[19]

[18] *Summa Theologica*, tr. 1, de scientia theologiæ.

[19] H. Lauer : op. cit., 21. In any future research into Albert's Moral Theology the three MSS. discovered by Mgr. A. Pelzer, *Quæstionen zur nikomachischen Ethik*, will have to be consulted. Grabmann, who discovered a fourth MS., sets a high value on these. (*Der Einfluss Alberts des Grossen auf das mittelalterliche Geistesleben*, 16.)

In the works under discussion there is to be found the Catholic doctrine on man's mission and destiny, as has, since Thomas, been united into one unsurpassable system : God, eternal perfection, is man's goal and at the same time the highest norm of his actions, both of them indeed beyond the confines of nature. Man, raised up again by the grace of redemption, can and must conform his will to the Divine Will. It is by this conformity that the degree of perfection of the rational creature is measured. The natural law and the positive commandments set before man this Will of God. Conscience is the judge in the individual case. Man's mission is consummated by free will aided by Grace. The good exercise of this assists the growth of virtue ; inconstancy disfigures the soul. Grace is dispensed principally by means of the Sacraments instituted by Christ. The final end of the good is eternal happiness, of the evil damnation.

Albert's greatest service to Christian moral philosophy lies in the fact that he took the Ethics of Aristotle, and gave a deeper foundation, a wider development, and a sharper delimitation, both to the system as a whole and to particular conceptions and tractates. Michael expresses this view as follows : 'For purely ethical questions he drew on Aristotle's philosophy more than did any of his predecessors, and by rigorous definition built a sure substructure for his researches in the field of Christian moral philosophy.'[20] He did this at a supremely important moment. It was just at this time that through the medium of the Arabs and Jews the ethical works of Aristotle were becoming known to Western Christendom ; but, owing to the false interpretations given by them to the Stagyrite's thoughts, it was precisely in the realm of morals that the greatest disorder threatened. We have only to think of the complete decline of responsibility induced by the doctrine of the oneness of intellect and the denial of immortality, and on the other side of the forlorn position of the human race if divine providence is eliminated. It was necessary here to fight the opponent with his own weapons, and this he brilliantly did by opposing to the false interpretation the true one, which endorsed the

[20] Michael : op. cit., iii, 245.

Christian claims, and by using these truths in the construction of a Christian moral philosophy. Lauer's judgement is that 'Albert may claim the credit for having carried out the great work as far as the essentials go.'[21] This credit is not lessened by the fact that there were previous labourers in this field. Without their work Albert could hardly have accomplished what he did. His work again paved the way for his pupil S. Thomas. Albert's renown will also not be diminished by the reproach that he followed Aristotle too closely; nor would this be justified, for although Albert rated Aristotle highly and insisted that a knowledge of him was indispensable to scientific work, he never shrank from correcting his errors, and indeed not merely the more gross ones, e.g. procuration of abortion and slavery, but also inaccuracies in his ethical teaching as in the case of the worship of God and pride. The Saint was also protected against overrating the wisdom of the Greeks by his *sentire cum Ecclesia* and his reverence for the Fathers. Among the latter he held S. Augustine in highest regard. Thus in the *Summa theologiæ* he answers a question with a decided 'yes,' because this is Augustine's plain teaching, adding 'cui contradicere impium est in his quæ tangunt fidem et mores.'[22] Consequently Albert's moral philosophy, in spite of the use made of Aristotle and of his Arabic and Jewish commentators in the solution of many difficulties in the first principles of ethics, is just as Augustine had propounded, only broadened and deepened and made to suit the needs of the times. The development and extension of Augustine's teaching is Albert's second great service to Christian moral science. Writings of Plato and Plotinus with which the Bishop of Hippo had not been acquainted, and to the study of which Albert felt himself specially drawn in the last years of his life, were useful to him in this.

The third benefit for which moral philosophy has to thank Albert is his own personal contributions to its further development. Lauer names in particular two points on

21 H. Lauer: op. cit., 9. This praise will have to be enhanced if the tractate *De bono* is also taken into account.

22 II *Summa Theologica*, tr. 14, q. 84, ad q. 3.

which Albert is a final authority: the exposition of the relations of love to the Holy Spirit and the doctrine of simple and solemn vows. For the further development of moral science the following were also of importance: the deeper comprehension of the nature and activity of conscience, the introduction of the principle of *epikeia* or equity, the shaping of a general ethical system, the more careful distinction between mortal and venial sin. The tractates on particular points in ethics, especially in the sections on usury, anger, and alms-giving, have never been greatly improved upon. By reason of the three great services named, Albert holds a prominent place among mediæval moralists, for they have only been surpassed by Thomas Aquinas. This is also acknowledged by Lauer, though this student of Albert's ethics is of opinion that he must be reproached for a four-fold defect in it. According to him the Saint never treated moral science as a rounded-off, complete whole, nor did he even assign to it a place commensurate with the structure of his general theology, where, e.g. in the *Summa theologiæ*, he took his own line independently of Peter Lombard. Lauer clothes his view of this double defect in the words: 'It is to be regretted that Albert paid so little attention to the uniform arrangement of the subject matter. He failed to give a uniform, comprehensive structure to his moral philosophy, even within the framework of his general exposition of the theory of the Redemption.'[23] Connected with these is the third defect, that Albert in his ethics quite overlooked certain important parts of the subject and failed to give others a treatment commensurate with their importance. Lauer here thinks it necessary to make the point that, because in Albert's works there are many gaps in the subjects properly belonging to Christian ethics, Alexander of Hales surpassed him, at any rate, as concerns the fullness of the subject matter. He cites as particularly imperfect his treatment of law, and almost the whole of the special ethical doctrine with the exception of the sections dealing with the three supernatural virtues and the sacraments. These three defects concern the completeness, the choice,

[23] H. Lauer: op. cit., 16.

and the arrangement of the subject matter ; all things which are most readily subject to dispute. The fourth and last reproach is directed against the treatment of the selected matter itself, and therefore reflects the more heavily on Albert the teacher. The parts of ethics treated are, he claims, wanting in the desired solidity, partly because the ideas are not clearly enough defined, partly, too, because the arguments are often very sketchy. Lauer is conscious of the severity of this reproach when he says : 'The defects attaching to the substance of the subject matter are accentuated by the lack of clear and concise definitions, frequent changes of opinion, and by the indefiniteness of the solution to many problems.'[24] And again : 'The actual solution to the questions put is frequently insufficiently developed, and the further argument is for the most part too much broken up into a citation and discussion of the reasons pro and con.' These four defects really do attach to the manner in which Albert has treated ethics in his printed works ; but this judgement is entirely changed if the still unpublished ethical writings of the Saint are taken into consideration.

For it must at once be pointed out that a large part of Albert's works which are concerned with moral doctrine have not yet been printed. In the year 1912 Professor Grabmann called attention to three unprinted parts of the *Summa de creaturis* in a fifteenth-century manuscript belonging to the Bibliotheca Marciana in Venice, of which the memory had not entirely perished, for Petrus de Prussia had mentioned them, while Mandonnet and Weiss have both referred to them, though not without some misapprehension.[25] The first of the unprinted parts—it is the third part of the complete *Summa de creaturis*—treats of ethics and is in full correspondence with the doctrine of the Good (*de bono*), whence the tractate derives its title. In this book the four cardinal virtues receive thorough treatment. Fortitude and temperance with their corresponding auxiliary virtues first come under discussion, and attached to this the teaching

[24] H. Lauer : op. cit., 15.
[25] M. Grabmann : *Drei ungedruckte Teile der Summa de creaturis Alberts des Grossen*, 47.

on the passions, with the regulation of which the said virtues are principally concerned. Next prudence is considered, and in this connexion the classifications given by Cicero, Macrobius, and Aristotle are reviewed. The whole work is brought to a close with a treatise on justice. This part begins with an investigation on the conception of right and the theory of law. The expression 'justificatio impii,' which has only an external relationship with justice, serves Albert as a bridge and pointer to the tractate *De Sacramentis* which follows.

Grabmann gives a very detailed table of the contents of the tractate *De bono*,[26] and his survey of the work is quite sufficient to make it clear that precisely those parts of moral philosophy, of which the omission in Albert's printed works occasioned Lauer's severe criticism, are to be found in these unprinted writings, and are in fact treated with a thoroughness and at a length which must certainly satisfy any demands. Thus the third reproach levelled against Albert as a moralist falls to the ground. In the wealth of material handled he takes an honourable place not merely beside Alexander of Hales but also beside S. Thomas. Still more, however, emerges from Grabmann's discoveries. The learned scholar could prove that the said tractate *De bono* dates from the time preceding Albert's teaching days in Paris, i.e. before 1246, and from this he draws the conclusion that, 'the work *De bono sive de virtutibus*, which, like the *Summa de creaturis*, belongs to the earlier years of the great school man, was composed a good twenty years before the *Secunda* of S. Thomas's systematic ethic, which deduces the whole of moral philosophy from the idea of the bonum.'[27] Here, therefore, we have a work, absolutely independent of Aquinas, which aims at a uniform conception of the whole ethical field and its systematic elaboration. Grabmann again emphasizes this thought in two other passages: 'All three unprinted parts of the *Summa de creaturis*, and in particular the *De bono sive de virtutibus*, are important precisely as systematic productions, and are also the best proof of the systematizing ability of the great German

[26] M. Grabmann: op. cit., 51.
[27] M. Grabmann: *Der Einfluss Alberts des Grossen*, etc., 15 *sq.*

scholastic ';[28] and in the same paper: 'It is in the *Summa de creaturis*, and particularly in the three unprinted parts under discussion, that we can best establish Albert's taste and talent for synthesis and systematization. This is perhaps most true as regards the tractate *De bono sive virtutibus*, in which the complete teaching of moral philosophy is collected and organized.' With the establishment of these points the first two reproaches are sufficiently invalidated. They could only have been raised on the basis of the insufficient knowledge of Albert's production in the field of moral philosophy permitted by his printed works.

The fourth reproach, based on the want of precision in the definitions and the lack of sufficient completeness in the final demonstrations, is not negatived by the newly discovered tractates. These are defects which would seem to be grounded in Albert's method of collecting, combining, and balancing his material. They were overcome by S. Thomas. If, however, we are properly to judge this merit of Aquinas's, which above all distinguishes his ethical works, we must remember that it is precisely in this field that the previous labours of his Master were of the greatest use to him. Grabmann thinks it incumbent on him to point out that the composition of the most important ethical work of Albert, the *De bono*, dates from the time when Thomas was sitting at his Master's feet.[29] Thomas had therefore the whole advantage of what Albert had achieved before him, and his lofty intellect easily soared beyond his Master. When it is said in praise of Thomas that he never reveals his peculiar gift for systematization in so brilliant a light as in the field of ethics, a substantial part of this praise reverts to Albert, for if the articulation and mastery of the matter in Albert's great ethical work does not reach up to the genius displayed in the wonderful plan and execution of the *Secunda pars* of S. Thomas, it yet furnished the latter a useful model, without which that master work itself could hardly have come into existence.[30]

[28] M. Grabmann: *Drei ungedruckte Teile*, etc., 80.
[29] Ibid., 83.
[30] 'In the library of Gonville College, Cambridge (and also in the Vatican, and at Vienna) there is a thirteenth-century

The dependence of the pupil on the master in these parts of theology is much greater than is to-day generally recognized. The well-known Dominican Lector, Johannes von Freiburg, who did good service in the field of practical ethics, wrote in his *Summa confessorum* : 'Thomas and Albert have almost the same vocabulary. Thomas, in fact, created his work out of Albert, who was his master in the Studium at Cologne.'[31]

Now that the reproaches levelled against Albert's work in the field of moral philosophy, which were not without justification based as they were exclusively on the printed works, can be shown to be in part wholly ungrounded, in part less suspicious, the services of the Saint to moral philosophy stand out in all the clearer light. Albert enlisted the aid of Aristotelianism in giving a new foundation to Christian ethics ; he gave prominence to Augustine's importance and propagated his incomparable teaching ; on many points by his special researches he made possible a deeper insight into pending moral problems ; and through all this Albert created for S. Thomas the possibility of giving from the speculative point of view a definitive exposition of Christian ethics as a whole. Thus in this domain also the Saint deserves the title of the Great.

Yet one more thing may here be said to Albert's honour. His age was one of objective observation and judgement. Albert, however, displays in his towering intellect something of that which only found expression in later times, namely consideration of the personal element in the ethical estimation of human actions. Lauer, too, makes this point. 'The great discerner of souls does not belie himself here. More than once his vast experience of life, his charity

manuscript which is one of the most romantic in the history of human culture. It is the *Nicomachean Ethics* of Aristotle, with a commentary on the text, and marginal notes on the text and commentary. Now the commentary is that made by S. Albert the Great when lecturing at Paris or Cologne ; and the marginal notes on Aristotle and Albert are those of Albert's student, Aquinas.' (Vincent McNabb, O.P. : *Catholic Church and Philosophy*, 77.) [Ed.]

[31] Joannes Lector, O.P. : *Summa confessorum*, lib. 3, tit. de consecratione, q. 17, quoted by Grabmann in another place.

in judgement, his just and wise weighing of all the circumstances, manifest themselves. This is especially the case when Albert, as for instance in his teaching on anger, or on the spiritual works of mercy, descends to the particular, and gives advice on the proper ordering of life, for he then reveals a unique greatness, a rare combination of high scientific training and a practical wisdom born of his own experience of life. . . . We can then catch a glimpse of his own soul, as in moving speech his loving heart sings the great canticle of love for God.'[32] But with this we are already in the presence of Albert the mystic.[33]

3. *Albertus Magnus as Mystic.*

Wherever Christianity is a living thing, there to a greater or lesser extent will flourish practical mysticism, the complete development of the state of grace, the intimate friendship of the soul with God, leading to the mysterious perception of His indwelling and working in the person thus favoured. The speculative investigation, however, of these facts and experiences, namely the science of mysticism, has only been cultivated at certain definite periods. The first to treat of these questions in Germany is held to be the Franciscan David of Augsburg, the teacher of the celebrated preacher Berthold of Regensburg. He was soon followed by the Dominican Albertus Magnus, who in the succeeding period was far to surpass him in importance and influence. Emil Michael thus describes Albert the mystic : 'Albert the Great was a deeply spiritual nature. Because of his superior intellectual gifts he was entrusted with transactions and offices which in themselves were sufficient to claim absolutely his whole energies. Yet neither his scientific and literary

[32] H. Lauer : op. cit., 15.

[33] According to Aristotle, political science (politica) belongs definitely to ethics. Albert also commented on this work of the Stagyrite. Accordingly, Wilhelm Arendt (op. cit., 87) groups Albert's treatises on the political and social sciences together. He is of opinion that in these Albert's services do not lie in the carrying of the problems a step further, but in holding fast to and handing on the doctrines which had come down to him.

activities, nor his repeated employment in the practical affairs of life were able to distract his spirit or to disturb his faith. In the accidents and incidents of exterior phenomena he fixed his eyes steadily on the centre of all being and all truth ; his heart belonged to Him who alone is love. It is no wonder that a state of mind such as this found natural expression in his works, even when they dealt with scientific or philosophical questions. Some of his writings in particular are dedicated to mysticism, e.g. the great Commentary on the Pseudo-Dionysius the Areopagite and many smaller works. The best witness to Albert's mysticism is the golden booklet, *De adhærendo Deo*, which he composed towards the end of his life on the words from the seventy-second psalm : "It is good for me to adhere to my God." '[34] Michael's further remarks are based solely on this little book, whose contents he describes in great detail. Beyond this, he only points out that Albert goes the reverse way from David. The latter began with instruction how to strive after virtue and ends with contemplation as the goal. Albert on the other hand begins with a penetrating description of the goal and ends his exposition with what man has first to do, with the practical exercise of trust and penance.

Easy as it was in the then state of research for Michael to describe Albert as a mystic with the aid of the *Libellus de adhærendo Deo*, this task is become as difficult since Grabmann, in the year 1920, pronounced against Albert's authorship of this precious little book, which had been honoured as the exquisite fruit of his mysticism and as his swan-song. On the ground of positive and negative, of exterior and interior, criteria Grabmann believed it should be ascribed to the Benedictine Johannes von Kastl. He cites as a negative argument that all the manuscripts of this libellus belong exclusively to the fifteenth century. A positive interior argument is supplied by the difference in style between this little book and Albert's works. The decisive, positive exterior argument is the express ascription of the book to Johannes von Kastl in three Munich and one Melk MSS. 'With the joy over the find, which,

[34] Michael : op. cit., iii, 143.

moreover, concerns a theologian of my own home town, there is mingled a feeling as of separation from Albertus Magnus, from whose scholarly life work the crown has had, as it were, to be broken off.'[35] Doubts had very early been cast on the Saint's authorship, and these were repeated in the course of the centuries down to Denifle and Mandonnet, but the deciding word on the matter was first spoken by Grabmann. However, his position has also lately been severely shaken, for the Dominican Théry has brought to light proof of the genuineness of the work as Albert's ; and Grabmann, in re-testing his arguments, acknowledges that Johannes of Kastl may well have worked over and extended a genuine work of Albert's. Whatever the end of the dispute over the authorship of this small and yet so celebrated mystical work may be, one thing is certain, that Albert cannot be exhibited as a mystic on the strength of this little book. We are therefore thrown back on the other works of Albert for our demonstrations, and primarily to his Commentary on the works of the Pseudo-Dionysius. These writings differ completely both in language and style from the little work *De adhærendo Deo*, but the conception of mysticism is also so strongly differentiated that Grabmann's arguments against the genuineness of this little work are but strengthened. True, that in considering this interior evidence, it must never be lost to sight that because of his universality and his constant endeavour to rescue from every given subject whatever truth it contained which might serve in the extension of knowledge, Albert found occasion in other fields to adopt a similar variation in method. It cannot therefore be ruled out of court that in his conception and exposition of mysticism he also varied, particularly as the little book *De adhærendo Deo* has been regarded by all as the closing work of his long scholarly activity. Whether this variation implies an improvement may be reasonably doubted both in this and in other cases.

Albert's commentaries on the works of the Pseudo-Dionysius fill Vol. XIV of Borgnet's edition. But in this

[35] M. Grabmann : *Der Benediktinermystiker Johannes von Kastl, der Verfasser des Büchleins De adhærendo Deo*, 189. Cf. also his article *Neue Funde.*

volume there are only to be found the *De cœlesti hierarchia*, the *De ecclesiastica hierarchia*, the *De mystica theologia*, and *XI Epistolæ*. From this it is at once seen that one of the most important works, the Commentary on the *De divinis nominibus*, is missing. So far this has not yet been published, though the manuscripts are well known and several attempts have been made to publish it. Quite recently Théry has been at pains to edit it, and we can only hope that he may succeed in overcoming the difficulties which have wrecked the previous attempts. For a final judgement on Albert as a mystic this edition is every bit as important as the solution of the question of the authenticity of the *De adhærendo Deo*.

Of the printed commentaries on the writings of the Pseudo-Dionysius the two *De hierarchia* contain scarcely any mystical matter, so that essentially only the work *De mystica theologia* remains for us in our investigation. This is, however, of all the more importance since its subject is the true mystical practice, namely *contemplatio*. Since, however, according to the traditional conception, the collective spiritual life forms a whole, and the highest stages of contemplation are normally a development from ascetic beginnings, we must in Albert's case have a look at the works which treat of these foundations. A number of smaller ascetical works are ascribed to the great teacher, in which he set himself the task of leading man to perfection by the practice of the Christian virtues. The most important of these works is the *Paradisus animæ*, or, to give it its full title, *Enchiridium de virtutibus veris et perfectis, quod et paradisus animæ dicitur*. Unfortunately this little work, which contains a quite remarkable practical treatise on ethics, and somewhat unusually begins with charity and ends with perseverance, can also hardly be regarded as an authentic work of Albert's. Berthier has made the attempt to claim the authorship of this little book for Bl. Humbert, who was Master-General of the Dominican Order in Albert's day ;[36] the question is, however, not yet settled. In the second place there comes under consideration the work *De mulieri forti*, an exposition of the thirty-first chapter of the Book

[36] Beatus Humbertus de Romanis : *Opera de vita regulari*, xvii.

of Proverbs. The commentary is made to apply not only to the Church but also to the individual soul. The work is carried out entirely after the manner of his Commentary on the Psalms. Again the *XXXII Sermones de Eucharistia* give us almost the same picture. Exteriorly both books readily pass the test as Albert's work, while interiorly they conform to his other writings. In them the Saint reveals himself as the experienced and prudent guide to the spiritual life, one who knows how to paint the sublime goal in clear and shining colours, who spurs men on to ceaseless effort, now from the point of view of personal development and perfection, now by the motive of faithfulness and gratitude to the Greatest of Benefactors. In all this he moves in a supernatural thought-world. His first and almost sole authority is Holy Scripture. Hardly a thought is expressed but it is at once verified and explained by various passages from the Sacred Books. The number of times when a *motif* appears which is treated psychologically is infinitesimal. This method gives the writings an objective and extremely serene character. In those days they may well have had an excellent influence on souls ; to-day their influence, at least in wider circles, would probably be almost *nil*.

It is in the Commentaries on the Pseudo-Dionysius that we really meet with Albert as a mystic. He had one great advantage over his great contemporaries, Alexander of Hales, Bonaventure, and Thomas Aquinas, that he alone had commented on all the works of the influential Greek : the Two Hierarchies, the Mystical Theology, the Epistles, and also the work on the Divine Names. Neither Alexander nor Bonaventure had ventured on the interpretation of these writings, and Thomas confined himself to the work *De divinis nominibus*. As in the case of Aristotle so also in that of the Pseudo-Dionysius, it was again Albert who had the vision to recognize the importance of these writings, and who attempted to make the truths they contained accessible. The undertaking was more difficult than in the case of Aristotle, since the thoughts were more lofty, the mode of expression more obscure, and the danger of error greater, due to their relationship to the pseudo-mysticism of Plotinus. Accordingly Albert does not write a mere paraphrase of these writings but a regular commentary, in which he analyses, corrects, and amends the text, exposes and solves difficulties, all, moreover, in harmony with sound theological doctrine. The work again was all the harder since little had been done on it before. Thus of the Mystical Theology only Scotus Erigena had written a paraphrase, but had not touched, let alone solved, the difficulties. The simple fact that Albert commented on all these mystic writings of the Pseudo-Dionysius gives him a special place in the history of mysticism. The influence which the Areopagite had on Christian mysticism at that time was unique, and this it was to preserve for the future. Heiler has aptly summed up the situation thus: 'An equally continuous curve of development leads from the Orphic-Dionysian mysticism, through Plato and the late Hellenic mystery-cults, to Plotinus's Neoplatonic mysticism of the infinite, which is the source of the mystic theology of the Pseudo-Dionysius Areopagite. His writings became the great treasure-house whence all the later Christian mystics took much of their material. It is not without justice that he is called the father of Christian mysticism. Dionysius nourished the whole mysticism of the Eastern Church; brought to the Church of the West by Scotus Erigena and the Victorines, he exercised a decisive influence on her piety and on her theology.'[37] Dionysius does not merely provide the preliminary conditions necessary to mysticism, but almost continuously expressly directs us to the most essential elements of all true mysticism, to union with God, to contemplation, to that *occulta cognitio*, which he describes in the brightest colours, but which he shrouds with the veil of mystery and wishes to keep so shrouded. This mystery is not to make it unattainable, for it forms the consummation of all perfection this side the grave; it is intended only to illustrate a sublimity which no human tongue may express. Dionysius also divides men into three classes; he speaks of the three ways; he gives directions for the more close preparation for the mystical union, and instructions on conduct during the mystic vision: all elements of mystical theology. Unfortunately he does not

[37] Friedrich Heiler: *Das Gebet*, 233.

clothe his teaching in carefully measured, clear, unambiguous language, but prefers, one might almost say intentionally seeks, obscurities in diction and picturesqueness in description, at the cost, however, of lucidity. His writings gave rise to the most momentous errors in the mystical field. An explanation of his practice, and some excuse for him personally, may be found in the fact that he himself was steeped in Neoplatonic ideas and was not altogether free from the influences of pagan mysticism. His fundamental error lies in the false conception of the relation between the body and the soul. He did not conceive of them as forming an absolute entity, but as having been united fortuitously. Whence he infers that the soul can at least know itself quite independently of the external world ; in fact she does not even need the assistance of the senses, whether exterior or interior.[38] It is thus that Dionysius will have understood his oft-repeated exhortation to detach oneself from all phantasy and all impressions. In order, however, to attain to the mystical knowledge of God, he makes the further demand that all intellectual activity be given up, so as to advance on the road to the super-intellectual plane. Herein lies the danger of passivism. Appealing to the Pseudo-Dionysius, the quietists have drawn obviously false conclusions. They make as a condition for the reception of mystical grace the absolute renunciation of all human activity. The more moderate excluded all conative activity with the exception of the acts of love. All quoted in their support the words of the Pseudo-Dionysius : 'If thou, beloved Timotheus, dost wish to prepare thyself to enter the highest possible plane of mystical experience, leave aside the senses and also the activities of the intellect, forsake whatsoever happens under the senses and whatever may be perceived by the intellect, whatsoever is and is not, and raise thyself with manly thought to intimate union with Him who surpasses all being and all knowledge.'[39]

[38] Albert, though he has the right conception of the relation of soul to body, teaches something similar : I *Sententiarum*, dist. 3, a. 29. Cf. Doms : op. cit., 53.

[39] *Mystica Theologia*, cap. 1 ; Zahn : *Einführung in die christliche Mystik*, 276.

Albert held the author of the Two Hierarchies, the Mystical Theology, the Epistles, and the Treatise on the Divine Names to be the true Dionysius Areopagite, the disciple of the Apostles. In this Albert was a child of his time, and the view he held explains the exceedingly great respect which he had for these books. Their language is to him almost as sacred as that of the Holy Scriptures. This, however, does not mislead him into reinterpreting the Scriptures in the light of Dionysius's ideas ; indeed to each one of his words he tries to attach a thought which shall be in accord with Holy Scripture. The Commentary on the Mystical Theology can be regarded as actually a masterpiece of skilful interpretation ; for Albert omits literally nothing, not even the smallest sentence ; and assigns to every one, even the most obscure, a clear meaning which conforms to dogma. He pauses over his explanations now for a longer, now a shorter time, according to the difficulties met with. Sometimes a single word demands a thorough analysis. In what follows we shall call attention to the thoughts which are most important for a proper conception of true mysticism.

Albert had had acquaintance with the danger of quietism ; and in relation with it raised the difficulty : 'Without intellectual activity there can be no knowledge. Accordingly Dionysius should not constrain Timotheus, to whom he wishes to impart a piece of knowledge, to abstain from intellectual activity ; he must rather exhort him to take it up boldly.'

The answer to this fundamental objection runs : 'The exhortation of Dionysius to let intellectual activity alone, refers to our natural intellectual operation, not to that which is in us by virtue of the divine light.'[40] With this on the one hand quietism is ruled out, for Albert demands personal operation for the mystical experience ; on the other hand by that distinction there is indicated the essential difference which obtains between natural activity, including the operation of grace, which in the generality of people is accomplished according to the manner of the natural, and mystical activity properly so called. It is the distinction

[40] *Mystica Theologia*, cap. 1, §2 ad 4.

WOODEN STATUE, *CIRCA* 1500, BY AN UNKNOWN MASTER, POSSIBLY MEISTER RABE, IN THE PARISH CHURCH OF S. ALDEGUNDIS, EMMERICH

which he as well as his pupil Thomas connects with the expressions *gratia operans* and *gratia cooperans*.

The third objection which Albert makes concerns our dependence on the senses. 'One must needs begin with the sensuous, therefore Dionysius ought not to teach that the senses should be neglected.'

The answer to this is as clear as it is short. He lays it down that the senses should be neglected as far as they lead in themselves to obscuration, but not that it is unlawful to rise to God by the employment of what is known by the senses. With this Albert does not wish to assert that mystical experience is limited to the truths which we create out of the things surrounding us, for faith of itself affords us a much higher kind of knowledge of God ; his object is to call attention to the operation of the senses which accompanies every normal cognitive act. The greatest authorities in the mystical field of our day agree with Albert on this point.

Quite similarly the Saint takes up a multitude of difficulties and gives the solution conforming to sound reason and true theology. Above all, his point is, and this he repeats in the most varied passages of his Commentary, that no one in any mystical vision enjoys a direct vision of God. This beatitude is, and ever will be, reserved for the world to come. Here on earth the favoured soul may perceive the workings of God, even exceptional workings, but never directly God himself.[41] Albert in this goes to the length of denying to Moses the direct vision of God, although the majority of the Fathers and theologians concede to the leader of the people of Israel this experience, not as a mystical one properly speaking, but as a quite extra-ordinary manifestation of grace.[42]

In a way all his own, but quite answering to his interest in natural science, he attempts to explain how it is that in contemplation, that highest activity of the noblest faculty, the operations of the other faculties are checked, in fact almost seem to vanish. Here he sharply differentiates the activity itself from its intensity ; also the activity and the

[41] *Mystica Theologia*, cap. 1, §4 ad 11.
[42] Ibid., cap. 1, §6 ad 3.

period over which it is effective. He naturally tries also to explain how it is that contemplatives can fast more easily than others and can stand a more severe fast without detriment to themselves. He has in the *De animalibus* expressed himself on this subject in what appears to us almost too drastic a manner, when he calls attention to the hibernation of certain animals.[43]

We can see from these few examples how eminent were Albert's services to mysticism. He was the first to use the scholastic-Aristotelian rule in the exploration of the obscure forms of speech of the mystics. With a decision which nothing could daunt and with inexorable logic he set forth the pertinent definitions. Through this, much of its mysterious charm vanished ; but what was perceivable by the mind of man was brought out clearly and tangibly. Nevertheless in Albert's exposition there remains enough and more than enough of the mysterious in the domain of mysticism. Let us only take the act of contemplation itself. According to Albert it is experimental knowledge won under the special impulse of grace by the intellect perfected through the gift of wisdom. These are certainly valuable definitions of the principles contributing to the act ; but no one will wish to assert that with them nothing remains to be explained in the action of the person and that of grace. The same is true if we say with Albert that the immediate object of contemplation is not God in the abstract, but some special action of God. Even under this point of view the nature of the said act is not fully determined. To many it will even seem that the mysteries are only removed to another ground and increased. Be this as it may, one thing is certain, that even the least sure perception of those sublime truths is of the greatest importance. We owe Albert the greatest gratitude for what he has so conclusively written on mystical problems in his Commentary on the Mystical Theology. What authorities in the field of natural science have said about Albert's importance in these subjects, namely that natural science, if it had followed in his steps, would have spared itself a détour of some centuries, is equally applicable in the domain of

[43] *De animalibus*, 564.

mysticism. Much obscurity, much dispute, many really portentous errors might have been avoided if men had continued building on Albert's principles, instead of for ever reverting to the obscure and extravagant teachings of the Pseudo-Areopagite. Thomas never departed from Albert's side in mysticism. He only transferred his Master's teaching on the *donum sapientiæ* to all *dona*, and he assigned them to the virtues in another order. If in other branches of theology Thomas surpassed his Master in precision and clarity of expression, this is not the case here. In the Commentary to the Mystical Theology Albert attained to the precision of his pupil. It is almost incredible that in spite of Albert's calm and lucid exposition, the old, distorted notions of pure passivity, of complete elimination of all activity of the senses, should after all these centuries be continually cropping up. In the same way the attempt has been made again and again to represent the spiritual senses, by which God may be directly perceived, as special faculties, although Albert long ago gave the only rational explanation of this mystical expression.

That the Saint expounds the purification of the soul in the sense of salutary ascetism need scarcely be insisted on ; as it would also be superfluous to dwell upon his knowledge and description of the three ways. Ample has been said to show that in the field of mysticism also Albert not only achieved great things in individual problems, but also actually laid new foundations and set up sign-posts for the further development of the subject, in virtue of which he certainly deserves the title of Great. It is not without justice that in the preface to an old printed edition of the *Philosophia pauperum* he is called 'sacræ theologiæ professor profundissimus.'[44]

Since such lucidity of ideas and precision of language do not dominate the little work *De adhærendo Deo*, which is rather a reversion to the whole conception and style of the Pseudo-Dionysius, we need not grieve too much over Grabmann's discovery.

True, it must be admitted that it happened to Albert in mysticism as it did in many other branches of learning.

[44] Printed in Leipzig in 1498.

He wavered to and fro between different opinions. Thus even in his unquestionably genuine works we find thoughts and expressions which are quite in the spirit of Pseudo-Dionysian mysticism. Albert speaks of particular potencies of the soul as *imago Dei* ; he defends the teaching of innate ideas of God ; he lays extraordinarily sharp emphasis on the presence of God in man. This last teaching is, however, become, as Doms rightly remarks, a gushing fountain of genuine mysticism.[45] In the Commentary on the Sentences the fire of his mystically inspired soul flames up but now and then ; in the later works, however, especially in the Gospel Commentaries, it breaks out into a mighty blaze. In numberless passages we find variations on the *bride-motif*, and on it the Saint reaches a depth and a sublimity of thought which ranks him with the greatest masters of all time.[46]

4. *Albertus Magnus as Dogmatist.*

The task of Scholasticism was to bring together into one system, suitable for practical use in the schools, the truths of the faith and the explanations and comments of the Fathers. Scholasticism therefore differs from Patristics, not through new dogmas, nor again through any neglect of the Holy Scriptures, but in its desire to present the Christian teaching in its entirety, to this end disclosing, more strongly than the Fathers did, the connexion between the truths of the faith and the perceptions of reason. This in the mediæval schools was the ground for special philosophical and theological speculation, which is the main characteristic of Scholasticism. It was not content with merely exposing the connexion between the truths of the faith and of reason, but sought rather by applying the principles of philosophy to the truths of the faith to win a greater insight into them, and thus to make the supernatural truths more accessible to the human mind, and to defend them against objections. Anselm of Canterbury is regarded as the father of Scholasticism. However, as he, with all the Fathers, held by the

[45] H. Doms : op. cit., 51, 60, 70.
[46] Ibid. : op. cit., 109, 112.

Platonic philosophy, he could not quite succeed in reaching his goal; what was wanting was the complete disclosure of the connexion between the natural and the supernatural. The whole of Aristotle's philosophy had to become known and turned to account, in order to lead the work of Scholasticism to a worthy end. We have already seen how Albert, by collecting the best manuscripts and by elucidating the complete works of the Stagyrite, helped to throw open this treasury of truths to the West. All that remains here is to describe how he employed his philosophy to elucidate after this manner the loftiest branch of theology, namely dogma; and we shall see that the eminent service which Albert rendered by the introduction of the Aristotelian philosophy has its counterpart in a similar service in regard to the further development of theology.

It has already been pointed out, but, in order to avoid any exaggeration, it should be repeated here, that others before Albert had made the attempt to use the Aristotelian philosophy in the service of theology. Alexander of Hales in particular worked at this problem; but, apart from certain individual questions, he did not succeed in bringing about the necessary amalgamation. In his works the Aristotelian texts have the appearance of being alien matter, whereas with Albert's the case is quite different. Here the great amalgamation is consummated, even though in one point or another the true balance had not yet been found. In such places we get an impression as if the Saint were standing overwhelmed in face of the wealth of ideas which were sweeping on him. However, he did not let this detain him, but adopted the expedient of simply drawing up the arguments for and against. In such cases the solution given at the end leaves something to be desired in clarity and precision. Defects such as these are more frequently to be found in the Commentary on the Sentences, less so in the *Summæ*. Whoever contemplates the gigantic task which Albert set himself, will hardly be astonished at these imperfections. He will rather rejoice in the fact that the Saint did not spend his time in a long search after clarity in every detail, but preferred to suffer a certain want of balance in secondary matters in order to complete the plan of his structure by giving the main elevation. To be sure, the point is now bluntly made against Albert that in the broad plan and unity of design for the structure of the philosophico-theological sciences he was also unsuccessful, and that we had to wait for Thomas to achieve this. On which it may be remarked that this objection as it stands is certainly not pertinent. Just as the whole undertaking has its origin in the genius of Albert who conceived it, so too has the design for its execution ; and Albert's work can, and must, be set down as essentially successful. We have already made this clear in moral science ; precisely the same is true in dogma. For all this, the fact remains that Thomas carried out the amalgamation down to the last detail, that his construction is more compact, and that in consequence the whole gives the impression of a far greater unity than do Albert's works. However, we must not forget that Albert wrote first ; Thomas was the pupil who sat at Albert's feet and to whom the Master imparted all his ideas, ambitions, and plans. It was by Albert that Thomas's work was inspired, furthered, watched over, and defended, and through Albert his work found recognition, at any rate in the Order. Without Albert, Thomas would not have been what he became. That Albert was influenced by Thomas has not been demonstrated. While the latter was in his *Summa* finishing the work for which Albert had laid the foundations in his Commentary on the Sentences, the Master too was working at a *Summa*, in which, however, he diverged in many ways from the road he had himself broken in earlier days, and was reverting to the views of the Fathers. Michael, talking of the plan and elevation of this work, says : 'The interior structure is in both works (the *Summæ de creaturis* and *theologiæ*) the same. They are split up into tractates, questions, and articles or membra, which are often further divided into subsections. The legion of individual questions are unfolded and ordered, as in an organic pattern, with strictest logical consequence from a basic principle. The point at issue is invariably exactly defined. Then, as in Abelard, though the latter had not known Aristotle's Organon, the reasons for and against are adduced. On this follows the solution, the explicit settlement of the problem, in which in turn the indefensibility of the several objections brought forward is demonstrated. In actual fact this is the circumstantial method of establishing a truth. If the subject has been treated from these points of view, nothing remains to be said in regard to its scientific foundation.'[47] That this method is not to everyone's taste, that because of this minute dissection and analysis the perspective is sometimes lost, are defects which are irremediable, for they attach more or less to every earthly action.

The arrangement of the material in the theological *Summa* follows that of the Sentences. The same questions and solutions recur ; and yet there is a vast difference. Albert had in the Commentary itself become sensible of and suffered from what was doubtful in the arrangement of the material in the Sentences ; and the repetition of the same matter in the most varied connexions had been extremely irksome to him. In the *Summa theologiæ* he tried to remedy this drawback. To be sure, love for the traditional struggled in him with the impulse towards new ideas. Keeping essentially to the customary sequence, he sought by elimination and transposition to arrive at a methodically ordered, compact structure. A glance at the first part of the *Summa* shows us Albert's manner of procedure. Exactly like Thomas in his *Summa*, Albert begins with an inquiry into the nature of theology, and not like the Master of the Sentences with the question of the subject-matter. From the first tractate, which corresponds to the first part of the first distinction, he has rejected the whole inquiry as to whether the Sacraments of the Old Covenant were mediators of grace. In the second tractate, corresponding to the second part of the first distinction, he indeed still treats of *uti et frui* (use and enjoyment), whereas Thomas puts this completely aside ; but, at any rate, he shortened and recast the exposition. He treated the Distinction II on the mystery of the Trinity in tractates 7 to 12, having previously spoken on the knowableness of God, and of His simplicity, immutability, and eternity. If here, too, the Saint does not exhibit the same compact incisiveness as does S. Thomas

[47] Michael : op. cit., iii, 120.

in his *Summa*, he nevertheless gives evidence not only of an earnest intention, but also of great ability in the building up of a systematic structure, which raises him far above the Magister sententiarum and his followers.

We will now notice more closely some special points in Albert's dogmatics. Following Grabmann,[48] we may point to one of the most difficult and obscure problems in the sublime mystery of the Trinity, namely the procession of the Holy Ghost from the Father and the Son. As M. J. Scheeben[49] long ago remarked, Albert paid very special attention to precisely this point, and has exhibited it with a breadth and a thoroughness exceeding that of any other scholastic. The basis of his exposition, which occupies more than seven folio pages, is the saying of the Pseudo-Dionysius that 'in God also divine love induces an ecstasy.'[50] A very personal inspiration is wafted on these words. This can only be the utterance of one whom an extra-ordinary subject has gripped, who has been filled by it, and is compelled by it to speak his thoughts. It may be that the efforts which were being made, especially at the time of the Council of Lyons, towards the reunion of the schismatic Greeks with the Roman Church, led Albert to make a thorough study of this difficult question, for their answer to which the Greeks reproached the Latins with defection from the primitive Church. Thomas at that time was no longer among the living and Bonaventure died at that Council. Albert attended it and, moved by his interest, took part in the proceedings.[51] It is much more likely that the sublimity of the subject—that this profoundest mystery of Love—captured him for its own sake, and stimulated him to give of his best to its elucidation. At any rate, it is precisely this tractate which reveals the penetrating vision and sure, firm grasp of Albert's genius in the solution of the deepest scientific problems.

[48] M. Grabmann: *Der Einfluss Alberts des Grossen auf das mittelalterliche Geistesleben*, 27.

[49] M. J. Scheeben: *Die Mysterien des Christentums*, 98.

[50] I *Summæ Theologicæ*, tr. 7, q. 31, m. 1.

[51] Petrus de Prussia: op. cit., 245. In this passage the importance of Albert's intervention is probably overestimated.

The special merit of Albert's tractate on man's first state has been pointed out by P. Kors.[52] Until Præpositivus, it had almost universally been accepted in theological circles that Adam was not created in sanctifying grace, but only possessed the gift of impassibility, and that he had sinned before sanctifying grace had been bestowed on him. Præpositivus advanced the contrary opinion. Nevertheless the most important theologians, such as William of Auxerre and Alexander of Hales, held to the old view and sharply opposed the new idea. In the *Summa*[53] Albert also supported the old view ; yet in the Commentary on the Sentences, which most people regard as having been composed before the *Summa*, he had accepted the new notion, but, it is true, only unequivocally as relating to the angels. As regards our first parents, he too here sets out the old view out of respect for the Magister sententiarum, but says quite openly that he holds the opposite opinion.[54] It was Thomas who brought the new view into general recognition.

Albert's exposition of original sin is thus criticized by P. Kors : 'The explanation of original sin is not very clear.'[55] This criticism is, however, more applicable to Kors' notion of the nature of original sin than to Albert's. Kors departs in important respects from the conception traditional in the Order of S. Dominic ; whereas Albert had a part in establishing the latter. The Master of the Sentences, relying on S. Augustine, had transferred the nature of original sin to concupiscence, but our Saint, in agreement with Alexander of Hales, and following Anselm, differentiates a material and a formal element in original sin. In concupiscence, to which he gives a wider connotation than undisciplined affection towards every kind of transitory good, Albert sees the material element ; the formal element, and with it the nature, he refers to the *carentia debitæ justitiæ*, that is to absence of original justice, which ought to be present, but in fact is wanting. Here, too, Thomas has

[52] P. Kors : *La justice primitive et le péché originel d'après saint Thomas*.
[53] II *Summæ Theologicæ*, tr. 14, q. 20, m. 1.
[54] II *Sententiarum*, dist. 24, B. art. 1.
[55] P. Kors : op. cit., 69.

given more pointed expression to Albert's thoughts ; he states quite unequivocally what is to be understood by *carentia*, he makes clear the inner connexion between concupiscence and the lack of sanctifying grace on the one hand and the first sin of our first parents on the other, and thus settles a scientific problem which had vexed men for centuries. It was only after the Reformation that the dispute on original sin was resumed, but then, to be sure, more from the point of view of the guilt, that is to say of its connexion with Adam's first personal lapse. For the estimation of Albert's position it will be, we hope, sufficient to have been able to show that in the doctrine of original sin, as in so many other points, Albert prepared the way for S. Thomas ; in fact we can almost say that on this point their teaching was the same.

Dr. Herbert Doms has made Albert's teaching on grace the subject of a very thorough investigation, which appeared as Vol. XIII of the Breslauer Studies in Historical Theology. He did not limit his research to a detached inquiry on the tractate on grace, nor did he, after the usual manner of to-day, fence this off from the rest of Albert's writings, but attempted to discover his views on grace in all its aspects. He therefore begins with the doctrine of man's striving towards perfect possession of God. He finds here, or better in the desire for God common to all creatures, the key to Albert's contribution to the doctrine of grace. Everything tends towards God, although, by its creation out of nothing, everything is afar off from God.[56] Man, by reason of his spiritual nature, is stamped with the image of God, and thus the predisposition to the most intimate closeness to God and to familiar intercourse with him is his ; though surely from the nature of things only the possibility is present in the passive disposition. The realization postulates the temporal mission of the Divine Persons and, bound up with this, their indwelling in the soul. Grace brings about the condition necessary to their indwelling, the *effectus in creatura* with which the *missio temporalis* is bound up.[57]

[56] Cf. S. Thomas : *Summa Theologica*, I, motus a Deo ; ibid., I–II, motus in Deum. [Ed.]

[57] H. Doms : op. cit., 68.

Grace is always described by Albert as something definitely beyond man's capacity. Hence it can never be acquired by man unaided ; it is bestowed by God himself by means of a kind of creative act. On the ladder spanning the distance between the creature and God *gratia* has its place in the proximity of God ; it is never there except God be specially present, and, through the indwelling of the Divine Person who has been sent, it escapes the common lot of created things, that of being transitory by reason of their miserable state. As an Aristotelian the Saint characterizes grace as an accident ; yet, influenced by the Neoplatonists, and out of regard for Augustine, Albert in other places shows that he is not contented with this definition. Indeed he reaches the point of actually denying that grace is an accident and falls back upon the bare conception of perfectio.[58] The relation of grace to the virtues is defined after the manner in which the relation between the soul and her faculties is set out in the Aristotelian system. As the tractate proceeds, it is shown how the soul is purified, simplified, and exalted through grace, how she enters into a special relation with the Divine Persons, and how the image of God is in this life a relative one, and reaches ultimate perfection in glory. His teaching on Merit, on Gratuitous Grace, on Justification, and on Predestination is also very detailed, and comparisons with the teaching of Alexander of Hales, Bonaventure, and Thomas are not wanting.

In his closing discussion Doms sums up Albert's contribution to the doctrine of grace in the following commendatory passages : 'Among the school men Albert's special contribution to the doctrine of grace would seem to be the doctrine of the *perfectio* in the sense of the Neoplatonic *appropinquatio ad* and *reductio in Deum*, at any rate as so skilfully applied.'[59] The following quotations have quite a Platonic ring : 'Man is raised by grace and glory to a state which, first imperfectly, and then perfectly, gives him the capacity to escape from all deprivation, and finally, in glory, to possess himself in a single eternity. Thus grace

[58] IV *Sententiarum*, dist. 46, art. 5 ad 2.
[59] H. Doms : op. cit., 268.

becomes the means by which he is liberated from the impotency arising from sin. . . . Herein lies at the same time the leading back to God, responding to the action of the rational will, and approach to him.'[60] That any suspicion of Pelagianism may be obviated, it is expressly stated that 'the attainment to this state far exceeds the means given to man in the state of wayfarer ; it is definitely supra naturam' (supernatural). Nevertheless grace and glory are in Albert's doctrine of grace nothing other than the perfection answering to the spiritual side of human nature. It is only the actual *visio Dei* which assures to man perfect possession of himself. With this is also given perfect interpenetration and union of the personal human spirit and the personal God. To this Doms remarks : 'Albert's speculations have here reached a height such as is only scalable by really great Masters in Theology.'[61]

If we compare Albert's teaching on grace with that of Alexander of Hales and of S. Thomas, we shall find many similarities in the manner of treating and of applying the Aristotelian principles ; but on closer investigation a very great difference appears. Whereas Alexander builds up his teaching on a Neoplatonic foundation, and Thomas bases his on the Stagyrite's principles which he develops to their logical conclusion, Albert's teaching represents an attempt at amalgamating the two systems. Thus the unity of the picture which he sketches is prejudiced, but it displays traits which Thomas missed as the following characteristic titles show : Grace as participation in God's nature, and Grace as the actual perfector of Man.[62]

It was with special love and care that Albert dwelt on two sections of his Dogmatics, on Mariology and the Eucharist. Grabmann calls particular attention to the former. 'In the field of Mariology Albert among all the early scholastic theologians wrote the most. His Commentary on the Sentences, his exegetical works, his comprehensive *Mariale*, contain a wealth of dogmatic and ascetical thoughts on, and allusions to Mary ; while to his unprinted work, *De bono sive de virtutibus*, he appended a

[60] H. Doms : op. cit., 269. [61] Ibid. : op. cit., 273.
[62] Ibid. : op. cit., 275.

little treatise on the Virginity of Our Lady. In his smaller treatise, *De bono*, preserved in two Munich MSS., we come across a very detailed excursus on the same subject. Albert used every opportunity to express his veneration and love for Mary. Certain Mariological works of his, in particular a Commentary on the Ave Maria, are still unprinted.[63]

It is not only the number and extent of Albert's Mariological writings which astonishes us ; we also find on many a point a depth of conception and a thoroughness of treatment which surpasses all expectation. In wider Catholic circles to-day interest turns on the doctrine of Mary's mediation : whether a general mediation of grace is to be ascribed to her or not. On this question Albert stands out as a clear, fully credited witness to the conviction of his age on the dignity and influence of the Mother of God. True, he did not treat this question in his works on systematic theology, but in the *Mariale* and the Commentaries on Holy Scripture ; nevertheless in lucidity of expression and sureness of treatment his teaching is not thereby affected in the slightest degree. Albert explicitly speaks of general mediation of every grace in the sense that all grace, which flows to men by the merits of Christ, comes to them through Mary. As all have a part in the grace of Christ, so too this comes to them through Mary. It is in this sense that Albert in the *Mariale* expounds the titles : Fountain of Grace, Gate of Heaven, Star of the Sea ; he develops the teaching dogmatically from Mary's position as bride, and as co-helper of Jesus ; and finds this truth most clearly expressed in the title Queen of Mercy.[64] He draws, too, a sharp distinction between the intercession of the Saints and the mediation of Mary.[65] From all this it will be clear what a prominent place Albert holds in the ranks of the great Mariologists.[66]

Albert's writings on the Eucharist are still more copious. This mystery would seem to have lain closer to the heart

[63] M. Grabmann : op. cit., 27.

[64] In the thirteenth century the Salve Regina began thus : Salve Regina Misericordiæ. [Ed.]

[65] H. Albers : *La mediación universal de la stma Virgen según el bto Alberto Magno.*

[66] Thomas Esser : *Die Gnadenfülle der allerseligsten Jungfrau Maria nach der Lehre des seligen Albert des Grossen.*

of the pious Master than all the others ; and he devotes even greater attention to it than to Mariology. Apart from the expositions in the Commentary on the Sentences, which are purely scientific, we possess three further separate writings of Albert's on this mystery. The first of these contains *XXXII Sermones de Corpore Christi*, in which the doctrine of the most Blessed Sacrament of the Altar was, according to the fashion of the time, set out in discourses. For a long time these Sermons circulated under Thomas's name. They enjoyed a wide circulation and were very early translated into other languages, including German. The second work is entitled : *De Eucharistiæ Sacramento*, or alternatively *Summa de Eucharistiæ Sacramento.* Grabmann calls it : 'A book of great depth of thought and touching intimacy. It belongs to the best that has ever been written on the sublime subject, and influenced the Eucharistic teaching of German mysticism.'[67] The third work bears the superscription : *De Sacrificio Missæ.* It has in our day inspired Professor A. Franz to words of high praise.[68] He calls attention above all to Albert's independent attack on a mediæval aberration to which even S. Thomas paid tribute. The bad taste of Almerich of Metz's method of explanation found in Albert a doughty opponent. He cut himself absolutely loose from this then popular, but purely arbitrary, exposition of the ceremonies of the Mass, and took a road on which we are still glad to follow him to-day.

The doctrine of the Church is not treated by Albert in any particular work, nor even in any self-contained section of the great systematic works, and yet Dr. Scherer was able to put together the whole doctrine of the Church from Albert's writings. To do this he had, it is true, to search through all the Saint's theological works. This wearisome labour, however, resulted in his finding in him the true conception of the Church, even though the old definition which he used is inexact. Albert, however, following the taste of his day, sought to illustrate and circumscribe this definition by images drawn from the Old and the New Testaments. A defect in Albert's doctrine appears in the

[67] M. Grabmann : op. cit., 27.
[68] A. Franz : *Die Messe im Deutschen Mittelalter*, 469.

chapters on the power of the Church ; for, since he wishes to regard God as the sole cause of grace, he seriously detracts from the importance of the Sacraments, and especially the Sacrament of Penance. On the other hand he has treated very correctly and very thoroughly on S. Peter and the Primacy, on the infallibility of the Church and of the Pope. In his investigations Scherer found confirmation for what Ignatius von Senestrey, Bishop of Regensburg, had compiled and published in the year 1870 on Albert's teaching on the infallible magisterium of the Bishop of Rome : 'In this little work Peter is held up as the Visible Head of the Church and of its unity through the power of the keys. The Church, however, is the Body of Christ, since everything which is entrusted to Peter's keys traces back to the One, as Albert in his tractate on the Holy Sacrifice of the Mass says : in quo omnia ad unum rediguntur, quæ Petri clavibus subiciuntur. And the author of that little work draws the conclusion that the Pope possesses plenitude of power, therefore also the power of teaching ; hence the unity of the Church derives from him ; hence his supreme power of teaching within its limits and substance cannot possibly be dependent on the concurrence of subordinates, but anything which his magisterium submits, irrevocably and infallibly possesses the value of a law of the faith.'[69]

It will be seen from what we have quoted how right Grabmann is when he says that in any longitudinal section of the history of dogma we everywhere light upon Albert as an outstanding theologian.[70] It is true that he was in many respects surpassed by his pupil Thomas, and it is superfluous to repeat this again ; but it cannot be too strongly emphasized that Thomas presupposes Albert, his teacher and master, in everything. With heroic love of truth and rare unselfishness, the Saint to the end of his days worked for the reputation of his pupil, and in the theological

[69] Wilhelm Scherer : *Des seligen Albertus Magnus Lehre von der Kirche*, 114 *sq.* ; Ignatius von Senestrey : *Beati Alberti Magni . . . doctrina de infallibili Romani Pontificis magisterio.*

[70] Dr. Carl Feckes has recently confirmed this in the case of the fundamental problem of the relations of faith and knowledge. (*Zeitschrift für Kath. Theologie*, Innsbruck, 1930, LIV, 1–39.)

field he was in this so successful that he himself almost fell into oblivion. The genetic manner of looking at things has already made clear and will make yet clearer Albert's importance to theology. This much is already sure, that here too Albert deserves the title of the Great. It was no exaggeration when Johann Guldenschaff, in the edition of the *Summa de Eucharistiæ Sacramento* published in Cologne in 1477, styles him: 'Sacræ theologiæ professor eximius.'[71]

[71] *Gesamtkatalog der Wiegendrucke*, I, 383.

THE SPIRITUAL GREATNESS OF ALBERT

1. *The Foundation.*

THE Middle Ages considered saints almost exclusively in their perfect state and were amazed at their supernatural greatness. A few legends were enough to satisfy their desire to know something of the way they took to become saints. Modern man prefers the psychological method of observation; he makes researches into the natural disposition of his hero, and of the conditions under which he lived, in order to discover how he became what he did. If the old way of looking at things was exposed to the danger of ignoring the natural, it is easy in the modern way to stop at this and to neglect the supernatural. Moreover, it stumbles against difficulties the moment a person of antiquity or the Middle Ages is in question; for here we are thrown upon sources, which wholly preserve the spirit of the old conception, and tell us everything except what we so badly want to know. The date of birth is missing, so is the name and station of the parents, the place of birth, etc., in fact what in the case of every inhabitant of the globe to-day is registered ever so many times.

We have to complain of the same negligence in the sources for the life of Albertus Magnus, even if we have more information about him than of many others. We know that he was a German and a Swabian, that he was born in Lauingen, that he had an uncle in the Imperial service and a brother, Henry, who was Prior of the Dominican convent in Würzburg. These are valuable pieces of information, which throw, at any rate, a little light on the circumstances in which Albert passed his youth. What he was like outwardly has come down to us; in stature he was not above middle height, in fact was rather short than tall, but he had a powerful, thick-set frame, which would seem to have been created for intense exertion. Only a few episodes of his youth are known, incidents of the chase, such as the hunting of pigeons with wild hawks, the fight between a swan and an eagle, and barbel fishing in the Danube. Valuable as these indications are, for which for the most part we are indebted to Albert himself, the researcher has yet to deplore that they are too meagre and are insufficient to dispel the obscurity which surrounds this Greatness in the making.

Obscurity also broods over his spiritual disposition and over his entry into the Order. The legends have here spun such a rank growth of tendrils over everything, that the natural hypothesis to account for his greatness would appear to have been actually destroyed. And it is remarkable that these legends are known to the people and have made him loved by them. Even Sighart says: 'The legend is so pretty that we cannot quite pass it over'; and he goes on to tell it as follows: 'Albertus was in those days [during his stay in Padua] at honest pains to penetrate into the sanctuary of learning; but all in vain. What he learnt to-day he had forgotten on the morrow; what he thought to have grasped to-day was on the morrow veiled in impenetrable obscurity. In a despondent hour, thoroughly discouraged at his stupidity and ill-cultivated mind, it was in his thoughts to make the decision to say good-bye, once and for all, to all study and to return home, when suddenly a light lit up his chamber and he saw standing before him three maidens of wonderful beauty [in the spirit of mediæval symbolism these would be Mary, Barbara, and Catharine]. One of them thereupon asked him with great friendliness why it was in his thoughts to despair. He gave as his reason the stupidity of his mind. Then she comforted the despondent youth and bade him beseech her Mistress that his wishes might be granted. Wonderfully encouraged by these words, Albert now approached the Queen of Heaven, and when she asked him what he desired, he prostrated before her and prayed that he might be granted the knowledge of all the wisdom in the world. Whereupon the holy Virgin gently answered him thus: "Be of good cheer, thou shalt get thy wish and soon wilt make such strides

LEATHER BINDING OF AUTOGRAPH MS. OF S. ALBERT'S COMMENTARY ON S. MATTHEW'S GOSPEL

The picture of the Saint cut some time in first half of fourteenth century.

that there shall not be thy equal in philosophy. I will always protect thee and will never permit that, caught in the snares of the evil one, thou deviate from the way of the pure faith and go to thy perdition. But that thou mayst know that thou hast to thank for thy learning not the exertions of thine own mind but my favour, before thy death thou shalt be deprived of all this knowledge." '[1] This account we must regard as pious embellishment, as an ingenuous attempt to explain Albert's astounding knowledge, for none of the earliest chroniclers report this apparition, and we do not find it until we come to Flaminius and Leander. Moreover, it does not fit in with the historical facts ; for a twenty-year-old youth could not have remained unconscious of such an hebetudo mentis, and would assuredly on this account have refrained from undertaking the journey to Italy to pursue his studies.

Rudolf von Nymegen reports a similar version to account for Albert's entry into the Dominican Order. 'One day Albert was again praying in the church of the Dominicans in Padua before the image of the Mother of God, when it seemed to him that the holy Virgin called to him : "Albert, flee the world and enter the Order of Preachers, which I have by my prayers obtained of my Son for the salvation of the world. There, according to the directions of the Rule, strive eagerly after knowledge, and God will enrich thee with such abundance of wisdom that the whole Church will be enlightened by the books of thy learning." '[2] Others have combined the two accounts into one, and in later times the first legend was transferred to the Saint's first years in the Order,[3] and it is in this form that it has passed into the lessons in the breviary. But neither the one nor the other of these legends is of any use as revealing to us Albert's natural disposition ; rather do they obscure the picture which we get when we go the reverse way and try to arrive at some conclusion as to the Saint's disposition from his later life, which is not exactly poor in historically attested facts. We can then deduce that in the soul of the youth

[1] A. Sighart : op. cit., 13 A, 5.
[2] Rudolphus de Novimagio : op. cit., 9.
[3] Petrus de Prussia : op. cit., 301.

there lived a disposition to what is great, spacious, and extraordinary ; and if we are to give this trait the name of a virtue, though we are here concerned not with a virtue but only with a natural disposition, we shall have to think of *Magnanimitas*, that virtue which Aristotle described so vividly and again so specifically, as if he were wishing to portray his pupil, Alexander the Great.[4] The picture which the Stagyrite sketched may have been according to his view that of a virtue ; Albert in the corresponding commentary has, however, made many corrections, smoothed out many inequalities, and planed off many angles, and thus has sketched the picture of the true Christian virtue, namely that of the magnanimous soul. In the work he had to do in order to fashion out of this natural disposition, with its kinship to Aristotle's design, the image of Christ, he unconsciously drew a portrait of himself.

Aristotle gives as the marks of greatness of soul a dignified bearing (motus gravis), an impressive voice (vox gravis), and soundness in discourse (locutio stabilis) ; and these will apply to Albert, at any rate if we are to take literally the expressions Blessed Humbert used in his letter to him.[5] To be sure, these marks are not infallible. The three signa may be there without the magnanimitas, and again, where magnanimity has been most gloriously developed into a virtue, the three marks may be absent. There is, however, a certain connexion ; for if we think of the ideal embodiment of the magnanimous soul, we give it a distinguishable form by these three characters. The essence of magnanimity lies in greatness of soul ; it is the eye, the interest, and the labour for what is great. On this ground Albert has in his paraphrase given to the marks of Aristotle a spiritual application ; for the dignified bearing he asks maturity (maturitas), he sees the impressiveness of the voice in the ordered dependence on the reason, and he refers soundness in discourse to the sureness of the truth which is to be expounded. Thus he himself points the way which leads from the natural disposition to the virtue, from the unconscious impulse to the considered willing and fashioning

[4] *Ethicorum*, lib. 4, tr. 2.
[5] Petrus de Prussia : op. cit., 254 *sq*.

of what is great. This need not lie in the material order, it need not have reference to some imposing structure or to a mighty army; it may be concerned with the Great, as such, in any order whatever. Albert possessed the gift for this as a dowry of nature. In contemplating his life and work everything forces us to this disposition as to the solution of the riddle. Wherever we meet with him, whatever work he is attacking, everything is great, or at any rate takes under his hand the form of greatness. He stands there great as a teacher, as a writer, especially in the scientific field, and not less great in the administrative offices he held, when we regard him as Provincial, as Bishop, or as Mediator. Thus we are forced to accept as his characteristic mark Greatness of Soul in its noblest application and its widest conformation; a greatness of soul which has as its object not a single good or a single great thing, but what is great in general, the good wherever it may be found. Thanks to this glorious disposition, Albert throughout his life avoided all those ugly excrescences on Aristotle's magnanimitas; just as he had theoretically rejected these in his commentary, so he developed in himself the disposition to a true Christian greatness of soul. Rudolf von Nymegen thus expresses what was deepest in Albert's soul: 'He was a pattern of magnanimity.'[6]

An eye for the good, an interest for the noble, an enthusiasm for the great, well fit the little Swabian lad who gave a bird to each of the wild hawks that had helped him in his pigeon hunt. They had, though uninvited, helped in the work; therefore, his feelings told him, they ought also to have a share in the booty. Magnanimity in the child. This insight he preserved, and it enabled him in later years to find good everywhere, even where his contemporaries in their blindness passed it by, namely in nature.[7] His Christian faith told him that God is the highest and most beautiful Good, which must be prized and loved above everything. The same faith also taught him that the nature in us has suffered hurt though the sin

[6] Petrus de Prussia: op. cit., 68; Sighart: op. cit., 114.

[7] Cf. Natura fecit melius in omnibus, in *De animalibus*, lib. 25. [Ed.]

of our first parents, and that the nature which surrounds us spells a danger to our salvation, if we surrender ourselves to it too much. But Albert did not on this account close his eyes to the good and the beautiful which shone forth everywhere in nature. On the contrary he held these beauties in exceptional esteem, and therefore sought them, observed them, discussed them, and described them, and this at all times and in all places. His interest in them did not decrease with the years, but grew. Like the modern naturalist, Albert could watch for hours the doings of the ant or the spider. It was not in him to engage in even the most everyday occupation thoughtlessly. The apple which he ate as dessert at his midday meal excited his attention, and the rind and flesh, the form and colour, were accurately observed by him ; even the core claimed his attention, and he was the first to give a really classical description of it. The danger, to which the unbelieving naturalist so easily succumbs, of stopping at these things, of getting wrapped up in this miniature world, and thus of becoming himself petty and limited in outlook, did not exist for Albert, for to him all these phenomena were revelations of the Most High. The order which he found in Creation, the good and the beautiful which shone on him from it, ever kept pointing up to Him, of Whom they, in their very limited way, portrayed, however dimly, the image. To discover the infinite, as it were, in the traces of a countless number of things, and at once to grasp the relation of the smallest of them to the Highest, is evidence of the wide vision of a man endowed for greatness. It is astounding how the Saint sought out the good in all fields, how he found it everywhere, and knew how to describe it fittingly. It was not only to the concrete things of nature that he applied himself, for the abstract sciences of mathematics, philosophy, and theology also came within his field of vision. That the writings of the Fathers offered him a superabundance of riches is clear ; but the books of the philosophers, those of the ancient world as well as those of his own times, aroused his interest, and in all of them he found good. The eyes of this magnanimous man perceived the value of Aristotle despite the distortion to which he had been subjected. He also found good in the works of the Jews and Arabs ; yes, he did not wish to see even the books of the necromancers, which were banned by the Church, destroyed, since some good was to be found even in them.[8] An eye that could, as it were, measure the firmament and at the same time not overlook the speck of dust on the wayside, a vision which could attentively follow the meanest little creature in its doings and raise itself from it and through it to the Creator, this was the spiritual disposition of Albert the Great.

True greatness of soul is not content with merely observing the Good, but passes on to its realization, if its own exertion be needed. It furthers the labours of those others who are striving for its realization ; it recognizes the Great, by whomsoever it be realized. This, to be sure, is the picture of magnanimity as conceived in Christian moral science, for Aristotle's magnanimous soul strives only after what will conduce to his own honour ; he passes any other thing by without a thought. Albert possessed the disposition towards the true magnanimity which everywhere promotes the Good under the aspect of the Great, which in so doing is daunted by no obstacle, to which no danger appears menacing, no enemy attack formidable. Something courageous, chivalrous, resolute, industrious, self-sacrificing lay in his being, as his actions in later years disclose. That a youth of some twenty years should have left his beautiful Swabian home and started off for Italy, there, in a foreign land, to pursue his studies, says nothing in a time when the impulse to travel drove countless young people into the wide world. Again, such a journey meant little at that time, for it was the usual thing for students ; and German youths by the hundred were doing the same thing and with the same purpose. However, they returned home when their studies were finished and there enjoyed the fruits of their labours in honourable posts. Albert, however, while he was still abroad, attached himself to the new and unfamiliar Order of Preachers. This was the courageous act of the Magnanimous Soul. The Order of S. Dominic could not hold out for him a prospect of the peaceful life

[8] Petrus de Prussia : op. cit., 127.

of a monk in the old abbeys ; it only promised him labour, severe labour, self-sacrificing labour, though, it is true, labour for what was highest and most beautiful, for the propagation of the truth in the life and teaching of mankind. Albert took the step of entering the Order. He led a life of labour, no exertion alarmed him, no undertaking seemed to him too daring. We need only think of the so straightforward, and yet so weighty, announcement with which he introduced his paraphrase of Aristotle : 'Our intention is to throw open all these writings to Latinists.'[9] This was an undertaking so great, so prodigious, that its execution by one man seemed impossible. When Albert's intention became known, derision and scorn were heaped on him. Many a one likely accused him of presumption. But Albert finished the work he had begun and thus showed that true greatness of soul was his portion. Still greater was the undertaking which must be regarded as Albert's life work, to which that revision of Aristotle's writings was merely contributory, namely the introduction of Aristotelian principles into Catholic theology. Considered in itself, quite apart from every circumstance of the age, this represents an extraordinarily great beginning. But Albert conceived the plan for this at a time when in faithful Catholic circles misgivings about the Stagyrite's teaching had reached their zenith ; when, too, the danger which was threatening the Christian faith from the champions of the false Aristotelianism was at its highest.[10] This magnificent plan was not only conceived by the Saint but also carried out by him. Meanwhile, however, the sword in his hand was not allowed to grow rusty, or even to stay idle. All his life long he had to fight on two fronts, against the old-fashioned theologians, and the later philosophers, as Grabmann with his well-known thoroughness has shown in minute detail. If to the discoverer of new worlds we ascribe resolution, if in the Crusader we honour courage, then we must also in Albert, for the discovery of Aristotle was like that of a new world, and his fight like that of a

[9] *Physicorum,* lib. I, tr. I, cap. I.
[10] The general situation has been well described by Grabmann in *Die wissentschaftliche Mission Alberts des Grossen.*

Crusader.[11] However great the difficulties, though acts of hostility might multiply, there never came from his lips a word of despondency or of ill-humour. With firm resolution and unswerving perseverance he brought the undertaking to its conclusion.

Albert revealed the same characteristic trait during his tenure of the office of Provincial, and later when he was called to the episcopal chair of Regensburg ; again when at the instance of the Pope he preached the crusade, and also in carrying out the many requests made to him to mediate between hostile parties. These were all weighty tasks, great undertakings, which must have been felt by Albert as hindrances to the carrying out of his life's work. Nevertheless Albert set himself to all these tasks with the same resolution. He saw the Good under the aspect of the Great ; he realized it, furthered it, wherever this was possible to him, and thus revealed the noble disposition towards magnanimity which was his by nature.

A third mark proving that Albert possessed by nature the disposition to magnanimity, which, however, he moulded to the form of the true Christian virtue, is the large-heartedness with which he let others work alongside him, the delicate consideration he showed for their views, and the recognition he accorded to their work, even when this surpassed his own.[12] Natural magnanimity is capable of tolerating many subordinate workers, it will also leave them free to create, at any rate in little things, with which it is not itself much concerned ; but it cannot bear to see others achieve greater things, for thus its own glory would be lessened or actually eclipsed. In Albert's case we see, however, that he not only trained many minds and filled them with enthusiasm for the Good and the Great, but also possessed the largeness of heart which in everything allowed to them a freedom bounded only by the barriers set by truth and duty. We have only to think of Albert's pupils, how they differed as men and as scholars, how widely

[11] G. Théry, O.P. : *David de Dinant, Étude sur son panthéisme matérialiste*, 84.

[12] Petrus de Prussia (op. cit., 213) says of him that he was without envy.

divergent were their conceptions and views, and yet all of them held the Master in almost fanatical veneration. Here we have Albert's best-loved pupil, Ulrich von Strassburg, who in his 'monumental' theological *Summa* composed the greatest and most comprehensive work of the German Neoplatonic School which derived from Albert.[13] He says of the Master that he is 'vir in omni scientia adeo divinus, ut nostri temporis stupor et miraculum congrue vocari possit.' Then there is Thomas de Chantimpré, who has left a number of important notes on the Master. Then again there is Blessed Ambrose Sansedonius, who taught with honour in Cologne and Paris, reformed the theological studium in Rome, and then devoted all his powers to the practical care of souls. And now we come to his most brilliant and celebrated pupil, S. Thomas Aquinas, who by the sanctity of his life and his incomparable works has also glorified his teacher, even if he never gave verbal expression to his praise of him. Both Ulrich and Thomas predeceased Albert, and were deeply mourned by him. Both completed a great work begun by their master in a manner which it was not given him to accomplish. Albert saw this and rejoiced. No trace of envy or jealousy did he ever show. When, after S. Thomas's death, his teaching was attacked and certain propositions in them actually condemned by Bishop Tempiers, his old master could not rest in Cologne, but undertook the long, toilsome journey to Paris in order to defend the teaching of his great pupil. These are deeds which not only attest the Saint's natural disposition to magnanimity, but also its finest and noblest development under the inspiration of grace.

Two things in Albert's life appear to cast a shadow on his magnanimity ; his withdrawal from the direction of the Regensburg diocese and his indecision on several philosophical and theological questions. If we examine the matter more closely, not only do these reflexions on him disappear, but, on the contrary, these very facts throw his greatness of soul into an even more beautiful light. Albert was induced, in fact actually compelled, by the Pope to assume the episcopal dignity and the charge of the see of

[13] M. Grabmann : *Der Einfluss Alberts des Grossen*, etc., 33.

Regensburg, otherwise he would without question have yielded to the request of the Master-General, Humbert, that he refuse the dignity. Nothing that has ever been said of Albert does him more honour than this letter of Humbert's. We shall come back to it in the last section. The see of Regensburg had been thrown into utter disorder by the mismanagement of Albert I, who found himself finally forced to resign his office. The Pope, who knew the exceptional qualifications of the Saint, thought that by his elevation, this terrible state of affairs might be remedied most quickly. Accordingly on January 9, 1260, Pope Alexander IV conveyed to Albert the formal command to take the burden upon himself, and on March 30 of the same year the Saint took possession of his episcopal chair. The end of the following year found him at the Papal Court, and he there pressed for a relief from his office, a request to which Pope Urban IV acceded at the beginning of the year 1262. More precise dates have not yet been ascertained. Albert therefore held the post for less than two years. The fact that the Saint was, in his prominent position, exposed to a good deal of hostility, whether on the part of the ill-informed common people, or on that of the nobility and clergy, will have made it easier for him to beg for his relief; but we must not see in this his real reason, for it is not the part of greatness of soul to recoil before difficulties such as these. The knowledge that after the first thorough-going reorganization had been effected, whereby the bad state of affairs was essentially remedied, there would, in the routine of regular administrative work, no longer be opportunity of achieving any great thing, might have influenced Aristotle's magnanimous man to renounce the office, but not the man of faith, who saw the great in every good deed. The true solution is seen in the following consideration. Albert saw in the Pope's summons a call to a great task, one, however, which would hinder his life's work, the renovation of theology, which seemed to him to be of even greater importance. He obeyed the order, he entered upon the office, he exerted his whole strength to answer to the calls made on him, but from the very beginning he had been determined, as soon as this was possible, to return to his life's task. The opportunity soon presented itself, for the worst of the disorders were quickly remedied, and what remained to be done could easily be effected by a bishop chosen from the cathedral chapter. Recognizing this, Albert did not tarry longer in Regensburg, but journeyed to Rome in order to take up the matter in person. He acted as the truly magnanimous soul must act, he sacrificed a great thing in order to attain to one yet greater.

With regard to the second point it has to be admitted that Albert left many questions undecided. We have already seen that he not seldom simply sets out the reasons for and against, and in the final solution of the question expresses himself with great reserve. This hardly seems to fit the picture of greatness of soul, since there could be found in it a want of decision. We have, however, seen that Albert only demands of the magnanimous soul that settled decision when the clear cognition of a certain truth is in question. Where the Catholic faith has made no definition, and no clear and conclusive proofs are available, he leaves his readers freedom of judgement. When he himself is not in a position to solve the problem, the most he will say is what this appears to him, what he holds to be the more probable ; but he will not bind anyone with an apodictic pronouncement. This is surer evidence of a greater largeness of spirit and heart than any over-hasty decision or stubborn clinging to his own opinion. That Albert did not linger on every individual question until he could pronounce a final decision on it must not be attributed to any restlessness of mind ; he acted thus because he wanted to demonstrate in broad lines the importance of Aristotle's teaching. If he had tarried too long over individual problems his main purpose would have been hindered. Here the carrying out of the details had to yield place to the great whole. This also is a sign of true greatness of soul. Peter of Prussia sees in the expressions so often employed by Albert : 'this view seems to me the more probable,' 'without wishing to anticipate anyone's judgement, I would say,' 'with the Masters I hold that,' etc., a sign of his humility, and this, too, belongs to the picture of truly Christian magnanimity.[14]

[14] Petrus de Prussia : op. cit., 93.

2. *The Development.*

It is the general teaching of the Church that every just man possesses the full endowment of the supernatural virtues, beginning with charity, from which flow the cardinal virtues, down to the last and least significant of the auxiliary virtues. Many theologians go further and teach that in the righteous soul striving after perfection, all these virtues have a uniform growth, and indeed grow in such a manner that all are to be found constantly in the same grade of perfection, so that it might appear to be quite indifferent in which virtue the soul was exercising herself, since on whatever one she was bent, any success there obtained would spread to all the others. Nevertheless every saint sets his impress on the Christian ideal of virtue from a quite definite angle of vision. Some one virtue seems to be the special adornment of his soul, and forms the characteristic mark of his appearance. This virtue would be practised by the saint in question more than the others; by this persistent exercise the exterior and interior obstacles would here almost entirely disappear, the ancillary faculties would by this practice attain to a degree of completeness, the other virtues, even those which by their nature stand higher, would be practised with an eye to that one virtue, and enter, as it were, into its service. At times it might actually appear as if one virtue or another were being prejudiced for the sake of the one specially favoured, as if, for instance, someone were seeming to practise humility at the expense of prudence.

Which virtue was it that Albertus Magnus practised above all the others, so that it had a decisive influence on his spiritual greatness? It is the same question as: What did the Saint do to give its full shape to the noble natural disposition which, for no merit of his, had been bestowed on him? Did he build further on the foundation which he found laid in him? The disposition towards the great, towards the extraordinary, had been given to him. A yearning after the sublime possessed him. He had powers which clamoured for development, and faculties which only asked to work tirelessly, dauntlessly, until what was noble, what was great had been achieved. This is how we must picture the youth on his journey to Italy. Mediocrity could never have become this Swabian's portion ; for this his heart beat too boldly, too vigorously. He will become great, whether in good or in evil, according as his choice is made. And Albert sought the Great in the Good. But he did not seek it in negation, in the virtue of renunciation. He was no recluse like Paul the Hermit. He did not fast like S. Bernard, nor did he use the scourge and hair shirt like Blessed Henry Suso. It is true that Albert practised mortification, but in so doing he remained within the limits of his rule ; no special exercises of this kind are anywhere related of him. That the mere outward observance of the austerities demanded by the Constitutions of the Order did not satisfy him, that with him the spirit of mortification quickened every exterior act of penance and charged it with spiritual value, must be assumed as responding to his truth-loving character. From this point of view he will also have surpassed many of his brethren in renunciation. The same would appear to have been the case with his piety. A true piety, a literally childlike piety, graced this great scholar. Both the liturgical as also mystical piety engraved deep lines in his life picture ; but they were not his distinctive stamp in the way that liturgical piety was for a Gregory the Great or a Gertrude of Helfta, or that mystical piety was in such saints as Bonaventure and John of the Cross. The legends tell us also of touching features of compassion, of which the most beautiful is that set out in the saga of the miraculous goblet ; nevertheless we cannot place him alongside heroes of Christian charity of the Middle Ages like Thomas of Villanova and Elisabeth of Hungary.

What, then, was Albert's chief characteristic, not by disposition, but of the Albert in action, as a creative being, as a Christian, on whom the image of his Redeemer is stamped ? We find confirmed in our Saint the scholastic principle : 'Gratia non destruit, sed perficit naturam.' He was by natural disposition magnanimous, and magnanimous he remained in all his struggles and strivings, so that this virtue has set its stamp upon him. If we saw in the disposition rather *magnanimitas* in the vague outlines of an embryo natural perfection with its defects and weaknesses as sketched by the Stagyrite, we certainly now find in our Saint the picture of true Christian magnanimity, the unquestioned, complete perfection of this virtue. This takes its place among the other virtues in full harmony with them, and in our Saint stands out so markedly that, thanks to its operation and because it is free of all opposition, it outshines the other perfections and reveals him in his individuality as Saint.

Albert's disposition towards magnanimity was almost universal. As such it reached out for the Great. In his long life the Saint did, as a matter of fact, achieve great things in the most widely different fields. Did magnanimity remain his characteristic virtue in this universality? This could hardly be. He was human, and therefore limited both in his capacity and his activities. Albert achieved much, but not always with the same perfection. He showed his interest for the Great wherever it was, and kept that interest to the end, but under one definite aspect it wholly captivated him. When as a youth he journeyed to Italy, the ideal may still have been very indefinite. Perhaps at that time this still bore quite worldly features, such as the greatness which it is for the statesman or soldier to realize. Perhaps, too, it was a mixture of the worldly and the spiritual such as the greatness represented by the crusader or the prelate in the Germany of those days. And then, during the time of his stay in Padua, the Great appeared to the young student in the form of Truth, and it revealed itself in such sublimity, in such towering dignity, that Albert, despite the nobility of his natural disposition, hesitated. It was not natural wisdom, it was the truth enshrined in the divine revelation, the wealth of the mysteries, the contemplation of which will constitute our bliss in the world beyond the grave, and whose acceptance on God's authority is the first duty of a Christian here below. Truth now stood before him, not that he might give his assent to her, for this he had done as a child, nor again that he might seal his confession with his blood, for this would have ranged him in the ranks of the martyrs. She presented herself to him as the Greatness which it was for him to conquer. Not that he was by so doing to comprehend these mysteries in their entirety during this life, for that is and ever will be impossible ; but he was to penetrate deeply into these truths, using to this end all natural means, even such as had up till then received scant consideration. It was his task to demonstrate the harmony between natural truth and revelation, and to teach this to others.

This certainly represented an extraordinarily great act, but if all this had been kept within the bounds of abstract knowledge, Albert would have become an eminent theologian, but nothing more. Truth presented herself to him that he might comprehend her in charity, and in charity experience her, and thus, though she were wholly transformed, pass her on to others, so that they too, indeed all, might grasp the Truth and order their lives according to her. Before this vision Albert hesitated, and for long he vacillated in fear ; for the sublimity of the greatness drew him to it, while the extraordinary in it struck fear into him, until at last almost miraculously the decision came. Albert had got to know the Dominicans in Padua. The new Order, which differed essentially from the old monastic Orders, since it had substituted study for manual labour, and had taken as its object to proclaim the truth of the Gospel, to preach it, and to disseminate it, had excited Albert's sympathies. Thoughts of entering the Order obsessed him, but his uncle, with whom he lived, extracted a promise from him not to put his foot into the convent for a definite period. This man of the world, who seems to have stood in loco parentis to Albert, may well have regarded the matter as a case of mere youthful enthusiasm. When the time expired Albert again resorted to the convent, but still could not bring himself to make the definite decision to enter the Order. He was, on the contrary, tormented by the worrying notion that he would not persevere and would have ignominiously to return to the world. Harassed by such thoughts, which even disturbed his sleep, he happened to attend a sermon by Blessed Jordan of Saxony, the successor of S. Dominic. The Beatus, whose preaching awoke many an answering chord among the students, was describing how the Devil often tried to frighten young men from joining the Order by giving them the delusion that they would not persevere. It was precisely these difficulties which were tormenting Albert at this time. The sermon gripped him to such an extent that directly it was over he sought out the preacher and greeted him with the words: 'Master, who has laid bare my heart to you?' What the general sermon had begun in Albert, personal conversation completed. Fortified by Jordan's assurance that with the help of God's grace he would persevere in the Order, Albert begged to be given the habit.[15] It is probable that he received this at once in Padua. With this S. Dominic's ideal had become also his own, and from now on all his yearnings, his struggles, and his labours were directed to the truth. Blessed Jordan's assurance banished from him all hesitation and timidity in the years that were to come. The high ideal of truth stood immovable before his eyes. In sure faith he embraced her; as a theologian he opened new paths by which men might ever more deeply understand her; as teacher, preacher, and writer he guided countless numbers to the truth. Among the great ones of S. Dominic's Order Albert stands forth as great in his grasp and realization of the ideal. If we follow him in the development of his spiritual greatness, in the formation of his magnanimity, we find him pressing all his natural good qualities and powers, yes, and all the virtues, even those which in the abstract order far o'ertop magnanimity, into the service and attendance of this one virtue. The theological virtues of faith and charity perfected magnanimity in him.

The Middle Ages is the era of faith. A more fitting description of this unique and glorious period of the German race could not be found. Man's interest was centred in the supernatural, which was not avoided, but sought and embraced wherever it was revealed. The mysteries offered no difficulties. Miracles really acted as pillars of the faith. It was the first rapture of an impetuous, imaginative nation in all the freshness of its youth, one which was to rejuvenate the others. Albert was a child of this people, a true German, who, himself full of faith, lived in this age which was so

[15] Girardus de Fracheto: op. cit., 187 *sq.*

strong in faith. Mediæval Germany was not content with the mere acceptance of revealed truths. It did not merely embrace the Word of God with the understanding, nor did it merely confess it with the lips, but it made the fullness of these truths its very life, and took the supernatural revelations and their practical consequences in deadly earnest. This does not mean to say that all, literally all, the commandments were observed at that time, but that the commonalty and most individuals recognized the moral demands implicit in revelation as competent, and felt themselves bound by them and wanted them carried out, even if in actual fact much was left to be desired. This easily explains the glorious figures, the magnificent embodiments of the life of faith in those days; the whole-hearted conversions followed by terribly severe penances performed in the fullest publicity. The race erred stoutly, but even more stoutly expiated its sins. Thus may be explained the unique phenomenon of the Crusades, those finest blossoms of the joyousness of chivalrous, vivid faith. Albert sprang from knightly German stock; so here he had almost as a matter of course the prerequisite for the right development of greatness of soul, the faith, firmness of faith, the joyousness of faith, life based on faith. Even for him, however, the realization of all this took the form of struggle, of hard work, and at times, too, of combat; though he will never have known fights due to doubts concerning the faith, which are the lot of an enfeebled, nervous, and overstrung race.

Doubts about the faith could, however, well arise in a man who, like Albert, was busied with the writings of Aristotle; for were not these, as worked over by the Jews and Arabs, in not a few points directly hostile to the Catholic faith? Pious folk knew this danger very well, and legend could explain the steadfastness of the Saint's faith only by the special protection of the Blessed Virgin, and would also have it that before starting his reading of these dangerous books Albert always prayed that he might be true to the faith. We may well believe that the Saint often besought this of God. The prayers which he composed for the different Sundays in the year, and in which he expresses the fundamental thought in the form of a petition, certainly never have faith as their exclusive subject, yet this is often prayed for conjointly with the other virtues. The gift which he thus prayed of God he himself sought to assure by frequent, one might almost say unremitting, contemplation of the revealed truths. If in those days set meditation was not yet practised, contemplative prayer was all the more cultivated. We know from the old Constitutions of the Order that a special time was set aside twice a day that the brethren might quietly devote themselves to prayer. Individuals were left free to choose their manner of praying. Two children of S. Dominic, Blessed Henry Suso and the devout Margaretha Ebner, have described the exercises which were intended, and these only differ from our meditation in the greater freedom left to the individual. It is explicitly stated of Albert that he cultivated this contemplative form of prayer. Thomas de Chantimpré, his faithful pupil, tells as an eye-witness that Albert, after the lectures and disputations were over, always gave himself up to meditation and the contemplation of heavenly things.[16] Similarly Petrus de Prussia avers that 'day and night he continued in meditation. He listened eagerly for the sweet whispering of the Holy Spirit, with constant prayer he knocked at the fountain of life and thus procured for himself the water of the wisdom of redemption for which he so longingly begged.'[17] As fruit of this meditation, and so also as fruit of his spirit of faith, we may regard the pious homilies which he composed for all the Sundays of the ecclesiastical year, to which we have already referred. Sighart considers that Albert's manner of expressing his spirit of faith in prayer is typified by the following, which is given by Rudolf von Nymegen :

Hail, O manhood of the Saviour united with the eternal Godhead in the Virgin's womb.

Hail, most High and Everlasting Godhead that came forth unto us clad with our veil of flesh.

Hail, O Godhead mysteriously united with our unfallen flesh by the power of the Holy Spirit.

[16] Thomas Cantimpratanus : op. cit., 483.

[17] Petrus de Prussia : op. cit., 173.

Hail thou in whom the fullness of the Godhead had bodily dwelling.

Hail thou in whom the grace of the Holy Spirit abode and had no measure.

Hail, for the unsullied manhood of the Son of God begotten of thee was hallowed by God the Father.

Hail, O untainted Maidenhood now raised above all Angel choirs.

Be glad, O Queen of all the world, who wert honoured in being made the temple of the most pure Godhead of Christ.

Be glad and rejoice, O Maiden of Maidens, in whose sinless flesh the blessed Godhead chose to take unto fellowship the pure manhood.

Be glad, O Queen of the Heavens, in whose most holy womb this Manhood of the Son had a home most beloved.

Hail and exult, O most noble offspring of the first father of mankind, who has been given to guard this hallowed Manhood and to suckle him at thy maiden breast.

Hail, O Maidenhood for ever blessed and most fruitful, whereby thou hast been worthy to receive the fruit of life and the bliss of eternal salvation. Amen.[18]

The spirit of Albert's faith shines out, too, in his book on the Most Holy Sacrament of the Altar. His predilection for this theme, and the searching, scientific manner of his treatment of it, which never forces the ascetic, mystical note, reveal the man of robust and living faith. His contemporary, Bernard of Guido, in his review of the Saint's tractate *De Eucharistia*, says : 'In this he reveals in the clearest way the sweetness he felt when engaged on this subject, his great knowledge of the Scriptures, the purity of his faith, the liveliness of his hope, the fire of his charity.'[19] In similar terms Petrus de Prussia had already pointed out the originality of these Eucharistic writings, which surpassed in sincerity everything that had previously been written.[20]

[18] Petrus de Prussia : op. cit., Appendix.
[19] Bernard Gui, quoted by Petrus de Prussia : op. cit., 178.
[20] Petrus de Prussia : op. cit., 177.

The best known of his prayers to the Eucharistic Redeemer runs :

Hail, thou Saviour of the world, the Father's Word—true victim, living flesh—wholly God, truly man. Ingrafted with thee may we be worthily offered in the Majesty's divine temple. Brought nigh to thy body at thy Father's right hand, may we one day share thy eternity, have fellowship in thy bliss, be incarnate in thy Incarnation, for thine is honour and glory unto ages of ages. Amen.[21]

We may see yet another expression of his lively faith in his attitude towards Mary. The pictures which the earliest writers give of this are very touching. He himself erected an enduring monument to his veneration of the Blessed Virgin in his *Mariale*. The introduction to this comprehensive work reveals the spirit which runs through the whole, the spirit of the author's faith : 'It is written (Ecclus. xxiv, 29–31) : "They that eat me shall yet hunger, and they that drink me, shall yet thirst. He that hearkeneth to me, shall not be confounded, and they that work by me, shall not sin. They that explain me, shall have life everlasting." Trusting in this rich promise, I set my hand to the task, otherwise I would have raised myself too much above my small talent and knowledge. I know, however, that the hand of God has not been shortened, but that to him who believes, all things are still possible. The work which we are accepting, describing the beginning of the Incarnation of Our Lord and the mystery of our Redemption, we undertake to the praise and glory and honour of the most glorious Virgin, Mother of God, venerated above all creatures, trusting in the very special help and mercy of her who is the most sure anchor of my hope, and looking to her for a happy ending and reward for the work, who is the mover of my will, the cause of my labour, and the examiner of my intentions. In the first place, therefore, I beseech the mercy of God and the Almighty Father of all Mercies, who dwelleth in light inaccessible, that he banish from me by the light of his brightness the deception

[21] Petrus de Prussia : op. cit., Appendix.

of error, the cockle of falsity, the desire for vainglory, and grant to me to see the truth and to speak the truth concerning the Mother of Mercy and Truth. I also beg those who may perchance see fit to look at this little book, that if they should peradventure find in it something which because of its novelty strikes their ears as doubtful, they should not too readily ascribe it to our temerity, but have patience rather with our artless devotion. For we have no intention of embellishing the Glorious Virgin with lies, nor even in grandiloquent style to coin something novel and great for superior intellects, thus not praising the Most Glorious Virgin, but vaunting ourselves, but wish to render in simple words a service of devotion to untutored and simple people, such as I myself am. For I should be well content, though I shall produce from the mouth of my heart nothing worthy of consideration concerning our Most Blessed Lady, if I may nevertheless give occasion to wiser men to write and speak on her.'[22]

This faith of his, so childlike, so firm, so devout, qualified the Saint for his great, scientific life work, the recasting of Catholic theology by the application of Aristotelian principles. And this undertaking of genius sheds yet another light on the spiritual greatness of Albertus Magnus. But for his firm and homely faith, this continual absorption in pagan philosophy would have led to his destruction, as it has done to many both before and after him. Only a theologian who was wholly confirmed in his faith, and had in addition mastered the whole philosophical teaching of his age, could begin such an undertaking. If Albert had been a man of less keen intellect and had been less versed in the philosophical problems of his day, he would, like most of the theologians of the time, have condemned the pagan wisdom, and taken up a hostile attitude towards it, since he would never have become conscious of the fact that there was that buried in it which could be of special assistance to theology, and that by its means the faith could be more easily defended and its harmony with nature more beautifully illustrated. But mere keenness of intellect and firmness of faith are not sufficient to explain this. The

[22] *Mariale* : Prologus.

work postulates in the Master such a fine sense for the full bearing of the articles of faith and for the truths of pagan philosophy compatible with it, that there must certainly have been here a mystical unfolding of the faith through the co-operation of the gifts of the Holy Spirit. What in the Pseudo-Dionysius is said of Hierotheus applies here to Albert: 'Patitur divina.'[23] By virtue of the gifts of understanding and wisdom he could see where the light which lit the faith of the ordinary righteous man failed, and into which the abstract knowledge of the theologian could not of itself penetrate. Thomas seeks to illustrate this sense by the difference which obtains between the judgement of one who is theoretically acquainted with a virtue, and that of one who practises this virtue in the highest degree. The judgement of the latter is the finer and surer, although its scientific argument often escapes him.

Peter of Prussia makes the point that Albert owed his wisdom not so much to his personal researches as to his piety,[24] and quotes Albert's own words as witness to this when he says in the prologue to the *Summa theologiæ*: 'In the divine sciences more is attained by prayer and piety than by study.'[25] Again the epithet 'divinus' which Ulrich von Strassburg applies to Albert seems to have reference to this mystic unfolding of the faith in the Master: 'So divine was Albert, that he may rightly be called the astounding wonder of our time.'[26]

The mystical unfolding of the faith is a gift of God's grace, but it presupposes on the part of the recipient that he lives a life according to the faith, that the spirit of faith permeates his thoughts, words, acts, and omissions. His standard must be not the laws of natural cognition, but the higher principles of the faith, which are often in direct contrast with the desires of fallen nature, and project

[23] *De divinis nominibus*, cap. 2, lect. 4; S. Thomas: opp. (Venice, 1747), VIII, 133.
[24] Petrus de Prussia: op. cit., 86.
[25] *Summa Theologica*: Prologus.
[26] Ulrich von Strassburg, *Summa Theologica*, quoted by Petrus de Prussia: op. cit., 87.

beyond the lines of pure reason. Fallen nature sees the main principle in pleasure; reason measures everything according to its utility, and in fact with regard to the happiest present existence possible. The Faith, however, counsels renunciation, because there is danger bound up with the enjoyment of earthly things: renunciation as a penance, and out of love. Albert lived a life of supernatural faith, but not so patently as some other saints. Whereas, for example, the life of the Saint of Assisi is only intelligible from the highest principles of the faith, because his actions stood in obvious contradiction to his environment, Catholic though this was, Albert on the other hand stands out in the midst of the world, and spends his days amid the pulsating life of Paris and Cologne. He intervenes in the controversies and affairs of the day, and in most cases was called upon to give the decision, since no one was his equal in reputation. In spite of all this Albert lived a life of a faith that did not take second place to that of S. Francis. Albert organized his ordinary daily life as it unrolled in Paris and Cologne, and his activities as professor, superior, mediator, solely according to the highest principles of the faith. The pure intention, the 'soli Deo,' attests this. And with this we reach the consummation of his spiritual greatness, his practical, self-sacrificing charity, which forms the coping-stone to his greatness of soul.

3. *The Consummation.*

'First man, then Christian, and thus to the complete man,' writes A. Weiss in the fifth volume of his Christian Apologetic.[27] The natural individuality of the person is preserved in the Christian and is perfected towards the good. The disposition towards magnanimity was in Albert, the Christian, more closely determined, and developed, so as to be consummated in charity. In him the development was accomplished quicker, the consummation took a more glorious shape, because he was not only a Christian, but also a religious, a priest, and a bishop. At the age of thirty he joined the newly formed Dominican Order and

[27] A. Weiss: *Apologie des Christentums*, i, 809.

PEN DRAWING FROM A MS. OF S. ALBERT'S *DE PROPRIETATIBUS RERUM* OF 1366 IN THE BAVARIAN STATE LIBRARY, MUNICH

at once entered with his whole soul into the conception of the noble Spanish apostle, Dominic, because it responded to his own natural disposition. The Order has epitomized its mission in the motto : 'Contemplata aliis tradere.' It demands of its members that they contemplate the truths of the faith in the quiet of study and prayer, that they make these by contemplation their very lives, and then out of the abundance of the heart and the mind communicate them to others. The contemplation refers to faith, the communication to charity. Albert made the ideals of his Order to such an extent his own, that the chief characteristic of the man, the Christian, the Friar, the Bishop, became magnanimity perfected by a living faith and heroic charity.

According to Aristotle, the *Magnanimus* is actually by nature more disposed to give than to receive. To take, somehow, conflicts with his nature ; whereas to give, accords with his whole disposition. Where, however, he is compelled to receive, he cannot rest, his every fibre urges him to repay, and indeed two and threefold, for this is to act greatly and nobly. Albert himself teaches that magnanimity is an incitement to good doing, even in the sense of practical charity.[28] S. Thomas has reduced the Master's exposition to the short formula : 'Magnanimo competit esse beneficus.'[29]

It may at times befall the man who is magnanimous in the natural order that he has nothing to dispense to others, but this can never be the case with the magnanimous Christian. The faith in itself places at his disposal inexhaustible treasures of truth, which make man content and happy in this world and give him the prospect of sharing in the bliss of heaven in the next. The faith therefore affords a fresh stimulus to giving and imparting the good, for faith is not to be taken as mere acceptance of the revealed truths, but as a living embrace of the whole body of the faith, of the sublimest mysteries as well as of the moral precepts, including that precept which Our Lord has designated as his law, namely charity. As a religious Albert had bound himself to the obligation to

[28] *Ethicorum*, lib. 4, tr. 2, cap. 5.
[29] S. Thomas : *Summa*, II, II, q. 129, a. 4 ad 2.

strive after perfect charity by the observance of the gospel counsels to perfection. The assumption of the priesthood and of the episcopal dignity enhanced his sense of obligation. Every fresh promotion was an impulse to the wider growth and greater practice of charity.

The Constitutions of his Order lay down that the Dominican must work for the salvation of souls, especially by preaching and teaching, and this precept Albert put into literal effect. The content of the apprehended and meditated truths, the ardour of his love for Him whom these truths proclaim, and for the souls for whom they were revealed, opened up a field of activity for his magnanimity, than which none more ideal could have been imagined. Albert taught and remained a teacher his whole life long. According to all probability the office of Lector was conferred on him as soon as he had completed his theological studies which he pursued in the Order.[30] The earliest reference on this point goes back to Henry of Hereford, who reports that Albert had twice lectured on the Sentences at Cologne, and had been Lector at Hildesheim, Freiburg, and Regensburg, where he lectured for two years in succession, and at Strassburg, after which he had gone to Paris.[31] Scholars differ among themselves as to the proper order of these activities and as to the precise dates which should be assigned to them. Of one thing, however, we may be certain, since it was this which had occasioned the narrator's reference, namely Albert's employment in, and outstanding qualifications for, the teaching profession. From Paris the Master returned to Cologne with the highest degree open to him, namely Magister in sacra theologia. Here a Studium Generale was to be organized after the model of the one in Paris. Its direction was confided to Albert as Regent. In this distinguished position, in which he had not only to lecture on the most important subjects, but also to oversee the whole curriculum, Albert remained until his election as Provincial. When the Chapter held at Worms in the year 1254 entrusted him with the direction of the Teutonic province, he had to give

[30] F. Pelster: op. cit., 83.
[31] Henricus de Hervordia: op. cit., 201.

up teaching. When, in October 1256, he went to the Papal Court at Anagni to defend the rights of the mendicant orders against William of Saint-Amour's attacks, he did this with such success that the Pope kept him in Anagni for a time and caused him to ascend the cathedra there. According to the trustworthy report of Thomas de Chantimpré, he there lectured on S. John's Gospel and the canonical epistles.[32] It is with reference to this that later writers style him Master of the Sacred Palace. It was probably because of his special talent for teaching that the Chapter-General in Florence relieved him of his office of Provincial in 1257. In 1258 we find him again in Cologne as Lector. In the year 1259 the Saint with Thomas Aquinas and Peter of Tarantaise formed a commission, which by order of the Chapter-General was to draw up new regulations for the curriculum of the Order. His teaching activities had to be again broken off when the Pope appointed him to the episcopal see of Regensburg; but even after his resignation of this office he could not at once go back to his lecture-room, since at first he was kept at the Papal Court. Whether Albert there earned extraordinary distinction in the philosophical table-talk in which Pope Urban IV delighted, or whether he again gave a course of formal lectures, is not certain. In any case, his learning and skill in teaching created such a stir, that Henry the Poet, in his poem on the Curia, hails him as the universal philosophical genius, who, if all philosophical books were to be destroyed, would be able to recreate out of his mind the true philosophy in still more glorious form.[33] The mission to preach the Crusade which he carried out by order of the Pope occupied his time until 1264, and, of course, temporarily put a stop to his teaching; but it is probable that he at once resumed this when in that year he withdrew to the convent at Würzburg.[34] It

[32] Thomas Cantimpratanus: op. cit., 141.

[33] M. Grabmann: *Ist das philosophische Universalgenie bei Heinrich dem Poeten Thomas von Aquin?*

[34] P. Mandonnet: *Albert le Grand*, extends this stay till 1267. Pelster (op. cit., 88) would, with Henry of Hereford, make him return to Cologne in 1266.

is certain that in 1269 he was Lector at Strassburg.[35] In the same year at the request of the Master-General he betook himself to Cologne and taught there till shortly before his death. Not many scholars have occupied the professorial chair for so long a time or have been so persistent in returning to their teaching after serious interruption, as S. Albert. In the case of other celebrated men of that period, as for instance Bonaventure, Hugo de S. Cher, and Raymund of Pennafort, employment in teaching was only a passing episode. There must have been something in the Saint himself which impelled him to teach and to persevere in this activity ; and this was nothing other than his magnanimity, which in this profession could express itself in the giving, the persistent giving, the superabundant giving, responding to its essential quality. The Saint gave of the wealth of his knowledge with both hands, without stint and ungrudgingly ; he lavished it out of a love which never says : it is enough—a love which is ever giving yet is never exhausted.

Albert must have been a quite exceptional teacher. Legend has embodied this in the tale of the Place Maubert. The people, so the story goes, flocked in such numbers to his lectures that even the great aula in Paris could not hold them, so that he had to give them in the open square.[36] The designation of the square has nothing to do with Albert ; the point of the story will have been the great reputation the Saint enjoyed as a teacher. It is peculiarly significant that an old chair is still shown at Regensburg from which the Saint is said to have taught.[37] Even though this chair date from a later period, the fact that to-day people still speak in this way of it, attests Albert's greatness as a teacher. The universality of his rich learning, the genius which enabled him to recognize whatever truth there might lurk in error, his magnanimity in appreciating the views of

[35] J. A. Endres : *Eine beabsichtigte zweite Berufung Alberts des Grossen an die Universität Paris ums Jahr 1268* ; Pelster : op. cit., 90.

[36] Petrus de Prussia : op. cit., 96.

[37] Sighart gives an illustration of this, op. cit., 388 ; see too H. Chr. Scheeben : *Albertus Magnus*, Pl. 11. [Ed.]

others, above all the new matter in his teaching and the kindly enthusiasm of his delivery, will have assured him the attention of his listeners, and this attention in alliance with their gratitude and affection may well have lightened and sweetened for the Master the labours inseparable from teaching.

Albert did not rest satisfied with the spoken word. Magnanimity seeks to dispense of the treasures of truth in every way possible. The spoken word reaches directly only a very limited circle, even if the listeners in their turn pass it on, and its influence thus endures after centuries. To effect an influence of this kind, the written word is surer, and few people have plied the pen as did Albert. It is perhaps an exaggeration to describe him as the most prolific writer who has ever lived, but, at any rate, the number and size of his works, especially when the learning they contain is considered, even to-day excites the admiration of all who are capable of judging. We are not even yet fully clear as to the number of Albert's authentic works, and certainly not a few have been lost.[38] In measuring the immense labour involved in the composition of these writings, we must not overlook the difficulties facing the writer in those days owing to the slowness of communications, the scarceness of books, the corruptness of the texts, and a hundred other causes. Yet Albert in spite of this was indefatigable, for love of the truth and his magnanimity impelled him to give of his wealth without stint. He states his intention in the introduction to the various works. That to the Commentaries on Aristotle's works is put shortly and to the point. 'Our intention is to make all these books (partes) intelligible to Latinists.'[39] Roger Bacon sees presumption in this short phrase. But Albert in the event showed that he had not undertaken anything beyond his powers. Moreover, he had been impelled to undertake their composition by the prayers of his brethren in the Order. But he did not meet their wishes at once, and it was only after they had importuned him for years

[38] Melchior Weiss: *Primordia novæ bibliographiæ b. Alberti Magni.*

[39] *Physicorum*, lib. 1, tr. 1, cap. 1.

that he at last gave way, unable any longer to resist them. It was love that drove him to compose the books on the Eucharist and the Mother of God. These subjects had taken such hold of his heart that he had to give them again to others. He worked at these books all his life. The chronology of the several works has not yet been definitely established. The *De Eucharistia* may be regarded as the fruit of his old age. Albert is said to have worked with extraordinary speed. The Commentary on S. Luke is held to have been the work of his Regensburg period ; but as this work is very voluminous, earlier researchers have thrown doubts on this report. If, in fact, the Saint had in those days nothing else to do but compose this work, it would have taxed all his powers. We must therefore suppose that he had previously been engaged on this work and that he put the finishing touches to it during the time when, as bishop, he ruled over the see of Regensburg.

Albertus Magnus has remained a living presence among men in his books, and in them the greatness of his soul lives and works further. He dispenses of the fullness of his knowledge ; there are often deep thoughts which open up new roads into the realm of truth ; or there are vigorous words spurring men to action ; but without exception they are words which serve the Truth, that she may be perceived, meditated, loved, and lived. One may miss in the most of these writings that classical repose and magistral exactitude which are the property of the works of his pupil Thomas. His impulse to give, to impart to others, was too great to let him round off the gift. He would have lost time which might have been spent on giving. So he gave precisely what he had to give. Albert the Magnanimous had to write as he wrote. The very defects of his works proclaim the perfection of their author.

Peter of Prussia writes that Albert brought forth the richest fruits by teaching and preaching. We have already seen what he accomplished as a teacher and writer. That, in addition, he had any time left for preaching is hardly believable. And yet the account given in the earliest biographies is borne out by Albert's works, for among them there is also a large volume of sermons. As the introduction shows, Albert preached and published these sermons before he became a bishop. In allusion to the parable of the slothful servant who hid his talent in the earth, the Saint says: 'That I might not be reckoned as such I have at the persistent request of some friends published these sermons.'[40] They are principally explanations of the pericopes for Sundays, and almost always fall into three parts. In the first the substance of the Gospel for the day is recalled, in the second the allegorical and ascetical explanation is given, and the third enshrines a prayer which embodies the practical purpose, and is directed to God, in order by His grace to set in hand its accomplishment. The sermons were published in Latin, but it must not be concluded from this that he only preached in this language. As Provincial he will have spoken to his subordinates in Latin, since in this language all studies were at that time conducted, and consequently it was understood by all educated people. As Bishop he will also have used it in his addresses to the clergy, but to the common people he preached in the vulgar tongue just as did his countryman, Johannes von Wildeshausen. Of the latter, tradition expressly says that he possessed several languages and therefore could preach to people of foreign nations in their mother tongue; and we may well take this to have been true of Albert, though perhaps not in quite so general a sense. Talking of the sermons, Sighart says: 'We must admire the deep condescension of the great man! He who was accustomed and qualified to speak to the wisest men of his day, here forgets, as it were, all his learning, and speaks lovingly and with the utmost simplicity to these plain, uncultured people, like a father to his children. He expressly declares that he is here only speaking and writing for uneducated folk. In fact in all things Albert only sought God's honour and man's salvation.'[41]

Of the addresses which Albert delivered to the clergy, the homily on Luke xi, 27, published by Paulus de Loë, may serve as an example.[42] K. Bielmeyer describes it

[40] Prologus ad *Sermones de Tempore*.
[41] Sighart: op. cit., 56.
[42] Paulus de Loë: *Alberts des Grossen Homilie zu Luke xi*, 27.

thus : ‘ It is a moving sermon on Mary which treats of the power of the Word of God and of the dignity of Mary, who in the flesh bore and suckled her divine Son ; one may say a masterpiece of the homilitic art of the Middle Ages. Its special value lies in the fact that it has come down to us as it was delivered, which, as is well known, seldom happens in the case of mediæval sermons in Latin. Albert the Great is therefore here brought into much more direct touch with us in his character of homilist than in his numerous other sermons. And the sermon is worthy of him, revealing in the author, as the editor points out, the accomplished theologian, the deeply devout religious, and the ardent votary of the Mother of God. Exterior and interior elements all point to Albert, so that his authorship may be taken as assured. It belongs to his episcopal period and all indications point to it having been delivered at Trier before the benefactors and clergy of S. Mary's Church, who in one passage are very sharply admonished.’[43]

Again in the Commentary on S. Luke's Gospel, which is said to have been composed in the same period, we find passages which display the forceful language which Albert employed in his addresses to the clergy. He there scourges quite mercilessly their manifest faults and failings, and firmly insists upon their reform. The priests must instruct and edify the people entrusted to them not by words only, but by their example. How touching the complaint sounds in his mouth : ‘ Alas ! In these days no one gives to the people ! ’[44] For a man like Albert it must have been painful to observe that prelates looked after themselves, but showed neither care nor interest in relieving the people in their need. That he himself out of his magnanimity gave, and went on giving, that he never wearied of giving, is in accord with his disposition, and reveals him in the perfection of his sympathizing, practical, self-sacrificing charity.

Such was Albert as preacher of the Word of God before he was raised to the episcopate, such he was especially during the short time that he had charge of the see of

[43] *Theologische Quartalschrift* (Tübingen, 1918, 333).

[44] Petrus de Prussia : op. cit., 216 ; *Commentarii in Lucam*, xvi, 21.

Regensburg, such he remained to the end of his life. Aventin's assertion that 'Albert was the most eloquent man of his century,'[45] is probably an exaggeration, for Berthold of Regensburg, whom he begged of the Pope to assist him in preaching the Crusade, will surely have surpassed him in eloquence. Sufficient fragments from the sermons have, however, been preserved to show that Albert must as preacher also have achieved greatness. These fragments are to be found in sayings which are even to-day current among the people as dicta Alberti. Sighart[46] has quoted a number of them. Obviously their authenticity cannot be proved, but they point to a man who understood the people and could talk to them forcefully. We have room for only one of these sayings here: 'If we forgive those who have wronged us in body or possessions or honour, it is of more avail to us than to have crossed the sea and laid ourselves down in the Holy Sepulchre.'

Albert did not confine himself to the general exposition of the truth in sermons and addresses, but also saw to it that the rules of the Order were obeyed. During the time when as Provincial he was responsible for the German Dominicans, he often intervened with great energy and severity. He insisted on his subordinates practising the poverty and humility prescribed by the Constitutions of the Order. No one was allowed private possessions, and when it appeared after the death of a lay brother that he had transgressed this rule, Albert, as Provincial, had his body exhumed and buried in unconsecrated ground, for this was the punishment prescribed for the offence. That in this proceeding, which to us to-day seems over-harsh, he had not the dead in his mind but the living, is clear. The latter were to be preserved from a similar transgression by a wholesome fear of the consequences. Even the superiors in the Order did not escape his disciplining. It was laid down that no one without a really valid reason should ride on a journey. In violation of this rule the Priors of Krems, Minden, and Hildesheim made the journey to Augsburg

[45] Quoted by Sighart, op. cit., 279.

[46] Sighart: op. cit., 209 *sq*. See for greater details of the many legends H. Chr. Scheeben: *Albertus Magnus*, 2002–30.

for the Chapter on horseback. Albert removed them from office and in addition imposed fasts and discipline. This made all understand that he meant his regulations to be carried out. Peter of Prussia, however, stresses the point that it was far from the Saint's mind to oppress his subordinates by too severe or too many rules.[47] Obedience, moreover, was made the easier for all, since they saw that Albert himself was most nice in the observance of anything he demanded of them. On his visitations he made the long journeys all over the German-speaking countries on foot, begging his way from door to door. As Bishop of Regensburg rich revenues were at his disposal ; he used them to remedy the disorders due to the mismanagement of his predecessors. Then, again, he spent money freely on the poor, made provision for convents and hospitals, and actually increased the revenues of his Cathedral Chapter. He certainly did not wish to encourage by this a life of careless luxury, but it was his intention that a suitable income should be an inducement to live a life conforming to the dignity of the post. For all these undertakings the revenues of the see, which had not sufficed for the personal expenses of his predecessors, were under Albert's regime sufficient. The reason for this lay in the poverty which the Saint personally practised, even as Bishop. It was not chance which took Albert, when entering the episcopal city, first to the Dominican convent. As Bishop he remained a religious both in his person and in his manner of life. The clogs, which were the footwear of the common people and were worn also by the Dominicans, and which he continued to wear even as Bishop, witness how faithfully he observed the rules of the Order, as far as these were compatible with his new office. One circumstance does, however, strike us at first sight as surprising, namely that the Saint, when giving up the bishopric, reserved for himself a portion of its revenues. This money he continued to use as he thought fit ; in fact he disposed of it in his will. In this document he expressly states that he did this by special papal permission.[48] In this Albert would appear not to have acted

[47] Petrus de Prussia : op. cit., 208.

[48] Quoted by Sighart : op. cit., 248.

magnanimously, for the magnanimous man may not be untrue to his principles; he may not, even with papal permission, allow to himself what he forbids to others. If we look at the matter more closely we shall see that the Saint here not only acted according to right, but again revealed the whole greatness of his soul. On giving up the bishopric he did not at once come again under the jurisdiction of the Order, but was kept in the papal service. For years afterwards he was engaged in preaching the Crusade. The revenues, probably reserved for him by the Pope himself, served for his maintenance. It was not until about 1266 that Albert, as Pelster shows,[49] again became subject to the rule of the Order. He did not, however, renounce the revenues, though this might give scandal to smaller minds. He retained them and used them for the good of the Order, as his testament proves. By his will three Dominican convents received legacies, and the residue was to be applied to the completion of the new choir of the Dominican church in Cologne. Personally the Saint lived among his fellow brethren as the poorest of them. Thus it is that the truly magnanimous man acts, one whom charity causes to brush aside petty prejudices, if by so doing the good of the whole may be the better served.

If it is the part of the magnanimous soul to overlook small acts of disrespect and even insults, charity impelled Albert to forgive them. Only once does he use forceful, even bitter words. In the Commentary on the Politics, when attacking those learned do-nothings who, to cloak their own indolence, sloth, or stupidity, can see in the works of others nothing but downright errors, he says: 'Men such as these killed Socrates and drove Plato from Athens to the Academy, and by their machinations forced Aristotle also to depart, as he himself tells us. . . . Such men are in the fellowship of learning like the liver in the body: for in everybody there is a gall-like liquor which, in dispersing, makes bitter the whole body. So in the learned body there are always some most bitter and gall-like men who turn all the rest to bitterness, nor will they suffer them to seek the truth in agreeable fellowship one with the

[49] F. Pelster: op. cit., 89.

other.'[50] We can see at the first glance that Albert is not here seeking to defend his reputation, but is saying in the interest of truth and in furtherance of his life work, that he is not going to let himself be hampered by such as these. This is quite in the manner of true greatness of soul.

When we contemplate the man whose whole life was given to the investigation and the propagation of the truth, when we see how under the spur of pure charity he was all things to all men, how in the small he saw the Great and practised it, the whole inconceivable breadth of Albert's magnanimity takes shape before our eyes as in an enchanting vision. To Frater Albertus, and in later years to the Dominus Frater Albertus, the whole of Cologne ran with its troubles. Like the humblest Mass priest he sat in his confessional and reconciled the poor contrite souls to God. How they also came to him with their thousand petty, everyday cares, and never came to him in vain, is better remembered in legend than in history, in the tales of the miraculous goblet with which Albert could cure all sicknesses, and that of the shoemaker's apprentice who wanted to see an exhibition of Albert's art.

The great of this world turned to him no less than the others with their often difficult and troublesome affairs. Then again this contemplative, this man of learning, was dragged into the turmoils of his day, with its feuds and disputes, and never turned a deaf ear when his help or his advice was sought. Everything that could serve his neighbour, certainly therefore everything that could benefit the community, counted as great in his eyes. He attacked the work and had with hardly an exception astonishingly great success. Parties which were at daggers drawn made peace at his word. Where interdict and excommunication could not bring the stiff-necked to submission, Albert's intervention succeeded. Most important of all probably was the peace which was concluded on Albert's advice and proposals between the Bishop of Würzburg and the citizens of that town in 1265, and, on repeated occasions, between the Archbishop of Cologne and this city.

The Saint, as an old man of eighty, rendered a quite

[50] *Politicorum*, lib. 8, cap. 6 *in fine*.

COPPERPLATE ENGRAVING BY WOLFGANG KILIAN, 1623, SHOWING SCENES FROM S. ALBERT'S LIFE.

inestimable service to the whole German Empire when, in the year 1274, he hastened to the Council of the Church being held at Lyons, and in a brilliant speech advocated the recognition of the newly elected German King, Rudolf of Hapsburg. According to Peter of Prussia the Saint took as the text of his discourse the words: 'He shall send them a Saviour and a defender to deliver them.'[51] In the event Pope Gregory X accorded recognition to Rudolf of Hapsburg, and thus with the co-operation of our Saint a dynasty assumed the most important throne in Europe, and held it longer and brought more blessings to it than any other. It was then with justice that Anselm Ricker, as Rector of the University of Vienna, said of him: 'We venerate in Albertus Magnus not only one of the greatest men, one of the greatest geniuses our country has ever brought forth; he is also, as it were, the ever-living, enduring embodiment of that brilliant epoch in our national history, to the intensity of whose spiritual life the august figure of an Albertus Magnus testifies as loudly as do the soaring cathedrals on the Rhine and on the Danube.'[52]

* * *

In this book some hint has been given of the universality of S. Albert's genius and influence. All knowledge was his province and he excelled in every field of learning; in truth no one so many-sided has ever been raised to the altars of the Church. For centuries, from the very moment of his death, he was regarded as a Saint, and, *quod semper, quod ubique, quod ab omnibus* he has been thus venerated, it is singularly meet that he should now have been accorded the almost unique honour of equipollent canonization, and thus *de jure* as well as *de facto* join the company of the Saints of the Church, to whose glorious ranks he has ever belonged. As a brother Dominican says of him:[53] 'Albert the Great, like Augustine, was a philosopher and theologian of genius;

[51] Is. xix, 20.

[52] Anselm Ricker: *Ein Kranz schuldiger Verehrung von der Alma Mater der Wiener Hochschule dem Andenken Alberts des Grossen gewidmet*, 7.

[53] Angelus Maria Walz, O.P.: *Zur Heiligsprechung des seligen Alberts des Grossen.*

like Ambrose or Jerome, Leo or Gregory, he was remarkable for his penetrating study and fruitful exegesis of the Holy Scriptures ; like Hilary, Isidore, and Bede he used his talents for the furtherance of education and culture ; like Peter Chrysostom he enjoyed no mean reputation as a homilist ; he was a reformer like Peter Damien, a scholastic like Anselm, a religious and a mystic like Bernard of Clairvaux, and like him preached a Crusade ; he was a mendicant, a teacher, and a Prior Provincial like Bonaventure of Bagnoregio ; with Thomas Aquinas he won renown as a consummate teacher, master, and systematizer. Those who were straying he led back into the way of truth ; he confirmed those whose faith was wavering and he possessed the true ecclesiastical sense, as did later a Peter Canisius. In the practice and teaching of piety he was a forerunner of men like John of the Cross, Francis of Sales, and Alphonsus Liguori. Among the saints and the most eminent teachers of the Church Albert the Great bears an impress all his own, that of a wonderful universality, of a many-sidedness and a thoroughness which revealed themselves in the magnificence of his achievement and the vast range of his influence. As he appeared to men, so they named him ; from the very beginning they called him *doctor universalis.*' Truly on all counts he deserves his title of the Great.

THE UNIVERSAL GREATNESS

THE CULT OF ALBERT THE GREAT

IN a picturesque article, *Albertus Magnus Redivivus*, which appeared shortly after the canonization of the Saint, a German writer[1] compared Albertus Magnus to a mighty city long swallowed up by the sands of the desert and at length laid bare by the labours of archæologists. How far from the literal truth this comparison is may be gathered from the following brief account of his cult based on various papers by Fr. Angelus Maria Walz, O.P.,[2] than whom no one has worked more fruitfully and perseveringly for the cause in recent years.

1. *From* 1280 *to* 1483.

Albert the Great died on November 15, 1280, sitting in an arm-chair in his cell in the Dominican convent at Cologne and surrounded by his kneeling brethren who had gathered in prayer round the dying Saint. The extraordinary regard in which the great friar, scholar, and bishop had been held in his lifetime found overwhelming expression at his death. His obsequies gave occasion for an imposing demonstration of heartfelt mourning and profound veneration. These took place on November 18. The Archbishop and Metropolitan of the Lower Rhine, Siegfried von Westerburg, himself officiated at the Requiem Mass and burial of his departed friend. A multitude of the faithful of every station in life thronged the church and its approaches in order to do honour to the great Master who had been to all both guide and friend, who had done so much to bring peace from warring factions to the city he loved, the

[1] Ferdinand Muralt ; his paper was published in *Hochland* for May 1932.

[2] A. M. Walz, O.P. : *Zur Heiligsprechung des s. Albert des Grossen ; De agendi ratione in causa canonizationis B. Alberti Magni ; Bestrebungen zur Heiligsprechung Alberts des Grossen in alter und neuer Zeit*, etc.

great Servant of God whose whole life had been spent in the service of his neighbour.

Albert's grave soon became a centre of prayer and pilgrimage. It was situated before the steps of the high altar in the middle of the choir of the Dominican church at Cologne. A stone slab, raised somewhat above the level of the floor of the choir, marked the spot where the Saint lay. On the stone was cut the simple inscription: *Anno domini MCCLXXX XVII Kal. Decembris obiit venerabilis frater Albertus, quondam ecclesie Ratisponensis episcopus, ordinis Prædicatorum, magister in theologia. Requiescat in pace. Amen.* To protect the gravestone from injury this was, soon after his death, surrounded by a railing bearing a tablet on which was set out the epitaph of which the following is probably the correct text:[3]

Phenix doctorum, paris expers, philosophorum
Princeps, verborum vas fundens dogma sacrorum,
Hic iacet Albertus, preclarus in orbe, disertus
Pre cunctis, certus assertor, in arte repertus,
Maior Platone, vix inferius Salomone,
Quem tu, Christe bone, sanctorum iunge corone.
Annis bis denis minus actis mille trecenis
Christi nascentis de corporis exit habenis,
Quinta post festum Martini luce molestum
Omne, petendo deum, transivit, agens iubileum.
Qui legit hos versus, mox ad tumulum retroversus,
Inclinans dicat Collectam cum Requiescat.

Signal evidence of the veneration in which Albert was held very soon after his death is the window presented by the Archbishop Siegfried von Westerburg which was set *circa summum altare, ubi ipse Albertus in pontificalibus depictus est*; the Archbishop himself appears in the window at Albert's feet. This window must have been put in before 1297. To his old companion and secretary, Gottfried von Duisburg, who was praying for the repose of the soul of his Master, the Saint appeared in glory, indicating to him that he was already in heaven. Similar consoling visions

[3] H. Ch. Scheeben: *Albertus der Grosse, zur Chronologie seines Lebens*, 131 *sq*.

were also vouchsafed to Theodoric, the Lector at Trier, and to Mechtildis of Helfta, while the faithful reported numerous miracles as the result of his intercession. It is therefore easily explicable that among all classes, the lettered as well as the unlettered, he should have been venerated as a Saint. It is possible that this title was accorded to him even in the thirteenth century ; it certainly was in the first half of the fourteenth. In fact in all the centuries succeeding his death he is not infrequently depicted in art with the halo of a Saint rather than the rays of a Beatus. Luis de Valladolid reports that Albert's was one of the three names submitted by the Dominicans to Pope John XXII, who had expressed the wish to canonize one of their Order. The names of the other two suggested to the Pope were Thomas Aquinas and Raymund of Pennafort. Both Albert and Raymund had to wait for the Church's recognition of their status, for the Pope chose Thomas, whom he canonized in July 1323.

At sometime in the fourteenth or early fifteenth century an Albert Chapel was erected in Lauingen, the Saint's birthplace, for Luis de Valladolid, writing in about 1414, reports its existence, and there is confirmatory documentary evidence in support of the Spanish Dominican's statement. Thus on December 12, 1444, the Burgomaster and Councillors of Lauingen submitted to the Bishop of Augsburg for his approbation a bequest they had recently made for the altar dedicated to All Saints and Blessed Albert the Great, which the bishop sanctioned two years later. Again in a document, dated January 16, 1483, concerning a bequest by one Ursula Rupp, the position of the chapel is specifically stated : 'It stands in the same building where Albert was born.' This explains how it is, as appears from ordinances of 1603 and 1604, that there was a corn-dealer's warehouse, i.e. business premises, above the chapel. The lower storey of the house where the Saint was born was in fact converted into a chapel, in which a specially appointed priest regularly held the liturgical services. The erection of this Albert Chapel may perhaps date back to the time of the movement in favour of his canonization during the pontificate of John XXII, and indeed Luis de Valladolid connects it with that movement. It is clear that there were ample grounds for regarding the promotion of the cause of the great teacher and prelate as promising success, in view of the acknowledged holiness of his life, his reputation as a miracle-worker, and the active veneration accorded to him.

The year 1480 is of especial importance in the cult of the Universal Doctor on account of the remarkable cure of a Dominican in Cologne, which was ascribed to Albert's intercession. This may have been a blessing on the devotion to the great Servant of God, which had in one form or another always been practised in that city; it may have been an outcome of the veneration for their Master fostered by the Albertists at the Rhenish University. At any rate it opened up new prospects for an official liturgical recognition of Albert's memory, to which possibly the triumph of the Franciscan Bonaventure before the Church Militant which Sixtus IV conferred on the Seraphic Doctor in 1482 may have provided a further stimulus. The Albertists now took energetic steps to secure papal approval for public liturgical honours to be paid to their spiritual leader, and in this they were helped by the Dominican Order. It was proposed to give the great Servant of God a more magnificent tomb, and on January 11, 1483, by direct authority of the Pope, Salvo Casetta, the Master General of the Order and at this time papal legate to the Emperor, opened the old tomb in the presence of the Provincial, Jakob von Stubach, the Prior of the Cologne convent, Jakob von Barch, Ulrich von Esslingen, the Rector of the Cologne University, and of numbers of professors, students, priests, and delegates of the town. The sarcophagus was opened: in it was the wooden coffin in which the Saint rested. The body was clothed in pontificals with mitre and ring; his right hand held the crozier. On a ribbon round his neck was strung a cross, as well as relics and pious mementoes. Body, clothing, and the rest showed hardly a sign of corruption. As may be expected, those days witnessed numbers of miracles, striking cures, answers to prayers, which resulted from the Saint's intercession. The right arm was removed from the body and was taken to the Holy Father by the Master General, who gave it to the

Dominicans of Bologna. With all the insignia of the episcopal dignity, the body was translated to its new resting-place in the magnificent tomb which had been prepared for it.

2. *From the confirmation of the cult to the extension of the feast* (1484–1670).

In 1484 Innocent VIII granted permission to the Dominican priories of Cologne and Regensburg to dedicate altars to Albertus Magnus and also to observe his feast yearly with a Mass and an Office. By this act, as Pope Pius XI remarks in his decretal letter *In thesauris sapientiæ*,[4] the official Beatification of the deeply venerated scholastic Master was accomplished. It was in fact a *Confirmatio Cultus*, in other words equipollent beatification, just as his canonization four and a half centuries later took the same form.

Why the Dominicans and the Albertists did not follow up Albert's cause more vigorously after this first success cannot now be determined. Certainly the wonderful cures effected at the Saint's tomb would of themselves have been ample ground for a formal process, and indeed in the sixteenth century astonishment that he had not already been canonized found open expression. Yet nothing definite was done. The times were, it is true, unfavourable. Neither in Cologne nor in Lauingen, nor indeed in any of the German lands was there, during those years of religious cleavage, either the calm or the leisure to follow up such a matter. The people of Cologne were in fact twice near to having to give up the faith of their fathers and to being forced to adopt the new religion ; while Lauingen from 1542 to 1616 was under Protestant civil and clerical jurisdiction. The Duke of Pfalz Neuburg's order that the Albert Chapel in his birthplace must be put to a more useful purpose, rings like the spiteful retort of a petty lordling to the resolution of the Chapter General of the Dominican Order in 1601 to follow up the cause of Albert's canonization.

[4] See Appendix A.

With the restoration of the faith, however, in Bavaria and the Empire the observance of Albert's feast was extended beyond the priories of Cologne and Regensburg.

Albert IV, Graf von Törring, occupied the episcopal chair of S. Wulfgang from 1613 to 1649. He was a tireless champion of the extension of liturgical honours to his great predecessor in the see, Albert II. In 1616 he proposed to introduce the observance of the Saint's feast in his own cathedral, and to this end approached the Holy See, and also certain notables at the Papal Court and in the Dominican Order in Germany and Rome. However, on July 13, 1619, and again on November 14, 1620, the Congregation of Rites answered that approval could not be given to the celebration of Albert's feast in Regensburg Cathedral. It is certainly curious that at the Papal Court the permission to keep the feast given by Innocent VIII to the Dominican convents in Cologne and Regensburg should not have been taken into account or discussed. Even S. Robert Bellarmine himself showed that he was ill-informed on the matter. Under Paul V there was nothing to be got, and it was only after his and Bellarmine's deaths that there was again hope, leaving on one side the purely formal aspects of the case, of getting a hearing for its actual rights. At the beginning of Gregory XV's reign Bishop Albert von Törring renewed his request to Rome. His action was supported by the Dukes of Bavaria and Pfalz Neuburg, who had returned to the Catholic faith, and, very strongly, by Cardinal Madruzzo. On September 21, 1622, two days after Tilly had forced Heidelberg to surrender, Pope Gregory XV gave his decision in favour of Albert's feast being observed in Regensburg Cathedral in the same way as was already done in the Dominican convent in that town. The consent, *vivæ vocis oraculo*, was attested by Cardinal Madruzzo.

For this extension of Albert's feast the Congregation of Rites give a delicious explanation. They now suddenly find it to be meet that 'iis qui vitæ sanctitatem longa temporis diuturnitate comprobarunt, non in soli natali vel in aliis locis dumtaxat, ubi corpora eorum asservantur, sed et ubique ab omnibus qui idem cum iis profitentur institutum venerationem debere.' It is curious that the Congregation of Rites did not realize this ten years before.

Shortly after this the Dominican Procurator-General requested that observance of the feast might be allowed to the whole Order. This Urban VIII refused. The *Brevis relatio apostolicarum gratiarum B. Alberti Magni Episcopi Ratisbonensis* of 1628 may well have been meant to prepare the way for this petition. Moreover, a new edition of the *Relatio* appeared in 1634. However, the petition presented by the Duke of Pfalz Neuburg that the feast might be kept in Lauingen was favourably received; for Urban VIII gave the required permission in 1631 for Lauingen, and in 1635 for the Dominican Order throughout the German dominions. The enthusiasm which this concession aroused is evidenced by a report of the Chapter-General of the Order in 1644 remarking on the magnificence of the celebration of the Saint's feast throughout the whole vast German province. Meanwhile Albert von Törring did not limit his efforts to supporting the request that the feast should be observed throughout the whole Dominican Order, but persevered for the formal recognition by the whole Church of Albert's claims. An edition of the collected works of the Master was needed to strengthen the cause. Such an edition had been discussed years before, in 1629, by the then Provincial of the German province. The work of preparation was now taken seriously in hand. In 1647 a collection was made by bishops in many countries and in the several Dominican provinces to secure funds to enable his works to be printed. These were finally published in Lyons in 1651 by Peter Jammy. Many individual works had been lost or remained buried, but what were collected made up twenty-one large folio volumes.[5]

Regensburg vied with Cologne in doing honour to the Saint. Relics of Albert which had been begged from the latter city were carried in triumphal procession to Regensburg, and the day, December 13, 1654, when these were taken from the Dominican priory to the cathedral was made a feast. On May 3, 1664, the privilege of liturgically observing the Saint's feast day was extended to the Venetian

[5] See Appendix D.

province of the Order, and finally, on August 27, 1670, at the request of the Master-General of the Order, John Thomas of Rocaberti, the same privileges were granted by Clement X to the whole Dominican Order throughout the world. With this an important chapter in the history of the liturgical cult of the Universal Doctor closes.

3. *From* 1670 *to* 1809.

For the next two centuries no fresh steps were taken to attain the goal for which Albert IV of Regensburg had struggled so hard. As has happened so often throughout their history, the Children of S. Dominic showed themselves curiously reluctant to take any strong initiative towards obtaining official recognition for their own brethren. Yet Albert was never forgotten. His feast continued to be kept in Cologne, Regensburg, and Lauingen, and throughout the entire Order of Preachers. Then came the revolutionary wars and the invasions of Germany by the French. On June 17, 1799, the Dominicans in Cologne were given two hours in which to evacuate their convent, so that the Saint's tomb was robbed of its devoted protectors. In the year 1804 the French ordered the closing of all religious houses on the left bank of the Rhine. The destruction of the old Dominican church in Cologne followed, and with it that of the magnificent tomb in which Albert's relics rested. These, fortunately, the Prior and brethren had just time to rescue, and they were given shelter in the Church of S. Andrew, where they were placed in a simple shrine beside the altar on the north side of the choir. In the first half of the nineteenth century little was done in Germany to extend the cult of the Saint, but south of the Alps a significant tribute was paid to his memory by King Charles Albert of Sardinia, who in 1839 built a church to S. Albert in the castle park at Racconizi and adorned it with fine glass windows in which scenes from the Saint's life are depicted. He also commissioned Hyacinth de Derrari to write a life of Albert, which was published in 1847. In 1857 there appeared the excellent life by Dr. Joachim Sighart. From 1856 on, the archdiocese of Cologne celebrated yearly the liturgical feast of the Saint, and in 1859 there took place the dedication of the new Albert altar in S. Andrew's Church in Cologne, in a reliquary above which the Saint's relics now rest. Devotion to the great Doctor steadily grew. On his feast day, November 15, in 1859, his relics were inspected at the instance of Cardinal Johann von Geissel and then placed in the beautiful reliquary prepared to receive them. The new altar was consecrated on the following day. In 1860 the Albert Chapel in S. Andrew's was further enriched by relics of S. Dominic and S. Thomas Aquinas. Meanwhile scientists like Alexander von Humbold, Meyer, and Jessen were discovering the great Scholastic's true place in the history of science, and the year 1867 saw the appearance of the great critical edition of the Saint's *De vegetabilibus*, the work on which was begun by Meyer and completed by Jessen.

4. *From* 1870 *to* 1931.

While the Vatican Council was sitting the German bishops got together and prepared a petition to lay before the Holy Father praying that Albert might be raised to the dignity of Doctor of the Church. The answer given them through Cardinal Patrizi was that such a request could only be met if Albert the Great had first been canonized. The soul of all these efforts was Bishop Ignatius of Senestrey. At the Episcopal Conference held in Fulda the bishops on September 2, 1872, signed a petition to Pius IX that Albert's Cause might be introduced. Much correspondence on the matter ensued. It seems that it was held to be a matter for the Postulator of the Dominican Order to pursue. Unfortunately the readjustment of the relations between Church and State in Italy, the forced evacuation of the Minerva in Rome, the unsettled housing conditions of the Curia of the Order, and then the Kulturkampf in Germany, all combined to cause the affair to be temporarily shelved. The Saint's Jubilee in 1880 was the occasion of great demonstrations in his honour, many institutions were placed under his patronage, and the German Catholic colony in

Rome petitioned Pope Leo XIII to canonize the Beatus and declare him a Doctor of the Church ; but information as to the steps taken to back up this petition is wanting. In the closing years of the century, 1890–1899, a new edition of the Saint's works edited by A. Borgnet in thirty-eight volumes appeared ; but for a really critical edition the world is still waiting.

A learned Dominican whose name will ever be held in honour by votaries of S. Albert, Paulus Maria von Loë, founded in 1906 the *Quellen und Forschungen zur Geschichte des Dominikanerordens in Deutschland*, now edited by Hieronymus Wilms, O.P. P. von Loë had a true devotion to his great brother Dominican. His researches into the life and writings of the Universal Doctor are fundamental, and the material he collected laid the ground for every future biography of the Saint. His labours stimulated others, within his Order and without, to strive for the realization of the hopes and prayers of centuries in the formal canonization of the great Scholastic. Things were beginning to move rapidly. In 1927 the Council of the German Catholic Academic Association, meeting in Aschaffenburg, decided to submit a petition to the Pope for Albert's canonization, the Episcopal Conferences at Fulda and Freissing followed suit. Fr. Angelus Walz, O.P., archivist of the Order in Rome, had enlisted the services of Dr. Heribert Christian Scheeben in the work of organization, and between them much was effected to bring all the various activities in support of the Cause into convergence. In the autumn of 1927 the Albert Committee came into being in Cologne, and an Albert Sunday followed in the same city. The Provincial of the German province, Peter Louven, O.P., sent out a special letter calling for the prayers of the Order that Albert might attain to the highest honours of the Church, and in the succeeding year faithful and unceasing intercession was made before God for this intention. A new edition of Rudolf of Nymegen's *Legenda beati Alberti Magni* was published in 1928 for the information of the episcopate of the whole Church. Many individual papers on Albert's person and teaching appeared, while proofs of the graces of which trustful votaries of the Saint had been recipients were duly chronicled. The matter was now not a national affair but one for the whole Church, to promote the glory of the Most High and the good of mankind through the example, pattern, and intercession of a perfect teacher and servant of God.

At last, on March 2, 1929, the Postulator General of the Order made an appearance in Albert's Cause as signatory to a memorial in favour of the proceedings. In August the first official steps were taken to get the Congregation of Rites to re-open the Cause. In the summer of 1930 there was published in Rome the *Esposizioni e documentazioni del culto del Beato Alberto Magno*, based on an article by Fr. Angelus Walz, O.P., which had appeared in a German Catholic review. On July 16 this was presented to the Pope by the Master General O.P., together with an exposition of the conditions which, according to Benedict XIV, must obtain for 'equipollent' canonization, and which were abundantly met in Albert's case. The Congregation of Rites, as is its wont, went into the matter with great deliberation. In the autumn of 1930 the historical section began, at the instance of the Pope, its investigation into the life and cult of the Universal Doctor. Its findings were set out in the *Inquisitio*, which was concluded on April 15, 1931.

The year 1930, the 650th anniversary of the Saint, was a busy year in the history of his cult. Prayers, memorials, individual literary studies, and other preparatory labours all contributed interior strength to the Cause. In his own Germany and throughout the world, honours, both lay and ecclesiastical, were paid to the Master. The gathering of students and votaries of Albert for the Görres Convention in Cologne in September of this year led to a supplementary volume to the *Esposizioni* being published. The special number of the *Revue Thomiste* devoted to Albert the Great deposed to something more than the mere celebration of the 650th anniversary of his death ; it was the expression of the hope that the highest honours of the Church would soon be bestowed on the Master of Thomas Aquinas. An Albert Week held in Rome from November 9 to 14, while not directly serving Albert's Cause, since it was his scientific importance that was commemorated, nevertheless lent it no inconsiderable weight through its impressive success, which surpassed all expectations.[6]

At a memorable sitting on June 22 the historical section of the Congregation of Rites declared in favour of the sanctity of the life and the cult of Blessed Albert. On July 15 the Holy Father in a conversation with the Promotor Fidei, Mgr. Salvator Natucci, laid down the steps to be followed to bring the matter to an issue : nomination of a Ponens (Cardinal Ehrle), arrangement for a regular meeting of the Congregation of Rites (December 15), designation of two theologians to review Albert the Great's teaching and the writings (Mgr. Martin Grabmann and Franz Pelster, S.J.). That it was possible to link the dignity of Doctor of the Church to admission into the ranks of the Saints speaks much for the scientific methods of the thirteenth-century scholar, which also met the requirements of the litteræ postulatoriæ wherein the double petition was made.

The Positio had now to be got ready for those taking part in the Session on December 15. For one reason or another the summer slipped by without the work of preparing this being attacked. In the end it had to be got ready and printed between October 10 and November 21. To produce this volume of 830 large quarto pages in so short a time was a truly Herculean task !

The Master General of the Dominican Order directed that prayers be said throughout the Order that the gift of light might illumine the session of the Congregation of Rites on December 15. The result of its deliberations was communicated to the Pope on December 16 by the Promotor Fidei with a petition that the observance of Albert the Great's feast be extended to the whole Church. This was at once graciously granted by the Holy Father, and thus December 16, 1931, became the day of the Canonization of Albert the Great and of his being raised to the dignity of Doctor of the Church. On December 24 Pius XI had in his hands the draft of the decretal letter,[7] and after it had

[6] See Appendix B.
[7] See Appendix A.

been engrossed by a 'scriptor apostolicus' in the Papal Chancellery, it was presented to the Master General of the Dominican Order at a special audience. The Fathers who witnessed the presentation of the decretal letter *In thesauris sapientiæ* will ever hold in memory the Holy Father's expression of satisfaction at the glorious issue of this great affair.

DOMINICAN FATHERS AT CEREMONY OF DELIVERING THE BULL OF CANONIZATION OF ALBERT THE GREAT

In the centre Cardinal Frühwirth, a former Master-General ; on his right P. Martin Gillet, Master-General ; second

APPENDIX A

Decretal Letter

OF OUR MOST HOLY LORD, PIUS XI, BY DIVINE PROVIDENCE POPE, REGARDING S. ALBERT THE GREAT, OF THE ORDER OF PREACHERS, BISHOP, CONFESSOR, AND DOCTOR OF THE CHURCH. PIUS, BISHOP, SERVANT OF THE SERVANTS OF GOD, FOR AN EVERLASTING MEMORY.

IN the treasures of wisdom is understanding and religiousness of knowledge.[1] In the book of Wisdom,[2] too, Solomon shows us in inspired words the reason why he sought from God the possession of wisdom—because it is wisdom that links the soul intimately with God and far excels every other good. A life which combines religious perfection with the study of wisdom has a marvellous power of arousing and lifting up the hearts of the faithful—*that their hearts may be comforted, being instructed in charity, and unto all riches of fullness of understanding, unto the knowledge of the mystery of God the Father and of Christ Jesus,* in whom are hid all the treasures of wisdom and knowledge.[3] Indeed, the more nearly a man approaches God by wisdom, the more the spiritual dominates his life ; for *wisdom is the teacher of the knowledge of God, and the chooser of his works.*[4] A man attains the divine wisdom in proportion as he imitates the life and deeds of Our Saviour, who said : '*He that shall do and teach, he shall be called great in the kingdom of heaven.*'[5] Gloriously eminent as a follower of Our Lord Jesus Christ was Albert the Great, friar preacher, master in theology, and at one time Bishop of Ratisbon ; marvellously combining the contemplative and active lives, he was a conspicuously great man in his own age and is still great in our day ; by his pre-eminent qualities as a teacher and his surpassing skill in so many departments of knowledge, he has won the special title of 'the Great.'

[1] Ecclus. i, 6. [2] Wisd. viii, 2. [3] Coloss. ii, 2–3. [4] Matt. v, 19. [5] Ibid.

Albert the Great was born at the end of the twelfth century of a distinguished military family, at Lauingen, in Swabia, in the diocese of Augsburg. He left his native land in pursuit of learning and went to Padua, where he studied the liberal arts, medicine, and science. There he came to know and love the newly-founded Order of Friars Preachers, and fell under the spell of the eloquence of Blessed Jordan of Saxony, Master General of the Order, and, when he had overcome his uncle's objections, was enrolled among the sons of S. Dominic. He was in all things wholly devoted to God, and he was especially remarkable for his tender devotion to Our Lady. Early in his career he was sent to Cologne to complete his theological studies. During this time he assiduously trained both his mind and his heart with a holy eagerness, and, mounting from strength to strength, *he resolved as a giant to run the way.*[6] Mingling and seasoning study with prayer, he fashioned his mind and shaped his whole manner of life so as to fit himself for preaching and the salvation of souls, and to make himself a useful and capable friar preacher. He was so keenly alert for the attainment of wisdom that he soon outstripped his fellows and took the heights of all the secular sciences with a masterly ease, and, as our predecessor, Alexander IV, said of him, *he drank so deeply and assiduously of the fountain of divine lore, that its fullness might be said to be stored up in his breast.*[7]

He was ordained priest; and in order that he might give to others the treasures of his contemplation and knowledge, he was appointed to teach at Hildesheim, Freiburg (Breisgau), Ratisbon, and Strassburg. His fame soon spread, and more widely still when he was made master in theology and professor in the renowned University of Paris. Later on, Albert was sent to teach at Cologne, where, at the bidding of his superiors, he founded and subsequently governed a *studium generale* of his Order. There, among many other famous disciples, his most illustrious pupil was Thomas Aquinas, whose genius he perceived and proclaimed; and all his life Albert held Thomas in a close friendship of holiness and learning; he stoutly defended his teaching when Thomas was dead, and always paid tribute to his greatness.

[6] Ps. xviii, 6.

[7] Bull of election of Albert as Archbishop of Ratisbon.

A model of prudence and justice to all, it is not to be wondered at that again and again Albert was called upon as an arbiter in public and private disputes : these he always settled with a strict sense of fair play and with rare skill and strength of purpose. His marvellous mastery of affairs, coupled with his zeal for religious observance and his love of Christian perfection, led the friars of Germany, assembled in chapter at Worms, to elect him as their Prior Provincial. The capitular Fathers were well aware of their need : they knew the times in which they lived. They knew how the vanity of the world can sometimes creep into the cloister ; they knew, therefore, that their ruler must be a man of holy life, of strong will, and conspicuous for prudence and every kind of virtue. Their hopes were not disappointed in Albert, who threw himself with indefatigable zeal into the work of ruling his province, which extended from the shores of Flanders, through Germany, to Poland and the very confines of Hungary. It was his custom to traverse the whole province, visiting convents, holding chapters, and, by example and word, urging his subjects to follow the way of regular observance, after the sublime example of his Master, who *began to do and to teach.*[8]

His prudence in management, his skill in civil business, and the fame of his learning and holiness, reached the ears of the supreme Pontiffs, who therefore specially chose him out to deal with important and difficult undertakings. It is specially worthy of mention that he was commissioned by Pope Alexander IV to organize, with the help of his friars, the defence and propagation of the Catholic faith among the heathens of Livonia and Prussia ; Alexander also confided similar duties to him in the kingdom of Brandenburg.

Albert was chosen by his Order to vindicate the rights of the mendicant Orders and plead their cause with the Holy See. For this purpose he appeared before the Papal Court, then at Anagni, and so successfully refuted his opponents and so impressed his hearers, that the Pope chose him to undertake a public disputation against the errors of the Averroists, and also appointed him to expound the Gospel of S. John in the school of the Papal Court. So deep was the impression of learning and virtue which he left behind him in Rome, that the same Alexander IV appointed

[8] Acts i, 1.

Albert Bishop of Ratisbon, a see at that time ill-favoured both spiritually and temporally ; and the task fell to him not only of tending the flock committed to him, but also of relieving the see of its heavy burden of debt. Notwithstanding his episcopal dignity, Albert observed religious poverty, and this proved an efficacious means of reforming morals and restoring ecclesiastical discipline. He in no way relaxed his love of study and contemplation. Ever zealous in rooting out vice and in reviving collapsed morals, discreet in settling quarrels, diligent in the administration of the Sacraments, he yet continued perseveringly in the task of writing, and ever worked to promote sound doctrine while watching over his flock.

With the permission of Urban IV, he resigned the see of Ratisbon ; and then, at the bidding of the same Pope, and armed with the authority of the Apostolic See, he preached a crusade through Upper Germany and Bohemia. When he had completed this mission, he returned of his own accord to the regular life of his Order, and spent the remaining years of his life preaching, teaching, and writing. In many dioceses, too, he was always ready to perform pontifical and episcopal functions, to undertake long and difficult journeys in the interests of religion. He visited Antwerp, Basel, and Strassburg, whence, after some stay, he returned to Cologne, which was to be his last resting-place.

He interested himself in the religious Orders of both men and women, made visitations under episcopal command, and worked with energy to stimulate communities to greater fervour by his own spirit of wisdom and holiness. Willingly and generously he gave his good services to all the faithful in the cause of religion, and he was never known to refuse anyone his counsel and help. And it is well known that he lived in terms of friendship with S. Louis, King of France.

Although his office and dignity entitled him to deep respect, it was not his way to overawe but to show himself a father, always inspiring confidence, never fear, after the example of S. Paul, who spent himself and was spent for the souls of his fellows.[9] Although worn out with age, he attended the second Council of Lyons, in which the Greeks made their profession of faith and happily returned to the

[9] 2 Cor. xii, 15.

unity of the Church. In that same council it was at Albert's instance that our predecessor, Blessed Gregory X, sanctioned the election of Rudolph of Hapsburg as King of the Romans, a matter in which it can be confidently affirmed that Albert was acting for the good of both ecclesiastical and civil society.

But all this life of business and activity was as nothing compared to the immense labour of his studies and his many learned written works, in which are gloriously displayed the force and acuteness of his genius, the fullness and depth of his mind, the overflowing wealth of his erudition, and his indefatigable zeal in defending the faith. Hence, historians and those who have written about him have rightly singled out for special praise the extraordinary universality of his mind; for he was occupied not only with divine things and the truths of philosophy, but also with all the other human sciences. Bartholomew of Lucca, a contemporary, declared that, in his knowledge of all the sciences and in his method of teaching, he excelled all the learned doctors of his day. Indeed, an examination of the mere titles of his innumerable works will show that no single science escaped his attention: astronomy, cosmography, metereology, climatology, physics, mechanics, architecture, chemistry, mineralogy, anthropology, zoology, and botany were some of the subjects he wrote about; and to these he added works on such practical arts as weaving, navigation, and agriculture.

As became a true Catholic teacher, Albert the Great did not let his mind dwell merely upon the consideration of the external world, as is so often the case nowadays with those who devote themselves to scientific research; but observing due order in all things, he passed from the natural things to the spiritual, and co-ordinating and subordinating the various spheres of knowledge, he proceeded by a real progression from things inanimate to things living, from living to spiritual creatures, and from the spiritual he mounted to God, the Author of all. And indeed God, the generous giver of all good things, had endowed him with the abilities needful for the accomplishment of his great work. Albert had an insatiable thirst for truth, a patient, tireless energy of inquiring into natural phenomena, a vivid imagination joined to a tenacious memory, a sane esteem for the established wisdom of the past. Above all, his was a religious mind, ready to perceive the matchless wisdom of God shining out through all creation. His was the spirit of the psalmist who invites all the elements of the world to sound forth the praises of the Creator, the spirit of which we read in the books of Job, Wisdom, and Ecclesiasticus, the spirit by which the Holy Ghost moves men to praise and bless God as the lavish giver of every gift.

It is especially noteworthy that he gathered together with painstaking industry every grain of the ancient wisdom, and gladly accepted whatever truth had been discovered by the innate power and ingenuity of the human mind, and, once he had separated it and purged it from all error, he made use of it to illustrate or defend the truths of faith. In particular he extracted such help from the works of Aristotle, which at that time were beginning to be disseminated throughout Europe. Putting aside all false interpretations of Aristotle, he not only warded off an impending peril to Catholic teaching, but, so to say, snatching a weapon from the enemy's hands, he used the ancient philosophy to support and defend revealed truth. Thus Scholasticism, enriched with the treasures of Aristotelian philosophy, entered upon a more excellent way and showed forth more clearly the wonderful accord that exists between right reason and faith. Albert was the forerunner; and it was given to Thomas, his chosen disciple, to take up the work and with happy daring plumb the depths of philosophy and scale the highest peaks of theology.

By Albert's efforts the whole of philosophy, and in particular the Aristotelian philosophy, was adopted to serve—under the light of revelation—as a sound and fit implement for the Christian theologian. All his intellectual activities were inspired by one high, steadfast purpose, namely to seek whatever of truth, goodness, or beauty was to be found in pagan wisdom, and to offer, nay, consecrate it to Him who is the First Truth, Supreme Beauty, and Essential Perfection. Albert it was who broke the shackles that held the natural sciences in bondage to the pagans, Mohametans, and Jews. At that time, owing to the prevailing misuse of the natural sciences, God-fearing men were inclined to look upon them with a certain suspicion, for they thought them a danger and a snare to the faithful. But the true theologian fears no evil in the works of nature or of natural reason, if only they are examined aright; for he knows that they bear within them the light of the

Creator. Among the teachers of the Middle Ages, Albert stands out as the scholar who gave to the schools of his time the riches of the scientific culture of the ancients, which he delivered systematically and excellently arranged in his great Encyclopædia, which begins from the simplest notions and rises to the heights of theology. Small wonder, then, that he was hailed as one who was *ignorant of nothing and knew all that was knowable*;[10] and could be said to be the wonder and miracle of his age.[11] Nor is it surprising that he was given the title of *Universal Doctor* and described of old as *the most resplendent sun of the philosophers of Christendom.*[12]

Non-Catholics, too, in our own time have praised him as the greatest scientific investigator of the Middle Ages. One well-known writer calls Albert *the most enlightened pioneer of the study of science in the West. Albert was the first to assimilate to the Christian religion the wisdom of the Greeks; the first to reconcile natural history with the doctrine of the Church; the first to describe nature in terms of art; the first to attempt to reduce forms of created things to morphological notions; finally, he first and alone gave us the complete account of the whole of nature and explained it in all its details.*[13]

To him belongs this great honour, that (excepting S. Thomas) there is scarcely another doctor of equal authority, whether in philosophy, theology, or the interpretation of Scripture. It would be an endless task to recount all that Albert has done for the increase of theological science. Indeed it was to theology that the whole trend of his mind was inevitably directed. The authority he had acquired in philosophy grew and increased, for, as we have said, he used philosophy and the scholastic method as a kind of implement for the explanation of theology. In fact he is regarded as the author of that method of theology which has come down in the Church to our own time as the safe and sound norm and rule for clerical studies.

Albert's numerous theological works, and, above all, his commentaries on the Sacred Scriptures, bear the marks not only of an enlightened mind and a deep knowledge of Catholic teaching, but they are stamped with the spirit of piety and arouse in souls the desire to cleave to Christ;

[10] Pius II in his Dogmatic Letter to the Emperor of the Turks, 1464.

[11] Ulrich von Strassburg: *Summa de bono*, lib. 4, tr. 3, c. 9.

[12] *Henricus de Hervordia: Chronicon*, 196.

[13] C. Jessen.

we readily discern therein the holy man discoursing of holy things. We need but call to mind his *Summa Theologica*, fragrant alike of piety and wisdom ; his *Commentary on S. Luke's Gospel*, which bespeaks a skilled and sound interpreter of Holy Writ ; his *Treatise on the Praises of Mary*, in which he reveals his burning love and devotion towards the Mother of God ; his incomparable work on the *Blessed Sacrament of the Altar*, in which appear his sincere faith and passionate devotion to the mystery of the Incarnation. Worthy of note, too, are his mystical writings, which show that he was favoured by the Holy Ghost with the grace of infused contemplation : these writings provided an inspiration and a guide for the German mystics of the fourteenth century.

All the works of Albert are of monumental value and of imperishable authority. With our predecessor, Leo XIII, we venture to say : *Although time will bring its increase to every kind of science, still Albert's teachings, which served to form Thomas Aquinas and were regarded in his time as miraculous, can never really grow old.*[14]

Let what we have said suffice to suggest something of the excelling holiness of life and marvellous teaching of Albert the Great, who, after a life of labour in the Lord's vineyard and after having deserved so well of the entire Church, on November 15, 1280, peacefully left this world for a blessed eternity. But since the setting of so great a luminary the glorious after-glow has never departed. Albert the Great still shines resplendent in the Church of Christ by the lofty fame of his science, the marvel of his holiness, the miracles he worked during life and after death—as trustworthy witnesses declare—hence we can make our own the words of S. Peter Canisius, Doctor of the Church, who, besides calling Albert the *light of Germany*, said of him : *He excelled in purity of life, in wisdom and science. . . . God has witnessed to his greatness and holiness by many miracles.*[15]

No wonder, therefore, that after his death public ecclesiastical cultus was granted to Blessed Albert with all its attendant circumstances and privileges. And it is a matter for rejoicing that several of our predecessors, *having due regard to the excelling merits of this holy man,*[16] have accorded

[14] Brief given December 10, 1889, to L. Vives, publisher of the works of Blessed Albert.

[15] The German Martyrology, under date November 15.

[16] Clement X in Decree, August 27, 1670.

special favours in order to extend his cultus; Innocent VIII, in 1484, granted to the friars preachers of Cologne and Ratisbon the faculty to erect altars in his honour and to keep his feast; such an authorization is equivalent to beatification. Gregory XV, in 1622, by word of mouth, granted the same privilege to the cathedral chapter and clergy of Ratisbon; Urban VIII, in 1631, gave leave for the celebration of his feast in the city of Lauingen, and in 1635, at the instance of the Emperor, extended the same right to all friars preachers of Germany; Alexander VII, in 1664, granted the same favour to the Dominicans in the province of Constance; and, lastly, Clement X, in 1670, authorized the celebration of the feast, with Office and Mass, throughout the entire Order of Preachers in perpetuity. Pius IX, in 1856, gave leave to the whole archdiocese of Cologne to keep the feast as a semi-double, and later, in 1870, he raised it to the rank of a double. Three years later, the same Pope, in the Church of S. Elizabeth, where a society of German Catholics had been formed, gave licence to all priests celebrating there to say the Mass of Blessed Albert the Great. In more recent times other dioceses of Germany, and in France, the archdiocese of Paris, have obtained leave to keep Blessed Albert's feast. A plenary indulgence has been granted at different times for his feast in various places: and Leo XIII granted a plenary indulgence to all who visited the church dedicated to him at Riga. Wherefore it is not to be wondered at that a man of such excelling holiness and learning should be considered worthy of canonization and of the title of Doctor of the Church. In particular his Cause was urged at the time of the solemn translation of his relics in 1483, and again with more energy at the beginning of the seventeenth century; but wars and the difficulty of access to the Roman Curia prevented this happy consummation.

During the Vatican Council the German bishops wished to realize the pious desire of the preceding centuries, and begged the Apostolic See to reopen the Cause of Albert the Great; but the troubled times the Church was undergoing in Italy and Germany prevented the fulfilment of these hopes.

At last, in our own time and with due solemnity, Cardinals, Archbishops, Bishops, and Prelates from all over the world, as well as Abbots and religious superiors, and especially universities, faculties, seminaries and colleges and learned societies, and personages of rank, fame, and learning all over Germany, have presented to us earnest petitions to honour Blessed Albert with the aureola of the Saints and the title of Doctor of the Church. We felt no reluctance in taking up a Cause which was already so much in accord with our own wishes, all the more because the present moment would seem to be the time when the glorification of Albert the Great was most calculated to win souls to submission to the sweet yoke of Christ. Albert is exactly the Saint whose example should inspire this modern age, so ardently seeking for peace and so full of hope for its scientific discoveries. Everyone nowadays is looking eagerly for peace, but there is no agreement as to the best way of attaining it ; indeed the very foundations of peace, namely justice and charity, are cast aside.

Let all then look with confidence to S. Albert the Great. For he with all his heart adhered to God, and *God is not the God of dissension, but of peace,*[17] of that peace which passeth all understanding and keeps the hearts and minds of the faithful.[18] Albert, who in his lifetime laboured strenuously and successfully for peace between princes and peoples and individual men, is put before us now as the perfect model of peace. His power and authority as arbiter and peacemaker were derived from his holiness and learning, which men respected and esteemed ; they reverenced, too, his innate dignity of person, which was further ennobled by his priestly character. He presented a living image of his Master, whom Scripture calls *the Prince of Peace.*[19]

Learning also is most conducive to peace, provided it is obedient to reason and supernatural faith ; indeed such obedience would seem to be necessary in order to assure to science its nobility, its security, and its truth. But how often it happens, especially in our own times, that this subjection of science to reason and faith is neglected and despised in scientific research ; indeed science is sometimes used against faith and reason, and *the Lord, the God of all knowledge,*[20] is set aside, and science, presuming upon its own all-sufficiency, leads to that deplorable state of materialism which is the cause of all those moral disorders and economic ills which have fallen as a bitter scourge upon the peoples of the whole world.

[17] I Cor. xiv, 33.
[18] Phil. iv, 7.
[19] Isaias ix, 6.
[20] I Kings ii, 3.

In Albert the Great the rays of human and divine science meet to form a shining splendour. His life is a standing proof that there is no opposition, but rather the closest fellowship, between science and faith, between truth and goodness, and between learning and holiness. Like S. Jerome, Albert, as it were with powerful voice, declares and proves in his wonderful writings that science worthy of the name, and faith and a life lived according to the principles of faith, can, and indeed should, all flourish together in men, because supernatural faith is the crown and perfection of science. It is not true, as modern atheists assert, that the Christian life and the pursuit of Christian perfection destroy the human spirit, weaken the will, impede civil activity, and rob men's minds of their native nobility ; on the contrary, grace perfects nature, develops, improves, and ennobles it.

Having maturely considered all Albert's titles and claims to saintship and to the worship of all the faithful, and with the desire that he should shine more brilliantly before the Universal Church, and in order to make up that which seemed to be still lacking to complete his glory, we have decided at length to fulfil our daily growing desire in his regard by equivalent canonization. Since, therefore, the time seems opportune, and since none of the conditions required by the most ancient custom and law of the Church in such matters are lacking, we have decided to follow a way of procedure which several of our predecessors have at times thought fit to use in the canonization of the Servants of God. Therefore, we entrusted the whole matter to the Sacred Congregation of Rites. Thereupon our dear sons, the Cardinals of the Sacred Congregation, met in ordinary assembly to hear the report of our beloved son, Francis Cardinal Ehrle, the Promoter of the Cause ; and when the historical investigation had been officially made into the sanctity of Blessed Albert's life and into the legitimacy of his cultus, and when the official written verdict upon his doctrine had been given by two learned men, well versed in his works ; and after taking the votes of the official prelates of the same Congregation of Rites, and all points maturely weighed and discussed, the large assembly unanimously agreed that we should be well advised to grant the favour. We therefore on the following day—that is to-day—having attentively heard a report of all these matters from our beloved son, Salvator Natucci,

Promotor Fidei, and in full agreement, most willingly approved the decision of the Sacred Congregation. Therefore, in virtue of our Sovereign Apostolic Authority, we order that the feast of S. Albert the Great be celebrated by the Universal Church on November 15 each year as a minor double, with the Office and the Mass of a Confessor and Pontiff, with the addition of the title of Doctor.

Let abundant thanksgiving be offered to God, who in the marvellous designs of his providence has, through our lowliness, deigned to perfect the glory of Albert in the sight of all the Church, and has revealed him in our age as a *shining light and morning star illuminating by his fecundity the whole body of the Church*,[21] and as one who truly laboured not for himself alone, but for all who seek out the truth.[22] May, then, S. Albert the Great be our intercessor, he who sought after wisdom and virtue from his earliest youth and bore the Lord's yoke cheerfully even as S. Paul the Apostle, who thought nothing could be more desirable than to bring into captivity every understanding unto the obedience of Christ.[23]

Therefore, having well considered everything that had to be examined, with full knowledge and with the fullness of our Apostolic Authority, we confirm, ratify, and again declare and order all that we have said above ; we publish it to the whole Catholic Church ; and we command that all copies, transcripts, or impressions of this present Letter, provided they are signed and sealed by a Notary Apostolic, shall be given the same reverence and acceptance as this Our Letter, wherever it shall be necessary for it to be exhibited and shown. If, however, anyone shall presume to infringe or rashly attempt to contradict this Letter of declaration, decree, command, and will, let him know that he shall incur the anger of Almighty God and of his blessed Apostles, Peter and Paul.

Given at Rome, in S. Peter's, in the year one thousand nine hundred and thirty-one, on the sixteenth day of the month of December, the tenth year of Our Pontificate.

I Pius,

Bishop of the Catholic Church.

[21] Anon. O.P. Sæc. XIV. [22] Ecclus. xxiv, 47.
[23] 2 Cor. x, 5.

APPENDIX B

THE ALBERT WEEK IN ROME, NOV. 9–14, 1930

'A GIGANTIC figure'—such was the expression used by the Holy Father to sum up the astonishing personality of Albert the Great. The phrase seems to go to extremes, and yet how else could one represent the feeling of exceptional greatness which overcomes us as we consider the Saint's person and work?

His life was rich. But, however weighty the charges laid upon him by the Church and by the Order, Brother Albert never forgot the one idea which ruled his whole life: his God. Before spreading the reign of the Master he lived it intensely, as saints do. He bent his intelligence, with all its exceptional gifts, before the whole truth, for he saw in it, always and everywhere, a reflection of the great divine Light.

Nothing is greater than this immense outlook on the whole universe by one who has understood creation.

His whole work is there. He disdains nothing. On the contrary, he has for all beings the boundless respect due to the works of God. He studied them all, for all branches of knowledge are worthy of the intelligence. He deserved to be the Master of S. Thomas.

Centuries have called him 'the Great.' Time has not diminished his greatness. It is fortunate that our twentieth century has been minded to set him once again in the full light of day, for is he not, with his beloved disciple, the witness *par excellence* of that unbelievable intellectual activity which marked the life of the Middle Ages?

The initiative of the Collegio Angelico and of the Dominican Historical Institute in favour of the Albertinian Week has enabled the Master's light to be shed still more brightly and far around. It was but 'just,' as Pius XI has said. Mgr. Ruffini, Secretary of the Congregation of Seminaries and Universities, and President of the Albertinian Week, opened the course of lectures on Monday, November 9.

The aim of his discourse was to show the place set apart by Albert the Great for philosophy and theology in the domain of science. Theology and philosophy cannot live as strangers to nature. In our present state we know God, naturally, only through our knowledge of nature. Scientific knowledge of nature will, therefore, be a condition of our progress in the knowledge of God. Blessed Albert is, perhaps, the greatest representative of this necessary union between the natural sciences and theology. Science and life have often greatly suffered from neglect of this union.

The teaching of faith, in its turn, when scientifically worked out, gives valuable help to our knowledge of nature. Is it not enough to know the dogma of creation to avoid any mechanistic notion of the world and the denial of all finality?

* * *

The next morning Mgr. Masnovo, Vice-Rector of the Catholic University of the Sacred Heart, studied 'Albert the Great and the Averroist Controversy.'

His penetrating and well-documented study laid stress on the value of Albert's intervention in the struggle against the Averroists, in 1270, when the controversy had reached its most acute stage.

The divergence of views between Averroists and non-Averroists came out in the question of the substantial union between the intellective soul and the human body, a union which, for the anti-Averroists, was one *in essendo*, whereas for their opponents it was *in operando*. To Master Albert we owe this clear statement of the problem, not in his 'De quindecim problematibus,' but in the course of 'De unitate intellectus.'

During the great strife of 1270 at Paris between Averroists and non-Averroists, Albert the Great, absent in body, is present in mind: it is from him that S. Thomas takes his inspiration. Thus when, in 1277, Albert returns to Paris to defend the memory of Thomas, attacked by the recent condemnation, it is himself he is defending as well as his disciple.

* * *

On the evening of the 12th Mgr. Grabmann, in a most interesting lecture, dealt with 'The Nature and the Aim of Speculative Theology according to the Teaching of

Blessed Albert the Great and S. Thomas.' Albert is usually celebrated solely as philosopher ; yet he wrote works of high theological value, some of which are unpublished.

In reply to the question, whether sacred teaching is speculative or practical, Albert replied that theology is neither a speculative nor a practical science, but an affective one, *secundum pietatem*, since its object is a beatific last end and a truth which is inseparable from the good.

Later on, S. Thomas was to revise somewhat this conception of theology : he considered theology as a speculative science. The speaker showed, however, that this difference is more one of method than of substance.

* * *

Dom Lottin, Benedictine monk of the Abbey of Mont César, Louvain, dealt with the moral system of Blessed Albert, and aimed primarily at determining whether reason is the immediate basis of morality.

The thought of Albert, when analysed, shows that he already possessed a very clear conception of reason as the basis of action, as standard for the will and as the foundation of the moral principle.

The lecturer showed, moreover, how Albert had clearly traced the plan of a systematic ethic which was then to be expounded in detail by Thomas Aquinas in his *Summa*.

* * *

On the 13th Fr. Fredegand of Antwerp gave a study of the 'Apostolic Life and Social Activity of Blessed Albert the Great.'

He well threw into relief Albert's true greatness, showing how he accomplished a great work of edification in the Christian world of his time by the example of a simple life, entirely animated by the love of God.

The vast extent of his work results from his close union with Christ, without which his activity would have remained barren like all human things.

The Father reminded his hearers that Albert, besides his scientific and philosophic works, had also published a volume of sermons for the people.

* * *

On the last day of the 'Week' Professor Seraphin Dezani, of the University of Turin, dealt with 'The Place of Blessed

Albert the Great in the Historical Framework of Experimental Science.'

The achievements of the 'Doctor Universalis' in this domain were overlooked until last century. Thanks to his assimilation of Aristotelian teaching and to his own experiments, Albert brought about so radical a revolution in the study of nature that he may be considered as the pioneer of modern experimental science. He has left us works of zoology and of botany carried out in the most rigorous scientific spirit. But all this activity is penetrated with the Christian spirit. Albert taught us to see the divine aspect of nature and to consider scientific truth as a continual confirmation of revealed truth.

* * *

An audience of the Holy Father brought the Week to a close. The Sovereign Pontiff congratulated the professors on having helped to recall and exalt the great character of Blessed Albert. They had thus done 'a work of supreme justice and of immediate usefulness.'

'Of supreme justice because Blessed Albert really deserves to have the rays of learning converge on his face and make a new halo around it.

'Such great figures suffice in themselves to remind a generation like ours that science and faith can and should agree.

'Blessed Albert deserved this tribute, which tends to bring him nearer to the contemporary mind. . . . He would seem to have gathered up in himself the very different temperaments of a metaphysician, a mystic, and a scientist. To-day as ever, it is easy to find empirical minds, men who skim over the various domains of learning, more to satisfy their curiosity than to contribute something to science.

'But it is much less easy to find people who, to study of a wide range of subjects, unite true depth and severe scientific precision. Such people are always a very rare exception. In the history of these great minds we have to jump from Aristotle to Albert the Great. Blessed Albert proved that he possessed in the highest degree that rare and divine gift, scientific instinct.

'In times when eyes and minds seem to be turned only to earthly things, not even guessing at the wonderful light that can come to us from heaven, figures like that of Blessed

Albert the Great stand out to remind us that no opposition exists between science and sanctity, any opposition between them existing only in the minds of those who do not feel the ineffable bond of kinship, the depth and the height of the bonds that unite truth and goodness.'[1]

[1] The papers read and discussed during this Albert Week have been published while the present volume was in the press under the Editorship of P. M. Cordovani, O.P., in *Alberto Magno. Atti della Settimana Albertina.* Rome, 1932; 282 pp.

APPENDIX C

CHRONOLOGICAL NOTE

THE precise chronology of S. Albert's life must always be a matter of dispute. Controversy has raged over the date of his birth. The traditional date, supported by Pelster and Scheeben, is 1193. This rests on the known date of his death, 1280, and the statement that he was eighty and more years, according to Rudolf von Nymegen and others, eighty-seven years old when he died. Endres and, later, Mandonnet have strongly supported a later date, namely 1206, based on the reference to him in the *Vitæ Fratrum O.P.*, as 'juvenculus' at the time of his admission to the Order of Preachers, and on a tradition reported by Jacobus de Soest and others that he was sixteen at the time of his clothing. It would seem to be easier to explain away this tradition than to account for the immense mass of scientific knowledge which he must have acquired before entering the Order, even if he added to it greatly afterwards, which must be done if the later date is accepted. Again, even the year of his admission is not absolutely certain. In fact Scheeben, who has done much careful research into the chronology of S. Albert's life, holds that 1228 or 1229 must be more probable than the generally accepted 1223. Those who wish to examine these questions as they stand are referred to *La date de naissance d'Albert le Grand* by P. Mandonnet, O.P., in *Revue Thomiste*, March–April 1931; and to Heribert Christian Scheeben's *Albert der Grosse; Zur chronologie seines Lebens*, his *Albertus Magnus*, and the article in the S. Albert number of *Divus Thomas* (1932) in which he answers Father Mandonnet's points.

The first date in S. Albert's life which can be exactly fixed, day, month, year, is May 15, 1248, when he was (probably) fifty-five years old! Even his family name is in dispute. The tradition that he came from the noble family of Bollstädt may be true, but on the other hand neither he nor his brother Henry ever appear as von Bollstädt, but they do as von Lauging, i.e., Lauingen, their presumed birthplace. It is possible that with the intensive research now being undertaken into things Albertian, more light may eventually be thrown on the many points still in dispute. At the moment Scheeben's book on the Saint's chronology must be taken as the most complete examination of the problem, and it is on this that the following skeleton is based. It is hoped that but few determined events and dates have been omitted.

Skeleton Chronology of the Life of S. Albert the Great

1193. Probable date of birth, presumably in Lauingen, since he called himself Albertus de Lauging. Possibly of the house of Bollstädt; but see Scheeben, op. cit.
Reigning Pope: Celestin III (1191–1198)*; Emperor, Henry VI* (1190–1197), *in succession to his father Frederick Barbarossa.*

1197. *Frederick II* (1197–1245) *Emperor succeeding his father Henry VI.*

1206. Alternative date of birth, supported by Endres and Mandonnet.

1198. *January* 8 *Celestin III died. Innocent III* (1198–1216) *elected Pope same day.*

1216. *July* 18 *Honorius III* (1216–1227) *elected Pope.* Dominican Order confirmed by papal bull dated December 22.

1221. August 6, S. Dominic died.

1222. May 23, Bl. Jordan of Saxony elected second Master-General.

1222–1223. Albert known to have been in Upper Italy; experienced the severe earthquake which devastated many Lombard towns.

1223. Date given by some for his entry into Dominican Order.

1227. *March* 19, *Gregory IX* (1227–1241) *becomes Pope.*

1229. Alternative and more probable date of admission to the Order of Preachers. (See Scheeben, op. cit.)

Received by Bl. Jordan of Saxony, Master-General, O.P. Probably sent at once to Cologne to go through his novitiate.

1233–1243. Lector, though not necessarily in this order, in Hildesheim (founded 1233), Freiburg im Br. (founded 1235, but perhaps not regularly established till 1236/7), Regensburg (founded 1229), Strassburg (founded 1224), and perhaps in other convents, including Cologne, where he may have lectured on the Sentences.

1238. Probably attended Chapter General at Bologna when S. Raymund de Pennafort was elected third Master-General in succession to Bl. Jordan. At this Chapter on first ballot, votes said to have been equally divided between Albert and Hugo de Saint-Cher; S. Raymund elected on the second.

Conrad von Hochstaden elected Archbishop of Cologne (1238–1261) in succession to Heinrich von Molenarken (1225–1238) and S. Engelbert (1216–1225).

1240. Saw a comet in Saxony.

1241. *Celestine IV* (*October–November* 1241) *becomes Pope.* Bl. John the Teuton elected fourth Master-General.

1243. Probably went to Paris this year to take the Doctorate in Theology.

June 25, *Innocent IV* (1243–1254) *elected Pope.*

1243/4–1248. In Paris. Lectured on the Sentences.

1245/6. Took the degree of Magister in Sacra Theologia.

1246. *Henry of Thüringen elected Emperor in succession to Frederick II, deposed by Innocent IV; died same year.*

1247. *William of Holland* (1247–1256) *elected Emperor.*

1248. On May 15 signed, as Magister S.T., report on the Talmud undertaken by order of the Pope by Odo of Chateauroux, the papal legate. Chapter General decided to open a studium generale et sollemne in the provinces of Lombardy, Provence, Germany, and England. Albert charged with establishing one at Cologne. Probably left Paris for Cologne after close of scholastic year, June 29.

1248–1254. Regent of Studies in Cologne. S. Thomas Aquinas his pupil till 1252.

1249. January 6 or thereabouts entertained William of Holland at the Cologne convent and induced him to complete the Dominican house in Utrecht.

1251. September 9 or 15, acting for Cardinal Hugo de Saint-Cher, the papal legate, confirmed the Teutonic Knights in the possession of the church of S. Nicholas in Utrecht.

1252. On Albert's recommendation Thomas Aquinas sent to Paris to teach there.

March 26 (Holy Saturday) drew up a judgement on the feud between Conrad von Hochstaden, Archbishop of Cologne, and the citizens, which was published on April 17 after arrival of the papal legate, Hugo de Saint-Cher, and confirmed by Pope Innocent IV December 12.

In June, in the Dominican Priory in Cologne, witnessed, as *frater Albertus lector fratrum Pred. Colon.*, document of Archbishop of Cologne and William of Holland laying down new statutes regulating the distribution, etc., of prebends by the Provost of the Chapter of Canons Regular in Kerpen.

1254–1257. Provincial of the Teutonia province, which included nominally the whole of Germany as she is to-day, Austria, Switzerland, Alsace, Lorraine, Luxembourg, Belgium, Holland, part of Poland, Lithuania, and Latvia. In 1229 there were in existence 14 houses for men; in 1254, when S. Albert was elected Prior Provincial, there were 40; at the time of his death in 1280 these had increased to 64, and in 1303 when the province was divided into two parts, Teutonia and Saxonia, there were in all 97 houses for men besides 74 for women.

1254. Elected Provincial at Provincial Chapter at Worms, which he attended as vicarius provinciæ, in succession to Hermann von Havelberg. Bl. Humbert de Romans elected fifth Master-General, June 1.

December 12, *Alexander IV* (1254–1261) *elected Pope.*

1255. February 17, in Cologne, witnessed, as *provincialis fratrum Predicatorum*, to a bequest by the Archbishop Conrad von Hochstaden.

March 11, urged by Pope to forward missionary work in Prussia and Livonia.

In February went to Alvoldinghusen near Soest to profess the first sisters in the Paradies Convent (founded 1253).

May 7, with the Abbot of Lehnin commissioned by Alexander IV to release from ban of consanguinity Johann I of Brandenburg and Jutta, daughter of the Duke of Saxony. Probably visited the Mark Brandenburg during the summer on this business.

In late summer presided over Provincial Chapter in Regensburg, whence he perhaps issued his letter on holy poverty.

1256. January 16, in Cologne, witnesses to a bequest by the Archbishop.

June 4, probably attended Chapter General in Paris. Perhaps on this occasion received from S. Louis the gift of a particle of the true Cross and a thorn from the Crown of Thorns, which he later (1271) gave to the Dominican convent in Cologne.

During summer presided at Provincial Chapter in Erfurt, issuing perhaps on this occasion his letter on confession.

September, called to Anagni to defend the Mendicant Orders against the attacks made on them by the Paris professors and embodied in William de Saint-Amour's book *De periculis novissimorum temporum*, which was condemned by the Pope on October 5 after a hearing before a commission of Cardinals.

(Albert's probable itinerary during the years 1255–1256 on his visitations as Provincial was: Cologne—Soest — Minden — Hildesheim — Halberstadt — Magdeburg — Seehausen — perhaps Lübeck — Stralsund — possibly Riga, and via Leipzig to Regensburg and perhaps Strausberg in Thüringen. After the Chapter in Regensburg (1525) visited some of the South German convents and thence down the Rhine to Cologne where he stopped January 1256; thence via Belgium to Paris for the General Chapter, visiting *en route* Maestricht, Louvain, Antwerp, Bruges.)

1256–1257. At the Papal Court. After the conclusion of the case at Anagni Albert kept by the Pope to lecture at the Curia (situate June–November 1256 in Anagni, December 1256–May 1257 in Rome, May 1257–October 1258 in Viterbo); lectured on S. John's

Gospel and the Pauline Epistles; also conducted a public disputation against the teaching of Averroes on the oneness of the intellect, later published as a book, and the subject also taken up again in his *Summa Theologica*.

1257. May 27, relieved of office of Provincial by the Chapter General at Florence. In late summer said to have presided at Provincial Chapter in Augsburg. (New Provincial not elected till 1258 at the Provincial Chapter in Vienna.)

1258–1260. Regent of Studies, Cologne.

1258. March 20, had vacated office of Provincial and assumed that of Regent of Studies, for on that date is referred to as *bruder Albrechte der lesemeister von den predigheren ce Colne*.

June 24, Albert by himself, or as president of a commission, other members being Goswin and Philip, respectively Dean and Provost of the Cathedral Chapter, Henry, Provost of S. Severin, and Henry, Provost of the Holy Apostles, published a settlement of the feud between Archbishop Conrad von Hochstaden and the city of Cologne, which was formally sworn to by the parties on June 28. Full peace was not brought about till a second intervention by Albert two years later.

In summer called to Lüttich to settle case of patronage of parish church of Dortrecht, claimed by the Abbey of Heisterbach, disputed by a royal widow and her cousin Wilhelm von Alvernia. Settled in favour of abbey.

1259. March, helped settle trade dispute between Cologne and Utrecht; finding published March 22 in Cologne and on following day in Utrecht.

June 1, took important part in revising curriculum of the Order at the Chapter General in Valenciennes, where he met Girardus de Fracheto, author of the *Vitæ Fratrum O.P.*, then Prior Provincial of Provence.

September 11 or later, called in with Henry, Provost of Church of the Holy Apostles, to end dispute between Dean Garsilius of Aachen, rector of the parish church of Rütten, and the Cistercian sisters of Burtscheid near Aachen on a question of emoluments. Case already settled, 1258, in favour of the sisters. Garsilius, obdurate, had retained funds, was excommunicated summer of 1259.

1260–1262. Bishop of Regensburg.

1260. January 5, date of Pope Alexander IV's decree appointing Albert Bishop of Regensburg in succession to Graf Albert von Pietengau who had resigned in 1259.

January 25, Rütten case settled by Albert; decision in favour of sisters confirmed; Garsilius capitulated.

March 29, entered Regensburg, having been consecrated bishop earlier in the month, perhaps on the Sunday *Lætare*, which this year fell on March 14; first going to the Dominican convent of S. Blasius and on following day being solemnly enthroned in the cathedral. On same day confirmed privilege, granted October 13, 1256, to Abbot Hermann von Niederaltaich by Albert's predecessor, that within the territory of the abbey two-thirds of the tithes from new-ploughed land should go to abbey, one-third to parish priest.

April 9, confirmed to Abbot of Waldhausen the indulgences connected with feast of dedication of the church and added others.

May 10, approved transfer of feast of dedication of church in Prüfenig to Sunday following the Assumption.

July 16, assigned to his Cathedral Chapter revenues of parish church in Cham, with obligation to give priest in charge a suitable salary.

July 30, helped the hospital of S. Catharina by grant of an indulgence and other concessions and created other means of increasing its income.

July 31, verified deed of conveyance of property to the house of the Teutonic Knights in Regensburg through Conrad von Hohenfels, commissary of the Cathedral Chapter.

July, second half, or August, consecrated an altar in the church at Lerchenfeld near Mintraching to the east of Regensburg.

September, attended conference of bishops of the Archdiocese of Salzburg at Landau, where agreement was signed making any censure delivered by a bishop of the diocese valid throughout the diocese. At same synod ordinances were passed that anyone guilty of unlawfully withholding Church property or levying tithe without authority, was to be excommunicated.

1261. February 22, certified to a document of February 1, 1252, in which Heinrich, Provost of Regensburg, and Heinrich the Dean had sanctioned the gift of land by Adelheid von Termannskirchen to the White Sisters of S. Mary Magdalen.

Before May 25 went to Italy to beg release from his bishopric.

Before or shortly after May 25, on which day Alexander IV died, arrived in Viterbo, bearing for the Pope some arrears of payment due him by the Abbey of Oberaltaich. As the Pope was dead these were returned to the Abbey, possibly delivered by Albert in person some time during 1261 or early 1262.

(May in the year 1261–1262 have visited Greece to consult with William of Mörbeke about translation of Aristotle's works.)

August 29, *Urban IV* (1261–1264) *elected Pope.*

September 28, Conrad von Hochstaden, Archbishop of Cologne, died, succeeded (October 8) by Engelbert II von Falkenburg.

Probably this year (not 1262 as given in *Monumenta Boica*) signed, with the Bishops of Freising, Passau, Chiemsee, and Lavant, protest against a demand made on the Archbishop of Salzburg by the College of Cardinals and the attempt to enforce it by the papal legate, Master Johannes de Ocra, by means of ecclesiastic censure. May have himself delivered the protest and laid case before the Cardinals. The petition failed as seen by Urban IV's decree of October 27, 1261.

During this year, possibly at the castle of Donaustauf, perhaps finished the great commentary on S. Luke, begun in Cologne. During this year S. Thomas Aquinas called to Rome by Urban IV.

1262. May 11, Urban IV confirmed choice of Leo, Dean of the Regensburg Chapter, to succeed Albert.

1263–1264. Preached Crusade in Germany.

1263. February 13 in Orvieto, appointed by Urban IV papal nuntio to preach the Crusade in Bohemia and all German-speaking lands.

April 1, celebrated Easter in Orvieto.

May 5 in Oberbayern, in Polling, granted indulgence of forty days to all visiting collegiate church on its dedication feast and on the feasts of the Invention and Elevation of the Holy Cross.

May 10 (Ascension Day) in Augsburg, granted indulgence in favour of the Dominican Sisters of S. Catharina in that city.

May 13 in Donauwörth, settled long-standing dispute between Bishop Hartmann of Augsburg and Graf Ludwig von Öttingen. Decision, announced in the Benedictine convent of the Holy Cross, was generally in favour of Graf Ludwig.

May 27 in Würzburg, granted an indulgence to all contributing towards the building of the oratory of the Cistercian nunnery of Himmelpfort.

June 5 in Frankfurt-am-Main, granted indulgence of forty days to all visiting church of the Teutonic Knights on the feasts of the Mother of God, Elisabeth, dedication of the church, and their octaves.

June 7, Joannes de Vercellis elected sixth Master General.

June 28 in Würzburg, granted indulgence to all contributing to the building of the cloister of the Augustinian Sisters ; thence to Cologne.

August 5, signed himself in a document promulgating three papal briefs predicator et promotor crucis . . . necnon provisor spiritualium in civitate et diocesi Coloniensi a sede apostolica constitutus, i.e. as possessing full powers of a papal legate.

August 25 in Cologne, witnessed compact between Archbishop Engelbert von Falkenburg and the city of Cologne, confirming and widening the one made, on June 16, 1261, between the city and Engelbert's predecessor. Perhaps from Cologne to Holland.

October in Magdeburg, outside his jurisdiction as preacher of the Crusade, to execute a papal mission : settlement of question of the bishopric. His decision nominating Heinrich, parish priest of Berge, to be Bishop of Brandenburg communicated to the Provost of the Praemonstratinians at Jericho near Havelberg by letter dated October 31.

December 16, no longer in Cologne, for on December 16, shortly after his departure, violent faction between Archbishop and city having led to Engelbert being made prisoner, was provisionally settled by the Bishops of Lüttich and Münster, and there was talk then, and later, on May 14, 1264, of calling Albert to come to raise the excommunication. Again proving that he was regarded as provisor spiritualium.

After leaving Cologne went perhaps to Holland or North Germany.

Towards end of year (probably) consecrated the parish church in Adelhausen, near Freiburg, going thence via Strassburg to Speyer.

During year given by Elisabeth, Abbess of the Ursuline convent in Cologne, the bodies of the 300 martyrs, of which he sent two, the relics of Candida and Florina, to the Dominicans in Freiburg, and the rest to their priory in Cologne.

1264. February 20 in Speyer, wrote to the Dominicans in Basel granting indulgence of forty days to all benefactors of their house and to all who visited their churches on the feasts of the Mother of God and SS. Dominic, Augustine, and Peter Martyr; on same date granted indulgence of forty days to all who visited the church of the Dominican Sisters in Klingenthal, near Basel, on the same conditions, with the feast of S. Leonard added.

March 18 in Regensburg witnessed agreement between Bishop Leo of Regensburg and his vassal, Zacharias von Hage, whereby latter in Albert's presence undertook not to marry his children without the bishop's leave, on penalty of fief reverting to the bishop and of paying penance.

Apparently remained in S. Germany for the rest of his time as preacher of the Crusade.

August 25 in Mainz, and in a document to the Augustinian nuns at Aldenburg, granting indulgences to all contributing to their building of the cloister, for the last time signed himself prædicator crucis.

October 2 Urban IV died; Albert probably got the news early in November, when his mission automatically came to an end. Then at once to Würzburg where he rested.

1264–1270. In Würzburg and Strassburg. Stayed in Würzburg from November 1264 till the summer of 1267, finding there probably his brother Henry, as prior, and his favourite pupil Ulrich von Strassburg, and spending what time he could in writing, but often interrupted by calls on him to settle disputes, etc., with occasional journeys afield to consecrate churches or altars or on other business. After leaving Würzburg spent some months on the Lower Rhine.

1264. December 4 in Würzburg, with Boppo, Provost of the Cathedral, settled a dispute between the Hospital of S. John in Haug and one of their wardens, Gottfried von Hohenlohe, concerning lands administered for them by the wardens, which the latter were apparently appropriating to their own use. Settlement witnessed by Prior Heinrich (presumably Albert's brother) and Br. Johannes, O.P.

1265. *February* 5, *Clement IV* (1265–1268) *elected Pope.*

April 10, with Bishop Iring of Würzburg settled another dispute between the Knights of S. John and Kraft von Hohenlohe. This settlement and that of the previous December, with another affecting Albert von Hohenlohe, confirmed by the Pope on June 16, 1266.

July 1, came to an agreement with Ulrich von Velleberg, commander of the Knights of S. John, that the walls of a stable of theirs in Würzburg were not to be so high as to obstruct the light of a neighbouring house.

August 26. With the Provost of Würzburg Cathedral, the Provost of Haug, and Graf Ludwig von Rieneck and Heinrich von Brauneck, witnessed and sealed agreement ending the feud between the Bishop of Würzburg and the citizens; with Heinrich von Brauneck commissioned to assess the indemnity due to the Abbey of S. Burkhard.

December 23, with others sealed a deed of mortgage between Luitpold von Nortenberg and the Dominican nunnery in Rothenburg.

1267. May 6 still in Würzburg; at request of the Dominicans in Regensburg granted indulgence of forty days to all visiting their church on the feasts of SS. Dominic, Peter Martyr, and Blasius.

During first half of year helped settle a dispute concerning certain measures of corn between the Knights of S. John in Würzburg and the Knight Marquard Crusen; also in this period consecrated an altar in or near the city.

June, left Würzburg for the Lower Rhine, first visiting perhaps Regensburg.

July 14, in Burtscheid near Aachen, consecrated a chapel and an altar in the Cistercian nunnery.

August 4, consecrated an altar in the indulgenced chapel of Our Lady in Cologne.

September 29. Sealed a deed of gift for the Teutonic Knights in Cologne, by which Dietrich von Heinsberg gave them the patronage of the churches in Niederkassel and Eitorf.

October or November, had probably arrived in Strassburg, where his beloved pupil Ulrich was now lector.

1268. Early in year consecrated the churchyard and an altar for the Knights of S. John in Schlettstadt.

April 29, in Esslingen to consecrate the Dominican church and High Altar.

June 4 in Schlettstadt again; consecrated chapel and altar for the Knights of S. John and granted indulgence of forty days to those attending the consecration, to benefactors of the order, and to those who visited the altar.

June 5, granted an indulgence to all contributing towards the building of church of the Knights of S. John in Colmar and to those visiting the church on Sundays.

June 15, back in Strassburg; consecrated an altar in the church of the Brothers of the Atonement of Christ, granting indulgence for visits to church on certain days, including Sunday next preceding the feast of S. John Baptist, on which day the feast of the dedication of the church was to be kept.

July 7, gave the Dominican sisters in Strassburg letter of indulgence applicable to benefactors of their convent of S. Catharina. At about this time must have executed papal commission (dated June 18) giving Conrad von Hohenlohe and his bride dispensation to marry. A special journey to Franken not necessary in this case.

During summer probably, went to Meclenburg on a papal commission, to reinstate the Knights of S. John in the enjoyment of lands, etc., given them in 1229 by Herzog Barnim von Pommern, which had been usurped by various nobles and by the Abbot of Colbaz. He was accompanied by Johann von Freiburg, probably a young Dominican who was a pupil of Ulrich von

Strassburg and was a well-known moralist, and by Albert von Havelberg.

Towards end of October went to Villigen.

October 26, stayed with the Knights of S. John in Colmar, to whom on the preceding June 5 he had given a letter of indulgence for the completion of the church, which, as he says, he had consecrated.

October 30 in Villingen again, on his way to Rottweil; granted the Friars Minor in Villingen an indulgence to those contributing to the building of their church and convent.

Early November, in Rottweil, where he laid the foundation stone of the Dominican church (the house had been founded the previous year), and consecrated the cemetery and granted an indulgence to those aiding in the building of the church.

November 29, *Clement IV died* (successor not elected till September 1, 1271).

During year, probably a few weeks before opening, on September 1, of scholastic year in Paris, Albert invited by Master-General, Johannes de Vercellis, to go to Paris to teach, it being his wish, in view of the trouble being stirred up by Gerhard d'Abbeville and Sigir of Brabant, that the Order be represented by its best and most distinguished teacher. Albert then *ca.* seventy-five, and since the Order could not give him a lector as assistant, asked to be excused. S. Thomas Aquinas then invited; reached Paris early in 1269.

During year, precise dates unknown, consecrated the Lepers' church in Adelhausen near Freiburg, perhaps on his journey from Villigen to Rottweil in October; also consecrated altar in the Liebfrauenkapelle in the Old Town of Rottenburg, perhaps on his journey to Esslingen in June; also consecrated an altar in Jung S. Peter's in Strassburg.

1269. April 7, in Strassburg ordained, in the Dominican church, 150 priests and 400 others to lower orders.

August 12, excommunicated the Abbot of Colbaz and others for again disturbing the Knights of S. John in Meclenburg in their possessions, in which by order of the Pope he had confirmed them the previous year.

End of August went to Basel.

September 9, consecrated Dominican church and

high altar in Basel, and on September 13 granted indulgence for visits to this church. During his stay in Basel probably sent letters of indulgence to the Friars Minor in Mülhausen (dated simply 1269).

During year, possibly on his way to Basel, consecrated the churches of the Dominican sisters in Unterlinden near Colmar and in Katharinenthal near Diessenhofen.

1270. Towards end of year invited by the Master-General to go to Cologne, at the instigation of the clergy and citizens of that city, who hoped he might settle the disastrous feud between Archbishop Engelbert and the citizens, which had led to the city being placed under an interdict.

Probably left Strassburg towards the end of 1270, arriving in Cologne at the end of the year or early in 1271, accompanied by the faithful Gottfried von Duisburg, *eius socius et minister* (perhaps assigned to him when, in 1268, he had to refuse the call to Paris as he had no lector assistant).

1271–1280. In Cologne.

1271. April 8. Increased the penalties he had, on August 12, 1269, imposed on Barnim von Stettin and the Abbot of Colbaz for attacks on the Knights of S. John.

April 16. By this date had successfully mediated in case of Archbishop Engelbert and the city of Cologne; the Archbishop had been released from captivity in which he had been held by Graf Wilhelm von Jülich since October 1267; but though a court of arbitration was set up to settle future disputes, the interdict imposed August 3, 1268, was not raised till after Engelbert's death on October 20, 1274.

August 31, sealed a deed of conveyance of the Burggraf Gernand von Werden.

September 1, *Gregory X* (1271–1276) *elected Pope.*

September 29, with others appointed mediator in a dispute between Wolfram, Dean of Kerpen, and his Chapter; cause of trouble unknown.

During the year consecrated Dominican church in Utrecht, which had been begun in 1248.

In this year the new choir for the Dominican church in Cologne, which Albert erected at his charge, was begun (condidit ipse chorum). Albert laid foundation stone and possibly sketched its design. He enriched it with many relics, including those presented to him by S. Louis years before.

In the first half of October of this or some other of his last years opened the Shrine of S. Evergislus.

1272. August 12 sealed an agreement between Gerhard Gyr, an alderman of Cologne, and the Abbey of Kamp.

December, with others declared for the authenticity of a deed of gift of the Abbess Geva of S. Cecelia in Cologne and seals a deed of gift of the same abbess. In this year Ulrich von Strassburg, Albert's best-loved pupil and friend, elected Prior Provincial (1272–1277).

1273. March, letter of Gregory X dated this month directed Albert or Bishop Hildebrand of Eichstätt to lay foundation stone of new Dominican church in Wimpfru. Probably done by Bishop Hildebrand.

September 7, consecrated new parish church in Nymwegen, Holland, to the honour of the Mother of God and S. Stephen, the high altar to the same saints, and two side altars to SS. Nicholas and Catharine, and ordered that the feast of dedication should be kept on the Sunday following the Nativity of the Blessed Virgin. As the new church, begun in 1254 by Otto Graf von Geldem, was within the city and replaced the old parish church outside the walls, Albert ordained that yearly on Trinity Sunday procession should be made with the Blessed Sacrament and an image of our Lady to the old burial ground.

October, with Dean Reimar of Aachen and others settled the dispute between the White Sisters in Cologne and the Provost General of their Order (of S. Mary Magdalen), Ditiko. This led to the reorganization of the Order.

October 24, *Rudolf von Hapsburg crowned in Aachen,* having earlier in month been elected emperor.

November (perhaps, but month uncertain) visited in Cologne by Ulrich von Strassburg, the Prior Provincial, and his secretary Hermann von Minden. Ulrich ill in Cologne, nursed back to health by Albert. Rudolf von Hapsburg probably in the city at the time of this visit.

1274. March 7, S. Thomas Aquinas died in Cistercian abbey of Fossanova.

May–June, in Lyons; attended council of the Church (begun May 7) and probably Chapter General of Order (begun May 13).

May 21, sent letters of indulgence in favour of benefactors of the Dominican church in Magdeburg, and at about this time, as reported by Bishop Leo of Regensburg, granted a similar indulgence for the Dominican convent in Regensburg.

June 6, attended consistory court at which the election of Rudolf von Hapsburg was confirmed; and spoke in his support to the text *Ecce ego mittam eis salvatorem et propugnatorem qui liberet eos.*

July 31, commissioned by the Pope to investigate procedure of appointment of Abbot of Fulda, with instructions to examine the proposed abbot and, if satisfied, to confirm his election and consecrate him, otherwise to order a canonical election. This commission executed late summer; the abbot proposed, Dean Berthaeus of Fulda, duly approved.

August, sealed a declaration of Frau Jutta von Hückeswagen for the abbess of the Cistercian convent in Dalheim.

October 20, Engelbert von Falkenburg, Archbishop of Cologne, died.

November 3, by authority of Wilhelm von Moerbeke, then chaplain and confessor to the Pope, released the abbeys of S. Ursula and S. Cecilia in Cologne from the penalties imposed in 1270, by the papal nuntio, Bernardus de Castaneto.

During year (perhaps in August) consecrated high altar (and probably church) in Vochem near Cologne; and at same time an altar in the Benedictine abbey of Brauweiler. It was perhaps while here on this mission that Albert was called upon to settle a dispute relating to certain property between Abbot Heinrich von Rennenburg and his Abbey of Brauweiler. Judgement reserved.

1275. February, verified copies of two papal briefs on protection to be given to Jews.

April 9, Siegfried von Westerburg (1275–1297) elected Archbishop of Cologne, and received from Gregory X permission to remove the interdict placed on the town August 3, 1268.

April 28, consecrated high altar in abbey church in München-Gladbach.

June 19, commissioned by Rudolf von Hapsburg to administer oath of allegiance to Eberhard von Diest, the newly appointed (April 20) Bishop of Münster.

September 7. Named as arbitrator in a new agreement between the Archbishop of Cologne and Gräfin Mathilde von Sayn, which replaced an old agreement come to between Mathilde and Conrad von Hochstaden and confirmed by the Pope Urban IV, January 8, 1263. The agreement concerned some property presented by Mathilde to the cathedral in return for certain revenues, and the coinage in which they were to be paid.

1276. January 3, verified transcription of a privilege granted, January 3, 1275, by Gregory X to the Knights of S. John.

January 10, Bl. Gregory X died, succeeded, January 21, by Bl. Innocent V.

May 27, granted letter of indulgence to the Cistercian nuns in Himmelpforte.

June 22, Bl. Innocent V died, succeeded, July 11, by Adrian V.

Sometime in first half of year in Soest.

August 18. Adrian V died, succeeded, September 18, by John XXI.

September 9, in Antwerp ; consecrated the Dominican church to S. Paul, also some altars, and granted indulgences to benefactors. At this time attended Provincial Chapter in this city (probably opened September 8) under Ulrich von Strassburg. On way back to Cologne consecrated two altars in Dominican church in Louvain (to SS. John the Evangelist and John the Baptist, and to S. Catharine) and granted indulgences to all visiting these altars on certain days.

In this year sealed the decision of the Provost and convent of Mechtern in Cologne to dissolve the cloister and hand over its possessions to the Archbishop on condition that he saw to the support of its members.

1277. March 7, 219 theses (including some of S. Thomas) condemned in Paris by Bishop Tempier at instance of the theological faculty. Albert, hearing rumour of attacks on his pupil's teaching, went early 1277 or end of 1276 to Paris to defend him. Since Robert Kilwardby on March 28 condemned the same theses in Oxford, it is clear that Albert's intervention saved them from the same fate in Paris.

April 6, delivered an opinion that levy of tribute on wax was admissable in law and by custom. The original document preserved in the Abbey of Saint-Trond.

May 20, *John XXI died.*

May 31, in Soest; gave letter to the Franciscans granting indulgence of forty days to all visiting their church on the feast of dedication and its anniversaries.

September 26, consecrated an altar in Cologne Cathedral.

November 25, *Nicholas III* (1277–1280) *elected Pope.*

During year again postponed judgement in case of Abbot Heinrich von Rennenburg and his abbey in Brauweiler, this time to 1282.

1278. October 20, said to have been present at constitution of Dominican priory in Colmar, but a mistake in the chronicle is possible.

During the year, with Gerhard von Andernach gave decision in the matter between the Archbishop of Cologne and Mathilde von Sayn (v.s. 1275).

1279. In January made his will.

February 14 or later, at invitation of the Prior of the Knights of S. John, Heinrich von Ratingen, solemnly translated the relics of S. Cordula to the chapel of the Knights.

May 4, verified a privilege granted June 4, 1248, to the Chapter of Kaiserwerth by Innocent IV, and, on August 18, the privileges granted September 1, 1248, by Innocent IV, August 29, 1277, by Rudolf von Hapsburg, November 25, 1193, by Henry VI, and December 6, 1224, by Henry VI, to the same Chapter.

September 8 (probably, if at all), said to have consecrated choir of the Victorskirche in Xanten.

1280. *August* 22. *Nicholas III died.*

November 15 died, and on November 18 was buried in the choir of the Dominican church, Archbishop Siegfried von Westerburg officiating at the Requiem Mass and obsequies.

1484. October 13, Innocent VIII gave permission to Dominican priories in Cologne and Regensburg to keep Albert's feast on November 15 with a Mass and Office. In effect a confirmatio cultus or equipollent beatification.

1622. September 21, same privilege extended by Gregory XV to Cathedral of Regensburg.

1631. April 2, same privilege extended to Lauingen by Urban VIII.

1635. March 6, same privilege extended to Dominicans throughout Germany by Urban VIII.

1664. May 3, same privilege extended to the Venetian Province of the Order by Alexander VII.

1670. August 27, same privilege extended to Dominicans throughout the world by Clement X.

1931. December 16, declared a Saint and Doctor of the Church by Pius XI.

APPENDIX D

BIBLIOGRAPHICAL

THE literature on Albert the Great is very extensive. Those who wish to consult a full bibliography are referred to the *Essai de Bibliographie Albertienne* by M. H. Laurent and M. J. Congar, O.P., in the *Revue Thomiste* for March–April 1931, and reprinted with some additions in the *Positio pro Canonizatione ac Doctoratu B. Alberti Magni* which appeared in Rome in the November of the same year.

Of the Saint's works only part have come down to us. The various lists compiled by the early biographers of Albert yield 138 separate works, varying in size from the *Summa Theologica* and the Commentary on the Sentences to little treatises. Of these only 65 are contained in the collected works, 5 others have been published separately, making 70 in all. Of the remaining 68 some were certainly wrongly ascribed to the Saint, others possibly; but many authentic works, for instance his several mathematical treatises to which he himself refers, are still missing. A thorough search among the manuscripts in convents and libraries should yield a harvest even at this date.

The following list contains the books referred to in the text plus the more important books and papers published since 1929.

Acta Capitulorum Generalium Ordinis Prædicatorum (ed. Benedictus Maria, Reichert, O.P. In progress Rome, 1898 etc).

Albers, Hilario: *La mediación universal de la stma Virgen segun el beato Alberto Magno* (La vida sobrenatural, XVIII, 244–264, 312–325, 370–377; XIX, 15–23, 171–176; 1929 and 1930).

Albert the Great, Saint.

Collected Works.

— *Beati Alberti Magni Ratisbonensis Episcopi Ordinis Prædicatorum, Opera quæ hactenus haberi potuerunt*, sub RR. PP. Thoma Turco, Nicolas Rodulphio, Joanne Baptista de Marinis Eiusdem Ordinis Magistris Generalibus, in lucem edita studio et labore

R. A. P. F. Petri Jammy, S. Theol. Doct. Conventus Gratianopolitani, eiusdem Ordinis (Lyons, 1651; 21 vol.).

— *Beati Alberti Magni Ratisbonensis Episcopi Ordinis Prædicatorum. Opera omnia*, ex editione lugdunensi . . . cura et labore A. Borgnet (Paris, 1890–99; 38 vols.).

Single Works.

— *De animalibus, libri XXVI.* (Nach der Kölner Urschrift . . . hrg von H. Stadler; Münster i.W., 1916 and 1921; 2 vols: xxvi+1664 pp.)

— *Tractatus de forma orandi, eiusdem legenda metrica premissa.* (Nunc primum in lucem prodit cura et labore A. Wimmer. Regensburg, 1902; xvi+116 pp.)

— *Liber de principiis motus processivi ad fidem* (Coloniensis archetypi, ed. H. Stadler; Munich, 1909; 56 pp.).

— *De vegetabilibus, libri VII, historiæ naturalis, pars XVIII.* (Editionem criticam ab E. Meyero cœptam absolvit C. Jessen; Berlin, 1867; lii+752 pp.).

— *B. Alberti Magni O.P. Commentarii in Librum Boethii de divisione.* (Ed. princeps rec. P. M. von Loë, O.P.; Bonn, 1913; 92 pp. and 6 pl.).

— *B. Alberti Magni . . . Commentarii in Job* . . . (Primum ex V codicibus manuscriptis, ed. M. Weiss; Freiburg i. Br., 1904; xi+567 pp. and 8 ill.).

— *Alberts des Grossen Homilie zu Luc xi*, 27 (zum erstenmal hrg. von P. M. von Loë, O.P.; Bonn, 1916; 56 pp.).

— *Mariale* (Cologne, 1473, Ulrich Zell).

— *Orationes B. Alberti Magni super IV libros Sententiarum* (ed. N. Thoemes; Berlin, 1893; xix+40 pp.).

— *Pædagogia Prædicatoriæ Familiæ a B. Alberto Magno . . . tradita ad Cultum Eucharisticum Sanctissime Celebrandum* (Biblia mystica Sanctorum O.P.; Diessen vor München, 1923; 552 pp.). Contains *De forma orandi; Sermones XXXII de Eucharistia; De adhærendo Deo.*

— *B. Alberti Magni Paradisus animæ sive Libellus de virtutibus* (ed. J. M. Sailer . . .; ed. nova cui accesserunt eiusdem De SS. Eucharistiæ Sacramento Sermones XXXII et De adhærendo Deo Libellus; Regensburg, 1878; xxvii +270 pp.).

— *The Paradise of the Soul* (Translation by R. Devas, O.P. London, 1921; 202 pp.).

— *Philosophia pauperum* (Leipzig, 1498).

— *Sermones B. Alberti Magni de sacrosancto Corporis Domini Sacramento* (ed. G. Jacob, Regensburg, 1893).

— *Theatrum omnium scientiarum artiumque collectum ex operibus Alberti Magni* (Venice, 1613).

Albert, Peter Paul: *Zur Lebensgeschichte des Albertus Magnus* (Freiburger Diözesan-Archiv, N.F. III, 203–298; 1902).

Albuerne, Nicolás, O.P.: *San Alberto Magno, naturalista* (La Ciencia Tomista, Sep.–Dec., 1932, 267–298).

Altaner, Berthold: *Die Briefe*

Jordans von Sachsen (Quellen und Forschungen, etc., XX ; Leipzig, 1925).
Analecta sacri Ordinis Fratrum Prædicatorum : Ad perennem memoriam Alberti Magni Doctoris (Anno 40, Vol. XX. fasc. 1, Jan.–Feb., 1932).
Archivum Fratrum Prædicatorum (edited by G. Théry, O.P. In progress, Paris, 1931–).
Arendt, Wilhelm, *Die Staats- und Gesellschaftslehre Alberts des Grossen* (Jena, 1929 ; viii +93 pp.).
Arts, Josef, O.P. : *De heilige Albertus de Groote en Kerkleeraar* (Ghent, 1932).

Bach, Joseph : *Des Albertus Magnus Verhältuis zu der Erkentnislehre der Griechen, Lateiner, Araber, und Juden* (Vienna, 1881 ; viii+212 pp.).
Bacon, Roger : *Opera quædem hactenus inedita* (ed. Brewer, London, 1859).
Balss, Heinrich : *Albertus Magnus von Cöln als Zoologe* (Munich, 1928 ; viii+147 pp.).
Barbado, F. M., O.P. : *Relations entre la physionomie, le tempérament et le caractère d'après le B. Albert et la science moderne* (Revue Thomiste, XXXVI, T. XIV, No. 65, 314–351 ; 1931).
Beltrán de Heredia, Vicente O.P. : *La producción literaria de San Alberto Magno y la labor futura de la crítica* (La Ciencia Tomista, Sep.–Dec., 1932, 147–172).
— *Comentarios de San Alberto Magno a los Económicos de Aristóteles* (La Ciencia Tomista, Sep.–Dec., 1932, 299–329).
Browne, M., O.P. : *Circa intellectum et eius illuminationem apud S. Albertum Magnum* (Angelicum, IX, 187–202 ; Rome, 1932).

Callaey, Fredegando, O.M. Cap. : *Voto sopra la vita del B. Alberto Magno.* (Printed in Positio pro Canonizatione ac Doctoratu B. Alberti Magni, Rome, 1931.)
—— also printed in Analecta O.P., XX, fasc. 1, Feb., 1932, pp. 475–530.
Cardauns, H. : *Konrad von Hohstaden, Erzbischof von Köln*, 1238–61 (Cologne, 1880 ; xi +164 pp.).
Carus, Victor : *Geschichte der Zoologie* (1872).
Casey, Hyacinth, O.P. : *Saint and Scientist : St. Albert the Great, O.P.* (Irish Rosary, Feb., 1932).
—— *The Scientific Work of St. Albert the Great* (Irish Ecclesiastical Record, April and May, 1932).
Chartularium Universitatis Parisiensis (ed. Denifle, Paris, 1889).
La Ciencia Tomista : Al nuevo Doctor de la Iglesia San Alberto Magno (Ann. XXIV, Nums. cxxxvii–cxxxviii, Salamanca, Sep.–Dec., 1932).
Colunga, Alberto, O.P. : *San Alberto Magno Expositor de los Salmos* (La Ciencia Tomista, Sep.–Dec., 1932, 214–241).
Cordovani, M., O.P. : *La Mariologia di S. Alberto Magno* (Angelicum, IX, 203–212 ; Rome, 1932).
Cuervo, Manuel, O.P. : *La teología como ciencia y la sistematización teológica, según San*

Alberto Magno (La Ciencia Tomista, Sep.–Dec., 1932, 173–199).

Delorme, Augustin, O.P. : *Albert le Grand : Sa vie, ses œuvres, son influence* (Juvisy, Seine-et-Oise, 1931 ; vii+57 pp.).

— *La morphogenese d'Albert le Grand dans l'embryologie scolastique* (Revue Thomiste, XXXVI, N.S., T. XIV, No. 65, 352–360 ; 1931).

Denifle, Heinrich, O.P. : *Die Handschriften der Bibelkorrektorien des 13. Jahrhunderts* (Archiv für Literatur-und Kirchengeschichte des Mittelalters, IV ; Freiburg i. Br., 1888).

— *Die Universitäten des Mittelalters* (Berlin, 1885).

Divus Thomas, Jahrbuch für Philosophie und spekulative Theologie : Albertus-Magnus-Festschrift (S. III, Bd. x, Hfte. 2–3, 304 pp. ; Fribourg, 1932).

Doms, H. : *Die Gnadenlehre des seligen Albertus Magnus* (Breslau, 1929 ; 303 pp.).

— *Ewige Verklärung und ewige Verwerfung nach dem hl. Albertus Magnus* (Divus Thomas, Albertus-Magnus-Festschrift, 143–161).

Drane, Augusta Theodosia, O.P. : *Christian Schools and Scholars.* (New ed. edited by Walter Gumbley, O.P., London, 1924 ; pp. xvi+742).

Ehrle, Francesco, S.J., Card. : *Die Ehrentitel der scholastischen Lehrer des Mittelalters* (Sitzungsbericht der Bayerischen Akademie der Wissenschaften, Philos.-philol. und hist. Klasse ; Munich, 1919).

— *Der selige Albert der Grosse* (Stimmen aus Maria Laach, XIX, 241–258 ; 395–414 ; Freiburg i. Br., 1880).

Endres, J. A. : *Albertus Magnus und die bischöfliche Burg Donaustauf* (Hist.—politischen Blätter für das kath. Deutschland, CXLIX, 829–836 ; Munich, 1912).

— *Eine beabsichtigte zweite Berufung Alberts des Grossen an die Universität Paris ums Jahr 1268* (Hist.-politische Blätter für das katholische Deutschland, CLII, 749–758 ; Munich, 1913).

— *Chronologische Untersuchungen zu den philosophischen Kommentaren Alberts des Grossen* (In Festgabe zum 70. Geburtstag von G. von Hertling, 95–108 ; Freiburg i. Br., 1913).

— *Das Geburtsjahr und die Chronologie in der ersten Lebenshälfte Alberts des Grossen* (Historisches Jahrbuch, XXXI, 293–304 ; Munich, 1910).

Esser, Thomas : *Die Gnadenfülle der allerseligsten Jungfrau Maria nach der Lehre des sel. Albertus des Grossen* (Theol.-praktische Quartalschrift, XXXIV, 273–288 ; Linz, 1881).

Fabricius : *Bibliotheca latina Mediæ et Infimæ Aetatis* (Hamburg, 1734).

Feckes, Carl : *Verhältnisse von Glauben und Wissen* (Zeitschrift für Katholische Theologie, LIV, 1–39 ; Innsbruck, 1930).

Fellner, S. : *Albertus Magnus als Botaniker* (Vienna, 1881 ; iii+90 pp.).
Fernández, Constantino, O.P. : *Alberto Magno y la Química Mediæval* (La Ciencia Tomista, Sep.–Dec., 1932, 242–266).
Franz, A. : *Die Messe im deutschen Mittelalter*, 466–473 (Freiburg i. Br., 1902).

Galguagnus de la Flamma, O.P. : *Cronica ordinis Prædicatorum* (Monumenta O.P., II ; Rome-Stuttgardt, 1897).
Garrigou-Lagrange, R., O.P. : *La volonté salvifique et la prédestination chez le B. Albert le Grand* (Revue Thomiste, XXXVI, 371–385 ; 1931).
— *De Sacrificio Missæ secundum sanctum Albertum Magnum* (Angelicum, IX, 213–224 ; Rome, 1932).
Gaul, Leopold : *Alberts des Grossen Verhältnis zu Plato* (Beiträge zur Geschichte der Philosophie des Mittelalters, XII, 1 ; Münster i. W., 1903 ; xii+160 pp.).
Gesamtkatalog der Wiegendrucke, (In progress, Leipzig, 1925 etc).
Getino, Luis, O.P. : *Manuscritos de San Alberto Magno en la Biblioteca Nacional de París* (La Ciencia Tomista, Sep.–Dec., 1932, 330–334).
Girardus de Fracheto, O.P. : *Vitæ Fratrum Prædicatorum* (ed. B. M. Reichert,O.P.Louvain, 1896).
Goblet, Heinrich : *Der selige Albertus Magnus und die Geschichte seiner Reliquien* (Cologne, 1880).
Gorce, M. M., O.P. : *Le problème des trois Sommes : Alexandre de Halès, Thomas d'Aquin, Albert le Grand* (Revue Thomiste, XXXVI, N.S., T. XIV, No. 65, 293–301 ; 1931).
Grabmann, Martin : *Der Benediktinermystik Johannes von Kastl, der Verfasser des Büchleins De adhærendo Deo* (Theologische Quartalschrift, CI, 186–235 ; Tübingen, 1920. Reprinted in Mittelalterliches Geistesleben, Munich, 1926).
— *Der Einfluss Alberts des Grossen auf das mittelalterlichen Geistesleben* (Zeitschrift für katholische Theologie, LII, 153–182, 313–356 ; Sonderabdruck, Innsbruck, 1928).
— *Drei ungedruckte Teile der Summa de creaturis Alberts des Grossen* (Quellen und Forschungen, etc., XIII ; Leipzig, 1919 ; viii+88 pp.).
— *Ist das philosophische Universalgenie bei Magister Heinrich dem Poeten Thomas von Aquin ?* (Historisches Jahrbuch, XXXVIII, 315–320 ; Munich, 1917).
— *Die Lehre des hl. Albertus Magnus vom Grunde der Vielheit der Dinge und der lateinische Averroismus* (Divus Thomas, Albertus-Magnus-Festschrift, 203–230 ; Fribourg, 1932).
— *Neue Funde* (Kölnische Volkszeitung, 1919, No.983).
— *Die wissentschaftliche Mission Alberts des Grossen und die Entstehung des christlichen Aristotelismus* (Angelicum, VI, 325–351 ; Rome 1929).

Graf, Thomas Aquinus, O.S.B.: *Die Lehre der hl. Albertus Magnus über das psychologische Subjekt der Gnade und Tugenden* (Divus Thomas, Albertus-Magnus-Festschrift, 162–194; Fribourg, 1932).

Guillelmus de Tocco: *Legenda sancti Thomæ Aquinalis* (Acta Sanctorum, Martii I, 660 *sq.;* Antwerp, 1668).

Haynal, Andreas M., O.P.: *Der hl. Albert der Grosse als Ausleger der Heiligen Schrift* (Divus Thomas, Albertus-Magnus-Festschrift, 195–202; Fribourg, 1932).

Heidingsfelder, Franz: *Geschichte der Verehrung des hl. Albertus Magnus in Stadt und* ***Diözese Regensburg*** (7ter Jahresbericht des Vereins zur Erforschung der Regensburger Diözesangeschichte, 37–62; Regensburg, 1932).

Heiler, Friedrich: *Das Gebet* (Munich, 1920).

Henricus de Hervordia, O.P.: *Liber de rebus memorabilibus sive Chronicon* (ed. Potthast; Göttingen, 1859).

Hertling, Georg von: *Albertus Magnus. Beiträge zu seiner Würdigung* (2nd ed., Beiträge zur Geschichte der Philosophie des Mittelalters, XIV, Hft. 5, 6: Münster i. W., 1914).

Hochwart, Laurentius: *Catalogus Episcoporum Ratisponensum.* (Printed by A. F. Oefele in Rerum Boicarum Scriptores, I, 148–242; Augsburg, 1763).

Humbertus de Romanis, Beatus: *Opera de vita regulari* (ed. Berthier; Rome, 1888).

Jessen, Carl. *See* Albert the Great: *De vegetabilibus.*

Joannes Lector, O.P., of Freiburg, *Summa Confessorum* (Regensburg, 1476; Lyons, 1518).

Killermann, S.: *Die Vogelkunde des Albertus Magnus* (Regensburg, 1910; viii+100 pp.).

Klaus, —: *Zur Geschichte der Klöster der ehemaligen Reichstadt Schwäbisch-Gmünd* (Württemberger Vierteljahrschrift für Landesgeschichte, N.F., XX).

Korner, Hermann, O.P.: *Chronica novella* (ed. Schwalm, Göttingen, 1895).

Kors, J. B., O.P.: *La justice primitive et le péché originel d'après S. Thomas* (Bibliothèque Thomiste, II; 1922).

Lang, Albert: *Zur Eucharistielehre des hl. Albertus Magnus: Das Corpus Christi verum im Dienste des Corpus Christi mysticum* (Divus Thomas, Albertus-Magnus-Festschrift, 124–142; Fribourg, 1932).

Lauent, M. H., and Congar, M. J., O.P.: *Essai de Bibliographie Albertinienne* (Revue Thomiste, N.S., T. XIV, No. 65, 422 *sqq.* 1931).

—— (Reprinted with some additions in Positio pro Canonizatione ac Doctoratu B. Alberti Magni; Rome, 1931).

Lauer, Hermann: *Die Moraltheologie Alberts des Grossen mit besonderer Berücksichtigung ihrer Beziehungen zur Lehre des hl.*

Thomas (Freiburg i. Br., 1911; xiv+372 pp.).

Lavaud, B., O.P.: *Les dons du Saint-Esprit d'après Albert le Grand* (Revue Thomiste, XXXVI, N.S., T. XIV, No. 65, 386–407; 1931).

Legenda Coloniensis, seu vita brevis et compendiosa Alberti Magni (ed. P. von Loë, Analecta Bollandiana, XIX, 272–84; 1900).

Lewin, Robert Kosmas: *Apostaten-Briefe* (Wiesbaden, 1928).

Loë, Paulus Maria von, O.P.: *Albert der Grosse auf dem Konzil von Lyon, 1274.* (Kölnische Volkszeitung, 1914, Literarische Beilage, No. 29.)

— *Alberts des Grossen Homilie zu Luk xi, 27.* Zum erstenmal hrg. von P. v. L. (Bonn, 1916; 56 pp.).

— *De vita et scriptis B. Alberti Magni* (Analecta Bollandiana, XIX, 257–284; XX, 273–371; XXI, 301–371; 1901, 2, 3).

— *Kritische Streifzüge auf dem Gebiete der Albertus Magnus-Forschung* (Annalen des historischen Vereins für dem Niederrhein, LXXIV, 356–362; Cologne, 1902).

— *Statistisches über die Ordensprovinz Teutonia* (Quellen und Forschungen, etc., I, 1907).

Luis de Valladolid, O.P.: *Vita Alberti Magni.* (Printed in Catalogus codicum hagiographicorum bibliothecæ regiæ Bruxellensis II, 95-105; Brussels, 1889.)

McNabb, Vincent, O.P.: *The Catholic Church and Philosophy* (London, 1927; xviii+124 pp.).

Mandonnet, Pierre, O.P.: *Albert le Grand* (in Dictionnaire d'histoire et géographie ecclésiastique, Paris, 1912).

— *La date de naissance d'Albert le Grand* (Revue Thomiste, XXXVI, N.S. XIV, 233–256; Saint-Maximin, Var, 1931).

— *Les idées cosmologiques d'Albert le Grand et de S. Thomas d'Aquin et la découverte de l'Amérique* (Revue Thomiste, I, 46–64; 200–221; 1893. Reproduced in *Les Dominicains et la découverte de l'Amérique*, 39–82; Paris, 1893).

— *Polémique averroiste de Siger de Brabant et de S. Thomas* (Revue Thomiste, V, 95–106; 1897).

— *Travaux des Dominicains sur les saintes écritures* (extrait du Dictionnaire de la Bible).

Manser, G. M., O.P.: *Albert der Grosse als Neuerer auf philosophischem Gebiet* (Divus Thomas, Albertus-Magnus-Festschrift, 19–40; Fribourg, 1932).

—*Alberts des Grossen Stellung zur Autorität seiner Vorgänger* (Divus Thomas, II, 75–85; Fribourg, 1915).

Meersseman, Gilles M., O.P.: *Albertus de Groote in de Nederlanden* (Thomistische Tijdschrift, II, 166–187; Ghent, 1931).

— *La contemplation mystique d'après Le Bienheureux Albert est-elle immédiate?* (Revue Thomiste, XXXVI, N.S., T. XIV, No. 65, 408–421; 1931).

— *Die Einheit der menschlichen*

Seele nach Albertus Magnus (Divus Thomas, Albertus-Magnus-Festschrift, 81–94 ; Fribourg, 1932).

— *De operibus B. Alberti Magni, O.P. Disquisitio critica.* (Printed in the Positio pro canon. ac doct. B. Alberti Magni ; Rome, 1931.)

— *De S. Alberti Magni postilla inedita super Ieremiam* (Angelicum, IX, 225–238 ; Rome, 1932).

— *Introductio in opera omnia B. Alberti Magni*, O.P. (Bruges, 1931 ; 173 pp.).

Meyer, Ernst F. H. : *Geschichte der Botanik*, IV, 9–84 (Königsberg, 1857).

— *See also* Albert the Great : *De vegetabilibus.*

— *Albertus Magnus. Ein Beitrag zur Geschichte der Botanik im 13. Jahrhundert* (Linnæa, X, 641–741 ; XI, 545 ; 1836 and 1837).

Meyer, Johannes, O.P. : *Liber de viris illustribus Ordinis Prædicatorum* (ed. P. von Loë, Quellen und Forschungen, etc., XII).

Michael, Emil, S.J. : *Geschichte des Deutschen Volkes*, III, 69–128 (Freiburg i. Br., 1903).

— *Wann ist Albert der Grosse geboren?* (Zeitschrift für katholische Theologie, XXV, 561–576 ; Innsbruck, 1911).

Œfele, Andreas Felix : *Rerum Boicarum Scriptores* (Augsburg, 1763).

O'Hanlon, Mary Ellen, O.P. : *Albertus Magnus, Chemist* (*The Torch*, July, Aug., 1932).

— *Saint Albert, Biologist* (*The Torch*, May, 1932).

Pacelli, Eugenio, Card. : *Nella luce di S. Alberto Magno* (Angelicum, IX, 131–146; Rome 1932).

— *Albertus Magnus* (German transl. of the above; Cologne, 1932).

Pelster, Franz, S.J. : *Die Ehrentitel der scholastischen Lehrer des Mittelalters* (Theologische Quartalschrift, CIII 37–56 ; Tübingen, 1922).

— *Kritische Studien zum Leben und zu den Schriften Alberts des Grossen* (Munich, 1918 ; xv+179 pp.).

Pelzer, A. : *Un cours inédit d'Albert le Grand sur la Morale à Nicomaque recueilli et rédigé par S. Thomas d'Aquin* (Revue néo-scholastique de philosophie, XXIV, 333–361 ; 479–520 ; Louvain, 1922. Also published separately, Louvain, 72 pp.).

Petrus de Prussia : *Vita beati Alberti Magni* (Cologne, 1487; Antwerp, 1621).

Pfeifer, F. X., and Platz, J. : *Kurze Geschichte der Stadt Lauingen und des seligen Albertus Magnus* (Donauwörth, 1881, 136 pp.).

Pflanzer, Dominikus, O.P. : *Albertus-Magnus-Handschriften in mittelalterlichen Bibliothekskatalogen des deutschen Sprachgebietes* (Divus Thomas, Albertus - Magnus - Festschrift, 246–276 ; Fribourg, 1932).

Pius XI, Pope : *Litteræ decretales de S. Alberto Magno : In thesauris sapientiæ* (Rome ; Scuola Tipografica Missionaria Domenicana, 1931).

— — Also printed in Analecta O.P., XX, fasc. 1, Jan.–Feb., 1932.
— — English Translation (Irish Rosary, May, 1932).

Positio pro Canonizatione ac Doctoratu Beati Alberti Magni (Rome, 1931).

Pouchet, A.: *Histoire des sciences naturelles au moyen âge ou Albert le Grand et son époque* (Paris, 1853; vi+656 pp.).

Puccetti, Angiolo, O.P.; *Sant' Alberto Magno dell' Ordine dei Predicatori Vescovo e Dottore della Chiesa* (Rome, 1932; xi+429 pp., with illustrations).

Quellen und Forschungen zur Geschichte des Dominikanerordens in Deutschland. (Founded by Paulus von Loë, O.P., 1906; now edited by Hieronymus Wilms, O.P. In progress, Vechta, 1906—.)

Quétif, J., and Echard, J., O.P.: *Scriptores Ordinis Prædicatorum*, I, 129 *sqq.* (2 vols, Paris, 1719, 1721).

Raymundus Martini, O.P.: *Pugio fidei* (Paris, 1651).

Revue Thomiste: Le Bienheureux Albert le Grand (XXXIIIeme Année, Nouvelle Série.—T. xiv, No. 65, Saint-Maximin, Var., Mars–Avril, 1931, pp. 227–468).

Ricker, Anselm: *Ein Kranz schuldiger Verehrung von der Alma Mater der Wiener Hochschule dem Andenken Alberts des grossen gewidmet* (Vienna, 1881; 32 pp.).

Ritter, Heinrich: *Geschichte der christlichen Philosophie* (Hamburg, 1845).

Rohner, Antoninus M., O.P.: *Kommentar des hl. Albertus Magnus zur Einführung in die Politik des Aristoteles* (Divus Thomas, Albertus-Magnus-Festschrift, 95–108; Fribourg, 1932).

Rudolphus de Novimagio: *Legenda litteralis de Alberto Magno* (ed. Cologne apud J. Guldenschaff, 1484; Cologne apud J. Koelhoff, 1490; Cologne, Kölner Görres-Haus, 1928).

Scheeben, Heribert Christian: *Albert der Grosse. Zur Chronologie seines Lebens* (Quellen und Forschungen, etc., XXVII; Leipzig, 1931; xv+167 pp.).
— *Albert der Grosse und Thomas von Aquin in Köln* (Divus Thomas, IIIe serie, IX, 28–34: Fribourg, 1931).
— *Zur Chronologie des Lebens Alberts des Grossen* (in the same periodical, X, 363–377).
— *Albertus Magnus* (Bonn, 1932, 238 pp. and 50 illustrations).
— *De Alberti Magni discipulis.* (In Alberto Magno: Atti della settimana Albertina celebrata in Roma nei giorni, 9–14 Nov., 1931, pp. 179–212; Rome, 1932.)
— *Les écrits d'Albert d'après les catalogues* (Revue Thomiste, XXXVI, 260–292; 1931).
— *Das Geburtshaus Alberts des Grossen* (Augsburger Postzeitung, Lit. Beilage, No. 42, 15 Oct., 1930).
— *Der selige Albert der Grosse* (Cologne, 1930; 32 pp.).

— *Die Tabulæ Ludwigs von Valladolid im Chor der Predigerbrüder von St. Jakob in Paris* (Archivum Fratrum Prædicatorum, I, 223–263 ; Paris, 1931).

— *Zur Chronologie des Lebens Alberts des Grossen* (Divus Thomas, Albertus-Magnus-Festschrift, 231–245 ; Fribourg, 1932).

Scheeben, M. J. : *Die Mysterien des Christentums* (Freiburg i. Br., 1865).

Schenz, W. : *Altes und neues über Albert den Grossen* (Augsburger Postzeitung, No. 57).

Scherer, Wilhelm : *Des seligen Alberti Magni Lehre von der Kirche* (Freiburg i. Br., 1928 ; ix+141 pp.).

Schneider, Arthur, *Beiträge zur Psychologie Alberts des Grossen, nach den Quellen dargestellt* (Beiträge zur Geschichte der Philosophie im Mittelalter ; Münster, 1903, 1906 ; 2 Parts : xiv+293 pp., vi+ pp. 294–559).

Schneider, Jakob M. : *Aus Astronomie und Geologie des hl. Alberts des Grossen* (Divus Thomas, Albertus-Magnus-Festschrift, 41–67 ; Fribourg, 1932).

Schrumpp, Meinrad M., O.P. : *Über zwei dem hl. Albertus Magnus zugewiesene homiletische Traktate* (Divus Thomas, Albertus-Magnus-Festschrift, 277–286 ; Fribourg, 1932).

Seibertz, J. Suitbert : *Geschichte der Stiftung des Klosters Paradies bei Soest* (Zeitschrift fur vaterländische Geschichte und Altertumskunde, XVII, 267–290. Münster, i. W. 1856 : Also published separately).

— *Quellen der Westfälischen Geschichte*, I, 4–13 (Arnsberg, 1857).

Senestréy, Ignatius von : *Beati Alberti Magni . . . doctrina de infallibili Romani Pontificis magisterio, testimoniis aliquot illustrata* (Naples, 1870 ; 14 pp.).

Sestili, G. : *L'universale nella dottrina di S. Alberto Magno.* (Angelicum, IX, 168–186. Rome, 1932.)

Sighart, Joachim : *Albertus Magnus, sein Leben und seine Wissenschaft.* (Regensburg, 1857, xvi+386 pp.)

— *Albert the Great* (translation abridged from the French edition by J. A. Dixon, O.P. London, 1876 ; xvi+472 pp.).

Simonin, H. D., O.P. : *La doctrine de l'Amour naturel de Dieu d'après le Bienheureux Albert le Grand* (Revue Thomiste, XXXVI, N.S., T. XIV, No. 65, 361–370. 1931).

Stadler, H. : *Albertus Magnus von Cöln als Naturforscher und das Cölner Autogramm seiner Tiergeschichte.* (Gesellschaft deutscher Naturforscher und Ärzte ; Verhandlungen, 1908 ; Sonderabdruck ; 249–254.)

— *Zur Tiergeschichte Deutschlands im Mittelalter* (Natur und Kultur, VI ; 1908).

— See also Albert the Great : *De animalibus.*

Stohr, Albert : *Der hl. Albertus Magnus über den Ausgang des Heiligen Geistes* (Divus Thomas, Albertus-Magnus-

Festschrift, 109–123 ; Fribourg, 1932).

Strunz, Franz : *Albertus Magnus. Weisheit und Naturforschung im Mittelalter* (Vienna, 1926 ; 187 pp.).

Théry, G., O.P. : *David de Dinant, étude sur son panthéisme matérialiste* (Kain, 1925).

Thomas Cantimpratanus, O.P.: *Bonum universale de apibus* (Douai, 1597).

Ueberweg, F., and Geyer, — : *Geschichte der patristischen und scholastischen Philosophie* (1928).

Ulrich von Strassburg : *Summa Theologica.*

Vosté, I. M., O.P. : *Sanctus Albertus Magnus Evangeliorum interpretes* (Angelicum, IX, 239–327 ; Rome, 1932).

— *S. Albertus in Apocalypsim* (ibid., 328–335).

Walsh, James Joseph : *The Popes and Science* (London, 1912 ; xii+431 pp.).

Walz, Angelo Maria, O.P. : *Albert der Grosse als Lector Coloniensis* (Angelicum, IX, 147-167. Rome, 1932).

— *Bestrebungen zur Heiligsprechung Alberts des Grossen in alter und neuer Zeit* (Divus Thomas, Albertus-Magnus-Festschrift, 287–304 ; Fribourg, 1932).

— *Compendium historiæ Ordinis Prædicatorum* (Rome, 1930).

— *Le culte du Bienheureux Albert le Grand aux xvii*e *et xviii*e *siècles* (Revue Thomiste, XXXVI, N.S., T. XIV, No. 65, 302–313 ; 1931).

— *De Alberti Magni et S. Thomæ de Aquino personale ad invicem relatione* (Angelicum II, 299–319 ; 1925).

— *De agendi ratione in causa canonizationis Sancti Alberti Magni* (Analecta O.P., XX, fasc. 1, Jan.–Feb., 1932 ; pp. 549–567).

— *Esposizione e documentazione storica del culto tributato lungo il corso dei secoli al B. Alberto Magno, Vescovo e Confessore dell' Ordine Domenicano* (Rome, 1930 ; 249 pp.).

— — II Supplemento (Rome, 1931 ; 223+iv pp.).

— and Scheeben, Heribert Christian : *Iconographia Albertina* (Freiburg i. Br., 1932. Text in German, French, English and Italian).

— *Statistisches über die Süddeutsche Ordensprovinz* (Quellen und Forschungen zur Geschichte des Dominikanerordens in Deutschland, XVII, 29 *sqq.* ; Leipzig, 1927).

— *Zum Kölneraufenthalt des Aquinaten. Ein Beitrag aus P. Denifles Nachlass* (Römische Quartalschrift, XXXIV, 46–58 ; 1926).

— *Zur Heiligsprechung des seligen Albertus Magnus* (Katholische Gedanke, II, 366–389 ; Munich, 1929).

Wasmann, Erich, S.J. : *Die moderne Biologie und die Entwicklungstheorie* (1904).

— *Zur neuen Ausgabe der Tiergeschichte Alberts des Grossen* (Stimmen aus Maria-Laach, LXXXIII, 282–286 ; 1912).

Weiss, Melchior : *Apologie des*

Christentums (Freiburg, i. Br., 1894).
Well, Alfons M., O.P.: *Der Vitalismus Alberts des Grossen* (Divus Thomas, Albertus-Magnus-Festschrift, 68–80; Fribourg, 1932).
— *Primordia novæ bibliographiæ B. Alberti Magni* (2nd ed., Paris, 1905; 88 pp.).
— *Reliquiengeschichte Alberts des Grossen* (Munich, 1930; 56 pp. and 15 ill.).
Wilms, Hieronymus, O.P.: *Albert der Grosse* (Munich, 1930; 237 pp.).
— *Alberto el Grande y la Teología moral* (La Ciencia Tomista, Sep.–Dec., 1932, 200–213).
— *Andacht zum sel. Albertus Magnus* (Vechta, —; 30 pp.).
— *Der heilige Lehrer.* Bilder aus dem Leben des heiligen Albert (München-Gladbach, 1932).
Wimmer, J.: *Deutsches Pflanzenleben nach Albertus Magnus* (Halle, 1908; 77 pp.).

Zahn, —: *Einführung in die christliche Mystik* (Paderborn, 1918).

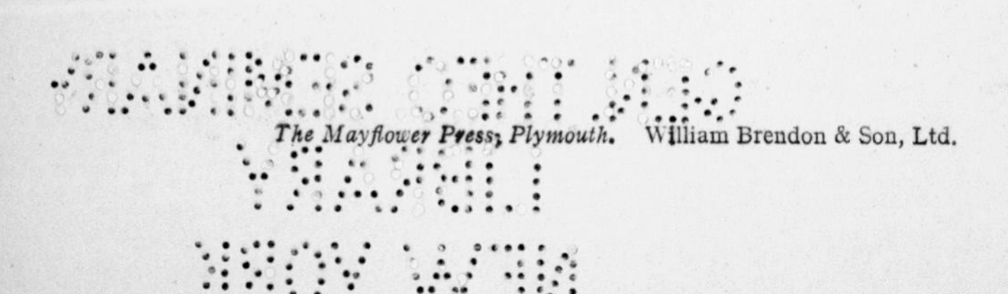

The Mayflower Press, Plymouth. William Brendon & Son, Ltd.